15

The Game of My Life

The Game of My Life

John Robbie

PELHAM BOOKS

PELHAM BOOKS
Published by the Penguin Group
27 Wrights Lane, London W8 5TZ, England
Viking Penguin Inc., 40 West 23rd Street, New York 10010, USA
Penguin Books Australia Ltd, Ringwood, Victoria, Australia
Penguin Books Canada Ltd, 2801 John Street, Markham, Ontario, Canada L3R 1B4
Penguin Books (NZ) Ltd, 182–190 Wairau Road, Auckland 10, New Zealand
Penguin South Africa, Amethyst Street, Theta Ext 1 Johannesburg

Penguin Books Ltd, Registered Offices: Harmondsworth, Middlesex, England

First published 1989
© John Robbie 1989

ISBN 07207 1936 4

Typeset by Industrial Graphics
Printed & bound by National Book Printers
Goodwood, Cape

Introduction

A couple of years ago someone sent me a rugby book for my birthday. It was very different from all the others I had read. The author was former England number eight forward Andy Ripley. It was a weird sort of work, containing poems, philosophies, stories. To anyone who knew Ripley, it was typically unconventional. I loved it, and still keep it beside the bed to dip into whenever I want to feel good.

In one of the chapters there was a section called 'Rugby is' — obviously based on the well-known 'Love is...' idea. There were lots of things that summed up rugby, but one of them really grabbed me.

It said that rugby is being the youngest player in the dressing room — and then suddenly you're the oldest. When I read it I couldn't go on. I know that sounds very dramatic, but that is the truth. It was talking to me. Here was John Robbie, the world's greatest rugby nut, the guy who had always been the youngest player — for my school, university, Ireland and the British Lions — realizing for the first time that his career is drawing to a close.

In my mind I was still a youngster, blissfully going from game to game and season to season, with never a thought to life outside rugby. From the moment I read that, everything was somehow different. News reports seemed more threatening; jokes about age in the dressing-room all seemed to be aimed at me. And, crazy as it seems, I suddenly began to feel that it was harder to get fit, and to keep that fitness. With hindsight it all seems a bit daft, but I suppose that was the time that I first started to look back at all the things that had happened to me as a result of my love affair with rugby.

It was Ollie Campbell, the Irish fly-half, who really put the idea of a book into my head. Ollie is my greatest rugby mate — he is also the best player I have ever come across. I really cannot speak about him in public, though, because I start spouting superlatives and going overboard (which usually has my audience wondering just what sort of a relationship we enjoy).

Anyway, I was in Ireland on a flying visit at Christmas 1987, and we were sitting in the New Jury's Hotel before going to watch the Irish trial. I was nursing a monumental hangover from a huge dinner at Greystones club the night before. Ollie had picked me up in the morning and had driven me to the trial.

All the way into Dublin Ollie had been quizzing me about life and rugby in South Africa. I told him about the training, the commitment, the crowds and the passion for the game that is everywhere. Ollie then surprised me by advising me to write this book.

I laughed at him. What could I write about that would make anyone vaguely interested enough to buy it? But Ollie seemed to make my life take on some sort of significance. Here I was, an Irish lad from the village of Greystones in County Wicklow, who (through the game of rugby) had become well known in Ireland, been to Cambridge University, toured all over the world and ended up — as a result of a major controversy — going to live in South Africa.

While it is one of the world's rugby powerhouses, South Africa is also among the most hated nations on the face of the earth. But what's it like to live there, Ollie wanted to know.

Since arriving in the country I had played provincial rugby for seven years, made the bench for the Springboks, and then just missed out on a full Bok cap when the 1985 All Blacks didn't tour. I got involved with the media, and through doing a sports reporting slot on Radio 702, the biggest independent station in the country, and presenting the Five Nations rugby broadcasts on TV, I had become something of a well-known person in South Africa.

Ollie had me believing that a lot of people in Ireland and indeed in rugby everywhere would actually be interested in what I had to say. He said he, for one, would buy a copy — God bless him.

I returned to South Africa in 1988, and never really thought about it again until, one day, I was having lunch with David Williams, my colleague at 702. Dave felt there were a lot of South Africans who, because they had been starved of rugby tours and overseas travel in general, would love to know about the game in Europe. He also argued that many people would like to find out a bit about the early life of this strange little talkative Irishman.

When I told Dave about my conversation with Ollie, we thought we might be on to something. Perhaps there were people in both places who had some idea of half of my career, and might be interested in the rest. But I felt that my lack of real fame ruled out the project. After all, rugby books are written by personalities like Colin Meads and Gareth Edwards. On the ranked list of international players in order of achievement, John Robbie was a long way from the top. David didn't agree but, for me, the subject was closed.

Isn't it funny how things just won't go away, though? A few months later I was contacted by the Penguin Group to discuss the possibility of me writing a book. We had a meeting. They explained they were keen to go from merely warehousing overseas books to actually knocking out a few themselves. They weren't rugby people in particular, but felt that I had a profile in South Africa that had possibilities. They were delighted to hear of my previous flirtation with the idea.

That was really it, I suppose. All through my life I had worked to a convenient philosophy that things are to a large extent predetermined; and that if something is to happen, it will keep on nagging at you until you give it a crack. Dave and I then planned a flexible proposal for the book. It was accepted, and hey presto! John Robbie is going to be an author.

That's the easy bit. Talk is cheap when you are a writer. Hitting the keys is hard.

You need motivation, which is a subject that has always interested me. In Ireland I was known as a successful team captain (which, as we shall see later, comes as a surprise to many in South Africa). The first thing I discovered about writing a book is that unless you believe in the project, you haven't got a prayer. My problem was that — despite Ollie, Dave, the Penguin Group and a lot of other enthusiastic responses to the idea — I still felt uneasy.

It became clear that my book would have to be rather different. I simply wasn't famous enough. I had read all the others, I had enjoyed them all — but with a few exceptions, they left me frustrated. Most of them had contained an awful lot of detail about the actual games. Although it was interesting enough to a fanatic like me, I felt that I really didn't know too much about the people behind the names. They remained ghosts to me.

Funnily enough, the one I enjoyed most was the one by JPR Williams, the Welsh full-back. Now JPR was a truly great player, respected by one and all — except possibly in Durban, where a lot of people still remember that controversial fight he had with Tommy Bedford on the 1974 Lions tour.

Before I read his book I had always believed that JPR was an out-and-out shit. Many rugby people had given me that impression, and it had been confirmed on the only occasion on which I met him. Also later, when writing for a newspaper, he had very cruelly dismissed my former Cambridge team-mate Eddie Butler, then the Welsh captain, as being merely a club player — which was nonsense. I started to read JPR's book with a very prejudiced mind. However, the book was very honest. Sure, arrogance did come through in places, but at least the reader felt that he was getting inside the man. I decided that the book I was going to write must try to do the same.

So I have attempted to be totally honest. Where I wanted to criticize, I have. But I would like to stress that these were my perceptions at the time. I am quite prepared to accept that someone can say, hell, John got it all wrong, it wasn't like that at all. But this is how I saw it, and this is what was inside my head, and why I acted as I did.

I found this approach quite scary. I noticed that in most of the other biographies, criticisms of players are few and far between, and the big issues — like politics and cash in rugby — are to a large degree side-stepped. Controversial headings disguise unremarkable chapters that only reveal a great ability of the writer in kicking for touch.

I have tried to avoid such evasions. The book does not set out to be controversial. I just want to give an idea to everyone, not just the rug-by fan, of how a boy from a certain background got hooked on a game that is a bit of a Victorian relic — and how it has affected almost every decision in his life so far. I want to get across that, despite giving an impression of control, there was often a little boy inside me who was as frightened as hell.

Finally, I would like to pay tribute to my friend and colleague David Williams, whose advice and assistance with this project has been invaluable.

1

My first confrontation of any kind with a journalist happened in Dublin. It was after the 1976 Irish tour to New Zealand. I had made the trip as a twenty-year-old and the verdict of the press, in its infinite wisdom, was that I had been a success: I was a Man with a Future. This resulted in quite a bit of interest from the media. It was all great fun, and I had this innocent idea that journalists were all on my side — in short, personal fans with typewriters. But this all changed after an interview with that infamous Irish character, Ulick O'Connor.

Now I had only known the man from his frequent appearances on *The Late, Late Show* on TV. It seemed to me that he was only there to antagonize and annoy the various guests and the audience, but it made for good television. He also wrote the odd sports article for one of the English papers, and it was in this capacity that he invited me for coffee at a Dublin hotel.

It all went well until Ulick started to press for details about dirty play on the tour. There had been scraps, and there had even been a suggestion that — perish the thought — the saintly Irish had started some of it. Faced with a contentious issue for the first time in my life, I clammed up, and Ulick lost his temper. He accused me of being a typical bloody rugby player, afraid to rock the boat and so on. I think he then realized that I was out of my depth and the interview ended on a very tame note.

It was all a bit of a disaster. At this time in my life, having achieved the only ambition I ever had owned, I was just beginning to realize something: that being a rugby player isn't enough to give you automatic respect. At the time it was only a suspicion; as we shall see later, it grew into a real inferiority complex.

I remember being quite worried about how the article would read, but Ulick wrote a very mild piece, mentioning nothing at all about the row. He did say something, though, that really annoyed me. He wrote that because of my Welsh mother and Scottish father, and because I was a Protestant, that in some way I was a bit apart from other Irish

5

players. The idea, I think, was to suggest that this put me at a distance from the mob, ignoring the fact that I had captained Trinity to great things that year and that I was a future Irish captain.

I was a bit hurt because I took it to mean that he was implying a certain aloofness — and that wasn't the case. A certain shyness in non-rugby situations I certainly had, but that was something else.

The point of this little story is that after all my travels and adventures, I suspect that Ulick's article wasn't too far off the mark in its implication that my Irishness was somehow 'different'.

I suppose that I wasn't a typical Irish lad growing up in the 1960s, and certainly the seaside town of Greystones was a very unusual place. It was known as the 'Protestant graveyard' or 'Little Belfast', because of the relatively large number of non-Catholic residents.

The town developed around two large estates owned by the La Touche and Burnaby families. It was also a fishing village; being about thirty kilometres south of the capital, many wealthy Dubliners built holiday homes there. A number of British army people, and Church of Ireland (Anglican) ministers, retired there. It all helped to create a very special atmosphere. It was and is a great place to live; for kids growing up, it was unbeatable.

It is separated from greater Dublin by Bray Head, a rocky headland that juts into the sea. This meant that travel to Dublin was difficult in the early days, and so the town stayed fairly small. We had the sea, but the two beaches were quite stony and gritty, which meant that we were not invaded by too many holiday-makers. Just inland, we had the beautiful hills and valleys of County Wicklow. And if you didn't mind the journey, Dublin and all the city had to offer was thirty kilometres to the north. It was great!

As a result of the early history, churches were built; I suppose more and more 'Proddies' (as Church of Ireland people were called) and 'press-buttons' (Presbyterians) decided that Greystones was a good place to live. There was never any religious trouble, and most of the societies which had sprung up from the various churches were open to all.

My mum was, and still is, a great one for the amateur dramatics. She was a founder member of the St Patrick's Players. Not only did they put on various plays, but for about twenty years Mum used to write, produce and direct the Christmas pantomimes. This kept just about every child in the village busy and out of too much mischief for the Christmas holidays, so she won the undying gratitude of all the parents.

We were in the Cubs, Scouts, Brownies and Guides, and played football — very casual stuff in the local park. There was also the Greystones rugby club, of course, and occasionally we used to go to their games. It was all juvenile stuff, though, and little did I know just how involved I would become there in years to come.

So what of my family? Well, I suppose it's a big cliché, but we have always been a very happy bunch. My late dad (also John Cameron Robbie) was a Scot from the town of Airdrie, just outside Glasgow. He used to joke that his father thought that the only good Irishman was a dead one. He grew up in fairly tough times. Although he was a very good soccer player, with offers of professional trials, he went to sea in the Merchant Navy and was for many years a confirmed bachelor. He served during the war on the convoys to America, and to me the fact that he had been to just about every country on earth was a thing of great wonder.

He met my mum — Dorothy Richards from Mountain Ash in the Welsh valleys — when he was about forty, and they got married after the war. Quite how they met I don't know. Mum always says it was at a party, and when she walked into the room he was the only one that didn't stand up. *He* used to claim that they went to the pictures one day, and when he came out he was engaged.

They had a couple of years of relative peace before producing four of us between 1953 and 1957. We are: Dave the eldest, Janie a year younger, then me next and Peter the youngest. Yes, we were baby boomers all right; with two kids of my own now, I have no idea how they managed at all in the early years.

Well, I do really, because there were two other people who made up our family, and they were just as dear as our parents. They were my mum's mother and father, our Nana and Grandpa, May and Bob Richards from the Welsh valleys; they lived with us until they passed away a number of years ago. We loved them to bits.

I think there were lots of things that shaped my life. First of all, Mum is a most extraordinary person. She is very bright, with a biology degree from London University. As a result of her dedicated teaching career, we were never allowed to neglect school work. None of us was brilliant, but with the love of sport that we all had during school days, and with the freedom of a small and friendly village, all of us could have got side-tracked.

That it never happened is almost entirely due to Mum. Many was the night we all spent (protesting loudly) working at the kitchen table, until she was satisfied that we were going to pass whichever exam was next in line. Of course, Grandpa was a retired teacher, and so she had a willing ally; between them they could cover the sciences, maths, English and history. The only real drama came in Irish, which was compulsory: without it, in our time, no state exam could be passed. Somehow, with a few failures along the way, we all managed to get our leaving certificates; Dave and I chose to go on to university. Without the extra pressures from home, I doubt we would have made it.

Another key factor was the theatrical input from Mum, and also the fact that she and Dad were extremely well-read. I think we were all endowed with a love of reading. Our house was packed with books, and it was completely normal to read before going to sleep at night. None of us considered this to be anything special; indeed, it's only now, when I meet people (including some Springbok rugby players) who have hardly read a book in their lives, that I realize just what a gift this love is. Mum started us off by reading books like Tolkien's *The Hobbit* and of course the 'Narnia' series by CS Lewis. I must say that I get a nostalgic lump in my throat when I read them to my kids — memories come flooding back.

Both Dad and Mum were very active in sports in their time. As well as being a good soccer player, Dad was also a keen cricketer while he was in the Merchant Navy. Mum was keen on hockey and athletics, and an extremely fast runner. We used to love it when she won the mothers' race at school (although I do recall that a certain Mrs Roberts, whose eldest boy achieved fame as one of the Boomtown Rats, used to beat her more often than not).

Grandpa also loved sport, and although I'm not quite sure to what extent he played, I do remember, when sitting horrified at the TV reports of the Aberfan disaster (a slag dump in Wales subsided and engulfed a village in the mid-1960s), him telling us that at one time he had played soccer for the town.

Anyway, presumably as a result of genetics, we all grew up with the raw materials to be players of sport — if we wanted to be.

Dave was very keen, and has a fantastic physique for many sports. However, I think he lacked a bit of confidence and although he was always playing rugby, soccer and lately renewed an interest in cricket, his real talent was in the swimming pool — if he'd had the right facilities and coaching, I'm sure he would have made it to the top. He has a marked ability to stick at things, more than the rest of us.

Janie is a bit of a beauty — at least that's the feedback that I got from my mates. She has the legs of a colt, and was a good hockey player and athlete. I don't think she really was that keen after school, though, and is now following Mum's example as a leading light in local amateur dramatics in the Cornwall village where she lives with her doctor husband and four kids.

Of us all, Peter probably has the most sporting ability. He also has the least dedication and ambition. I have absolutely no doubt that, had he shared my passion for rugby, he could have been an international fly-half or centre. About the only thing that Pete really had a passion for was reading about flying; at the age of twenty-nine, he recently qualified (top student for his year) as a pilot.

The main thing that our family gave us, though, was total support. For this I can never repay them. Bear in mind that, of our whole school, we lived the furthest out from Dublin — to most of our Dublin schoolmates, Greystones was as far removed as Cork or Belfast, and the tortuous thirty kilometres did take at least an hour by car, or up to two hours by bus. Yet I cannot remember taking part in any school activity, no matter how long it took or where it was, when my father didn't collect us, or which my whole family didn't support. We, of course, thought this was totally normal. It's only now that my kids are growing up that I realize just what an effort or a sacrifice it can be to support them in all their activities — and their school is just around the corner.

Mum and Dad, and in the early days my Grandpa, stood on muddy sidelines, in draughty halls during boxing tournaments, on hard benches at cricket matches, and in the chlorine-reeking buildings in which were the few public swimming baths that were shared by all but the very top schools in Dublin. I don't recall them ever complaining or not being there. They offered support, brought us down to size in victory, and built us up in times of crushing defeat.

I can remember us all heading off to the school boxing tournament one night in Dublin. Our school was one of the few that still practised the noble art, and the Robbie mob were (of course) involved. Peter, probably about ten years of age, was the first to lose; I was second, bursting into tears when the result was announced; and Dave was last. Three losses out of three, and it was a gloomy car on the way home. Peter broke the spell, though, by announcing that although he had lost, he had at least hit his opponent 'right in the balls'.

Dad informed Peter that the correct way of saying it was that he had been hit in the lower stomach. Pete thought for a moment, and then said that his way sounded better.

We all laughed, and my parents had the good sense to allow one of us to be a bit profane without punishment. It was a master-stroke, and this sense of being grown up helped us to get over the shame of the defeat for the family in the ring. (Woe betide the one who tried to repeat the exercise in less trying circumstances.)

Another very real influence in my life was religion. In Ireland at that time, our lives were to a large extent run by the church. It all was very natural, though. We went to Proddie or Catholic schools, totally identical except that *they* were taught by priests and religious instruction differed. A lot of the community organizations were affiliated to the local churches, but this was not an aggressive thing. We all hung around with our different gangs of kids, but these were totally mixed up. Most of my gang were Catholic, and the only jealousy that existed was because I didn't have to go to church every Sunday, and their parents made them.

We had, though, a very good Sunday school that was run by an incredible family called Evans. There were loads of them, mostly farmers, and they lived Christianity to the letter, but without losing the element of fun. They certainly helped us all to a belief that was based on good rules and a friendly approach.

Each summer the highlight of our early lives took place. This was the visit to Greystones of the Children's Special Service Mission: the CSSM. This is a Christian mission for children that travels to various places in the British Isles and Ireland, setting up camp for two or three weeks in the summer holidays. It was Protestant but anyone could attend, and the emphasis was on having good clean fun. As one got older, it encouraged more and more emphasis on matters spiritual. It sounds a bit like indoctrination, but it wasn't. In my day it had a leader from Wales called David Lewis, and we worshipped him. He was a natural comedian, a very devout man but above all a great believer in humanity, warts and all.

The CSSM would set up in a local house, and for a while it was the centre of our universe. Many people came down from Dublin and even Belfast for holidays in Greystones, just to go to the CSSM, so each year was like a big reunion. 'Volunteers', young men and women mostly from Britain, used to come and run the whole thing. It was Bible readings early in the mornings, a service on the beach before lunch, games in the afternoons, and films or discussions in the evening.

Recently Mum wrote to me to say that she had hosted a number of the visiting workers in our house, and that she kept crying at the beach service when she saw all the kids that we used to go with now attending with their children. I imagine I would also have a lump in my throat.

Please don't think that we were little angels — far from it. We grew up like all children, and lost our innocence early. We cursed and swore on our own with the best of them; fought, lied and bullied; and although I never partook, cigarettes and even the odd swig of stolen beer occasionally made an appearance. However, I really do think that the background we had gave a lot of us a very firm base on which to build our lives. I must say now that although I am a firm believer, I am an infrequent church-goer.

I have no doubt that my love of rugby came from my Grandpa. A great family friend of ours was Dicky Williams. He had been a fly-half in Wales during I think, the Cliff Morgan era; although uncapped, he had gone north to Rugby League and played for Britain in that code. One of my early memories is of him visiting us and playing with Pete and me in the garden of our big old house. We had little soccer balls and knew little of rugby; he tried, with little success, to teach us — I suppose I was about three or four.

Quite when I took an interest in rugby I don't know. I remember my Grandpa and me walking down to the house of our local vicar, Canon Elliot (a great friend who still writes), to watch Wales play in the Five Nations. Like most of my mates, we had no TV in those days. I also remember that Grandpa, who could speak Welsh, used to watch the Welsh news; an early hero was news reporter Dewi Bebb — Grandpa told me he was an international. And when I was small, I went into Dublin with Grandpa to watch Bective Rangers, our nearest senior rugby club in those days, playing in their annual home games against Cardiff, Ebbw Vale and Neath. I can remember seeing Keith Rowlands playing for Cardiff, and can hear my grandfather complaining that the Bective boys had tried to intimidate him. I wonder.

Because we had to go to a Proddie school, and because that meant Dublin, it was decided that we would all go to Dublin High School, a famous old day school in the city. So there was great excitement in 1963 when the school got to the Schools Cup Final against the mighty Blackrock College. Although I wasn't even at the school then, I can remember going to Lansdowne Road (for the first time) to watch that heroic defeat — and the cheer from the blue-and-white-clad supporters as 'The Rock' won 6-0.

My next memory is getting a rugby ball for Christmas. We used to get what we asked for, within reason, so I must have requested it. I can see it now: a Slazenger size 4, and Grandpa and I would practise passing in the garden.

Details are hazy. All the informal games of those early years were soccer in the park. But I know quite definitely that at the age of eight I was a rugby fanatic. I knew the Laws, had a hero — Fergus Keogh, the Bective full-back — and had only one ambition in life: to play rugby for Ireland.

2

Schools in the Republic of Ireland are classified by religion, but this is not forced or contrived — it just seems to be the order of things. A new friend would say: 'Hey Johnnie, how come you live in Greystones but go to school in town (Dublin)?' The answer would be simple: 'There is no really handy Proddie school nearby.' No problems, the message would be received loud and clear: John is a Prod, and now on to far more important matters, like 'Do you support Spurs or United?' That was the way of things, and where I lived religious differences meant very little. I suppose more of the Protestants in Greystones were 'middle class', as they used to call people who had only moderate difficulty in paying the bills at the end of the month. But my close friends were the guys who called in after school on the way to play football in the park — in fact, the park played a large part in our lives. It was really just a field, ringed by bushes, in the middle of Greystones; it had an open drain running through the middle of it. To us it was Wembley, Lord's, Lansdowne Road, and when we tired of sport and played soldiers, various battlefields of the world all rolled into one.

I went to the Proddie high school in Dublin, my friends went to the (Catholic) Presentation College in Bray, or its near neighbour, St Brendan's.

Normally the Proddie kids go to national school before going on to secondary school. These national schools are usually very good, giving an excellent basic education on which the secondary teachers can build. However, at the time when Dave was to go to school, Mum was not happy with the local national school and we were each sent to school in Dublin — Wesley College for Janie, Dublin High School junior school for us boys. Both were fine old schools with good histories. For us it meant an hour's trip by car into school in the morning and then two buses home in the evening; if there were school activities then Dad would always pick us up.

Once there was real drama. It happened at the time of my first exams,

13

which meant that, instead of getting out of school at 2.30 pm, we were let out at 12.30. My routine was broken, and a friend persuaded me to catch the train instead of the bus.

He got off in the suburbs of Dublin, but he assured me that the train went all the way to Greystones, about twenty kilometres further on.

All was well until the train stopped in Bray, the town on the Dublin side of the headland that divided Greystones from the Dublin area. I sat and sat, waiting for the train to start up on the last eight kilometres, through the tunnel on Bray Head to Greystones. It never started. A cleaner with a brush started his work, and the truth dawned on me — I was stuck in Bray.

Now what was supposed to happen was that all passengers going to Greystones got off at Bray, and a connecting bus took them the rest of the way. I suppose it was more economical or convenient. Which was all very well and fine, but somebody forgot to tell the eight-year-old kid, who was not a regular on the trip, about the arrangement. I had no money, and it was starting to get dark. Being shy with strangers, I would never have dreamed of asking for help, or even of getting on a bus and explaining things to the conductor. There was only one thing for it — I would have to walk home.

On Sundays, the family used to go on various walks, up the hills of Wicklow or along the beach — and sometimes Bray Head.

This was our favourite. It was a cliff walk of about eight kilometres, and the path climbed high up the Head and got very narrow indeed over some impressive cliffs. Often the path had been eroded, and you had to climb over into fields to skirt around the fallen bit before rejoining the walkway further on. I must say it was tricky enough in broad daylight when walking in a group. Anyway, it was the only way that I could think of for walking home from Bray, and so I set out.

It's amazing how things are so logical to a child — and how shyness can affect things. The first part of the walk from Bray goes past the fun-fair area, where we used to go on the ghost train and dodgems, before leaving the town behind. Then it led up onto the Head proper, and the fork that leads either to the summit, with its wooden cross visible for miles around, or to the cliff walk around the headland to Greystones. By the greatest of good luck, as I walked past the fair-ground area, I met a friend from school, a guy called Richard Ross. Although he lived in Dublin, he was there with his Dad — obviously on some treat or other for the evening. I remember asking if he had any money. He said no, I said cheers — and that was the end of it. He never thought of asking *why* I needed money, or why I was walking towards Bray Head with my satchel on my back. I never dreamt of explaining my predicament to him, or finding his father and bursting into tears, or something sensible like that.

The same Richard Ross turned up on holiday in Johannesburg a year ago, the first time I'd seen him in many years. To this day neither of us can really believe that I didn't ask for help. Imagine my parents. It's now dark and starting to rain, and eight-year-old Johnnie is not home. Three o'clock, four o'clock, seven o'clock. The police are called. No one has seen the boy on the bus. Various neighbours are driving the road to Dublin. Finally, school friends are contacted: it's learnt that I took the train. More frantic activity, but no sign of me.

At about nine o'clock, pitch-dark and lashing with rain, my Dad is driving up Church Road in Greystones on one of his frantic search trips. Then he must have seen this small, soaking child wearily walking on the footpath — he stopped, and I got in.

He just looked at me and asked: 'Where were you?' I burst into tears, saying 'Where were *you?*' I had walked over Bray Head, along that sometimes tiny path in the rain and the wind — all because I was afraid to ask for help. It really is incredible, looking back, and the thought of it happening to one of my kids fills me with terror. But I now know that kids can sometimes have a really different picture of the world. Although I'm not particularly good with young children, I do understand them, I think — and much of this understanding was gained during my Bray Head adventure, and from thinking about it afterwards. Certainly, with kids, you can never take things for granted.

I was good at school work early on. The preparation mum had done at home, and our very good nursery school (run by a Miss Buckley, who lived next door) stood us in good stead. I came first in J1 (or Grade I), then second in J3 (Std 1), having skipped a class.

But then I sank rapidly in the ratings. I suppose I became complacent, and every waking minute had become dominated by sport — and all the sports took a poor second to rugby. The prize I chose after coming first in J1 was a book, *Rugby for Schoolboys* by Donald Ireland. (He taught at the same public school that my cousins went to in England.) I still have the book, and it is still one of the best books on coaching schoolboys that I have read. My Grandpa helped me choose it.

At school I had a hero, David Jones, who was a good rugby player. To me he was a god. I think I had my first pangs of an inferiority complex when, having got my rugby book at the prize-giving, I watched him (having come first in the class two years ahead of me) descend from the stage with a copy of the Holy Bible. I suppose this only cemented further the Sir Galahad picture I had of him. (Another coincidence: his parents were very friendly with my future wife Jennie's family. Recently I had the chance to tell him that he had been my hero, and that I had always admired him for choosing a Bible as his prize. I must confess that I felt a bit let down — for all my experience — when he told me that he had made his choice under some pressure from his mother. We had a good laugh about it, though.)

Schools rugby in Ireland is, I think, pretty unusual. Firstly, there are a large number of schools playing the game; secondly, most have been doing so for many, many years. The schools play each other from Under-11s in friendlies, and by and large it's all pretty small-time stuff. But at Under-15 this all changes.

This is the Junior Cup year: at the end of the season, starting just after Christmas, all the schools in each province are drawn in a knock-out competition. There is great rivalry, and the Cup matches are well supported by singing, cheering, partisan (but always polite) crowds.

However, even this is tame compared to the Senior Schools Cup, which is for the Under-18s — the First Fifteen of each school. This Cup has been on offer for over a hundred years (I believe it's the oldest rugby cup in the world; certainly it's the oldest school trophy). The passion involved here is incredible. Some of the great names in Irish and even world rugby have cut their teeth in this Cup; most share my view that nothing the senior game can offer ever compares with the thrill of playing and succeeding here.

What made it so incredible in Ireland is that most school friendlies are played before very small crowds — certainly different to South Africa, where each Saturday crowds numbering several thousand regularly watch schools rugby rather than clubs. And South African schoolboys play in curtain-raisers before provincial or Test matches — they're quite used to playing in front of big crowds, and at major venues.

In Ireland — having grown up watching the junior and senior sides play Cup matches each year, travelling to Donnybrook (the ground on the site of that famous old fair in Dublin), singing the songs and waving the banners — your whole rugby life is geared to getting selected for the side in your senior year.

In my case, though, it was an annual pilgrimage in the singular just about every year. After that one appearance in 1963 (which I watched with Grandpa), High School had fallen on bad times. We had good sides now and then, but the giants — Blackrock, Belvedere, Terenure College and the hard midland schools of Clongowes Wood and Newbridge — were bigger, stronger and had more range and depth than the leading Proddie schools.

Once we had a great team, when I was about fourteen. Phil Orr was at prop; together with our scrum-half and centre, he'd even been picked to play for the Leinster Schools side. For High School to get one player into this provincial side was unusual — three was unheard of.

Anyway, for the first time in many a year, our side had a chance. Then the draw came out — disaster. In the first round we were to meet the mighty Blackrock College. Now to all Irish rugby people, the very name is synonymous with schools rugby. In the ninety-odd years (at that stage) of the Schools Cup, they had won it over fifty times. The names of their heroes through the years sounded like a Who's Who of the game in Ireland: Ronnie Kavenagh, Niall Brophy, Johnnie Quirke (who got a full cap for Ireland at seventeen) and the great Fergus Slattery. These were the men of Rock — and their supporters were the most numerous, vocal and (let it be said) fair. They were almost unbeatable.

For High School, who had hoped to have a good run until they met Rock at a later stage, the draw was a disaster.

But it was a great game. High School led 5-3 until near the end, when Rock scored and so took it by a point. High School had never won the trophy, although they had contested the very first match of the competition almost a hundred years before. As we drove home, I remember thinking that if our side of that year couldn't win then we never would.

When I was at Under-11 and Under-12 level we had fair teams.

Usually the tactic was to get the ball to Peter Gault, our big number eight, and he would score. If that didn't work, give it to me and I would. That succeeded against the normal schools, but playing big names we usually lost: instead of two 'stars' they had about eight.

However, when I was thirteen a new boy arrived in school — a little dark-haired chap called Ian Burns. I had met him once before when he visited Greystones for the CSSM. From the first practice we knew he was special. Every time he got the ball he ran through everyone else and scored. I had been operating at fly-half, but after he came it was the Burns-Robbie half-back combination. I have absolutely no doubt that if Ian and I had not teamed up, it would have taken me much longer to get recognized and make it to the top, if ever. At junior level we won our cup match — great jubilation, as it was High School's first win in about ten years — but in the next round we lost 16-3 to Castle-

17

knock College, one of the big boys.

In the next two years a number of things happened. At this stage I was a rugby fanatic. I don't think that an hour in the day went by when my mind didn't settle on a rugby day-dream. I watched all the games, collected programmes and even wrote all over the world for others. Alex Kellerman, the recently retired secretary of the South African Rugby Board, and I still laugh about the letter he once received from a young Irish schoolboy. It was addressed 'Mr Kellerman, SARB, Somewhere in South Africa'. I will never forget the excitement when I got a big bundle of programmes from Tests, trials and interprovincial games in South Africa in reply, with a lovely hand-written note. Of course, to those who know Alex that would be par for the course, and he remains a friend and a thorough gentleman. I devoured books as well, and although Grandpa had by now passed away, his grounding in the basics coupled with my love for him had made me a walking rugby brain.

Luckily there were a few at school who felt as I did, and this was to bind us together in our senior year. We were also lucky that we had two outstanding rugby masters: Derek Cole, a shrewd forward coach, and Jack Cornish, one of the old-style teachers who believed in discipline and sportsmanship, took the backs.

Jack, in particular, had a great influence on me. He loved the passing, running game, but above all he was steeped in the tradition and spirit of rugby. If you didn't know how to lose there was no point in playing.

Ian Burns and I both made the senior side as sixteen-year-olds.

We had a good year, reaching the semifinals of the Cup. For High School (and, I suspect, all the other less fashionable rugby schools) this was a marvellous achievement, and we had all the neutrals on our side when we played Belvedere College, the holders, at Lansdowne Road. We scored early, but in the end lost to a late try and went out 8-4. (At fly-half for Belvo was a certain Oliver Campbell. He was to play a big part in my rugby. They also had Frank Quinn at scrum-half and Ray Finn in the centre — I later played in Irish teams with both.)

I find it hard to describe what losing that game meant to me. My whole world collapsed. Half the team were in tears in the dressing-room. Had the scene been witnessed by 'educationalists' who are against competitive sport for schools, on the grounds that it places too much pressure on youngsters, well, they would have had a field day. That night I stayed in town, got horribly drunk for almost the first time in my life, and achieved a certain notoriety in school for being violently sick in the front of one of the guy's cars while we were stopped at a traffic light.

At that stage in my life I was a non-smoker (I still am), and, apart from a few teenage experiments with alcohol, a non-drinker. Most of the guys who lived in town were far more advanced. They used to go to dances, ride motor-bikes, drink in pubs and chase girls. I must say that I was very shy with girls; I was much happier talking rugby with the boys.

And for quite a while, at this stage of my life, I was heavily involved with religion. The CSSM had always played a great part, and at one stage I even contemplated a career or vocation in the church. I suppose, looking back, there was little chance of the Reverend Robbie ever making an appearance. But the experience was good for me, I think, and — although it's far less formalized now — I do have a belief, and in truth could not contemplate life without one. The thought that this life is it, with nothing to follow, would be enough to send me scurrying for the caffeine pills in an attempt to stave off sleep and avoid wasting a few hours of precious living time.

Alongside my religious feelings, I was also a young sportsman involved in rugby, in an environment where there was tremendous publicity around the cup competitions; and I lived in a very exciting summer holiday town. The combination meant that in many ways I was a bit of an oddball. Perhaps it's just hindsight, perhaps it applies to everyone, but I feel I missed out on a lot of the fun of growing up. My conversation was limited in the extreme: it was sport, sport and more sport. My reading had just about gone the same way, and there was only one thing in life I wanted to do: play rugby for Ireland. I knew the contents of my programme collection off by heart.

I used to have conversations with myself and God. He would offer me one cap for Ireland — guaranteed — or I would chance making it on my own, risking my skills and luck with injury. It was childish stuff, but I decided that I wanted to make it on my own — and then go on to many more than the one cap that my imagined God was offering.

My brother Dave and I were on good terms at this stage. For a long time we had not seen eye to eye — silly, but at one stage, following a hell of a row when I was about fourteen, we hadn't spoken for about six months. Can you imagine it? Living in the same house, attending the same school, having the same surname. I think it nearly gave Mum a nervous breakdown. In the end it all came right, and Dave and I have been very close. (When I go to Ireland now, the first thing I do is schedule at least one day with him to compare notes on the world.) Anyway,

Dave has told me that there was a time in my life when I couldn't watch TV without commenting that certain people would make good rugby players. For example, if we were watching a cricket match, I would comment that Tony Greig would have been a great number eight, with his height at the end of the line-out. This was the sort of stuff I came out with all the time, and it must have been very boring.

At school, I remained quite good at work — by which I mean that I passed most exams. I was very good at cramming. I think the terror of failure sharpened all my senses. I could study acres of notes the night before an exam and know them almost perfectly. And I actually enjoyed doing the papers: the weeks leading up to exams were awful, but when I got into the hall it was just like a game. (At university all the swots used to hate me, because with no work I always managed to do quite well, while many of them — having haunted the libraries all year — battled to get results. I would have battled to *find* the library!)

Because I was always young for my class, I did the leaving certificate (the Irish equivalent of Matric or A Levels) when I was sixteen. I got three honours, enough for university entrance, but everyone agreed that I was too young. So I returned for an Upper Sixth year. We had a Common Room to ourselves, plenty of spare time, and even a couple of girls who had joined from other schools to keep us company. And, of course, we had rugby. After the near-miss of the year before, all the key players realized that we could achieve a dream that for most of our schooldays had seemed impossible — winning the Cup.

We went through the first half of the season almost unbeaten, with wins against the mighty Blackrock (for the first time in living memory, I might add), Terenure College and Belvedere. We lost, though, to Mary's College who were unbeaten. They were situated close to us, and that year were undoubtedly the favourites. They had Rodney O'Donnell at full-back and Tony Ward at fly-half. I went on to become a British and Irish Lion with both of those guys; at school they were match-winners.

It's funny looking back at the schools game. I get sick of listening to people both in Ireland and South Africa extolling the virtues of schools rugby and condemning the senior game: 'Why can't they run the ball like the schoolboys? Why do the senior players kick so much? How come so-and-so doesn't make breaks like he did at school?'

Of course when we were at school we loved this type of talk. What we didn't appreciate then was that the excitement of the school game and the purity of it is due, in large part, to the naivete of it. Old lags know the great mental steps that have to be made in the transition to the senior game, where homework is done, angles are covered and it's generally much tougher.

There's no doubt that I was a good player. I also had the real hunger, the fanatical desire to succeed. But I was also lucky to come under the influence of the best rugby coach I have ever met — Oliver Bourke. He was a medical doctor in Dublin, and a single man in those days (though now he seems to be attempting to produce a hockey team of girls all of his own). He played for Trinity in his youth as a big, thick, unfit donkey (forward) — at least, that's what my spies tell me — and he was overshadowed as a player by his brother, the late Aubrey Bourke.

Then came the coaching revolution in Europe, and Ireland's contribution was the superb annual course for schoolboys, club players and coaches. It was held in late summer at the Butlin's Holiday Camp north of Dublin. With intense coaching, hundreds of players and the various temptations of Butlin's, it was an experience never to be forgotten. In the end, I think, it got totally out of hand, and for a few years now smaller courses have been held at different venues. But for many players now in their thirties, Butlin's was the watershed. Many a boy became a man, in many ways, during those weeks.

Despite all the shenanigans in the evenings, the coaching was always excellent. Carwyn James, Chalky White, John Burgess and many other greats attended, and I loved every minute of it. However, at my first course, the schoolboy co-ordinator was a certain Ollie Bourke, and he really needled me. I was good, and I suppose I knew it — but hard as I tried, I could get no praise or encouragement from him. The final ignominy was in the match, the climax of the week, when we all had a chance to show what we'd learned. I was substituted at half-time. I was very cross and not a little hurt. So I dismissed the man from my mind and loudly described him as an idiot.

A few months later, our school played against Clongowes Wood, a strong country side from west of Dublin. It was our big trip of the year (my first year on the senior side, when I was sixteen). Who should be at the game but one Oliver Bourke — he was their school doctor and also the coach.

Anyway, I had a blinder. I think I was trying to prove something to him, and we had a good win. After the match he came over, said 'Well done' and then proceeded to pick my game apart. He highlighted areas and options that I hadn't thought of, and mentioned parts of my game that needed special work. All this, I might add, was uninvited, and I

21

was totally bewildered. I didn't say much, but on the bus home I had a good think.

What he had said made sense — and I must confess I was shattered. Here was John Robbie, the world's greatest rugby brain and the next Gareth Edwards, suddenly realizing that he fell far short of the required standard. Gloom, doom and despondency followed for a few days. Then, one evening at about six, the phone rang. It was Bourke with comments, once again uninvited — but the approach was different.

He listed a number of really good things I had done. He pointed out real strengths and also potential strengths; and he ended by suggesting that, from time to time, he might make a few suggestions to me about the game. He told me he was doing this with a few players, in an attempt to raise the standard of schools rugby. He finished by saying he had selected players whom he thought had the ability to go to the top.

The call must have lasted an hour; at the end of it I was a disciple. Looking back, I realize that being involved with Ollie Bourke was a major factor in enabling me to achieve most of my rugby ambitions. Later our group used to meet occasionally to practise skills, moves and discuss the game, sometimes on a Sunday morning at eight o'clock and often in the height of summer — we lived for those informal sessions.

I was scrum-half, Ollie Campbell was fly-half, Tony Ward was in the centre with Ray Finn (a man who would have won many more Irish caps had he not concentrated on his career as a veterinary surgeon). Johnnie Fortune, a lanky sprinter who went on to play for Ireland B, was on one wing; Michael Hickey, who specialized later in Gaelic football, was the other wing; Rodney O'Donnell, another future Lion, was at full-back.

Had Ollie Bourke ever been persuaded to coach the Irish side — instead of his first love, Under-19 rugby — then Ireland would have enjoyed much more success. His big secret was that he made accurate assessments of players who had the raw talent, based on their desire to succeed and the willingness to learn. He then made sure they got regular coaching with lots of feedback. He had the right formula.

But back to school. In my second year on the senior side, Ian Burns was magnificent. While he never became a full Bourke disciple, he still had been influenced by Ollie; as a result we were hot. We had a very mobile pack of forwards. Ian and I at half-back were, thanks to Ollie, streets ahead in terms of tactical awareness. Our centres never missed a tackle; we had one flyer, a chap named John Reid, on the right wing. The rest was pure spirit and will to win.

It was a nervous day when the draw was made for the Cup. Unusually for football competitions, the whole draw was done at once — you could work out who you would have to meet in your half on the way to the final. It was amazing: almost all the big boys were in our half: Terenure College, Castleknock, St Mary's, Blackrock. To us it was a disaster.

It's strange looking back across fifteen years or more. I can remember just about every move in every game; I can almost taste the particular atmosphere of each tie. We beat Terenure 14-0 in a replay, three tries to nil, and we were on the road. We won well against Castleknock, and so we were through to the semifinals.

To anyone not Irish it must sound crazy to put so much emphasis on a schools competition that involved only four rounds, but believe me — to schools in Ireland, old boys and generations of parents, the whole thing has a rare importance and mystique. We were also the 'people's choice', being traditionally a loser school.

But we still had St Mary's at Lansdowne Road, and I never thought we would win. Well into the second half it was 6-6. Then a scrum about twenty-five metres out in front of the posts; a quick heel: next minute I was through and running at the corner. I can see the whole thing now, as clearly as it happened. Their left wing stayed out marking our right wing. I dummied the pass, and had just grounded the ball on the line when I was hit in a tackle by Rodney O'Donnell. The ref was John West (who went on to a brilliant international refereeing career); as he blew his whistle, I thought he had not given the try. I knew I had scored, and I screamed hysterically at him. He shouted back at me that he had given it. I felt so sheepish.

Then it hit home, and I was trotting back to the halfway line with our supporters going mad. To this day, I have never experienced anything to equal the pride of that jog back to my place to watch the kick. But it missed.

So with minutes to go, we were 10-9 up. Then we gave away a penalty on the halfway line — a long kick, but they had Rodney O'Donnell's big boot. Then, in a moment of emotion, our number eight Peter Gault cursed the ref — another ten yards. It was now a kick of about forty metres, straight in front.

You remember little things. I was on my knees behind the posts, almost in tears, praying aloud that O'Donnell would miss. (And I almost hit the touch judge, himself a senior club ref, because he was laughing at me.) The kick missed. We were in the final.

Some of the St Mary's boys were crying, lying on the floor in the

23

tunnel on the way to the old dressing-rooms at Landsdowne Road. My thoughts went back to the previous year when we had lost, and I felt sorry for them. It was the only game they had lost all year. Tony Ward still says the greatest disappointment of his rugby career was losing that match. He's not exaggerating. Such is the magic of the competition in Ireland that most players rank only an international cap as above a cup medal.

Well, the publicity was fantastic. Little Dublin High School was in the Schools Cup final against Belvedere, who had won it the previous two years. The newspapers made us underdogs, but everyone who really knew schools rugby tipped us to win. The papers also discovered that the surnames of High School half-backs made up the name of the famous Scottish poet: headlines such as 'Robbie/Burns — Poetry in Motion' started to appear. It was heady stuff indeed, and I suppose we all got a bit big-headed. But luckily we were all too aware of our appalling history of near-misses.

We beat Belvedere 19-7 in the final, on the Monday after St Patrick's Day. It was an easy game. Our pack was too good, I spent the afternoon chucking huge spin passes to Ian, and he did the rest: two brilliant tries and two drops. I kicked a corner penalty in the first minute and a conversion. It was over long before the end. At one stage in the game a scrum ball shot straight out the back. I ran to it, and as Ian ran left I gave a reverse pass to him. It was totally unrehearsed and it must have looked fantastic.

Anyway, the papers went mad. You would have thought that it was Robbie and Burns and no one else, which wasn't true. However, because the hacks in the papers had got it all wrong — we were outsiders, and because we were Prods — the whole thing was way overboard.

Why am I dwelling on it so much? Well, I believe that this event, more than anything else, cast the die for my life. Along with Ian, I experienced excessive publicity. We got written about by all sorts of journalists. Because I was going up to Trinity College, and because (with certain yieldings to temptation) I was avowedly a non-drinker, I was very much the clean-cut young academic with the Corinthian attitude to sport.

It was all nonsense. I was a very immature person, with a limiting fanaticism for rugby. I was very badly read, and uncomfortable in any company beyond sportsmen. I played cricket a bit, and with no real effort got a schoolboy cap against Wales. (I suppose I did try, but I must have been the worst spin bowler ever to have achieved such eminence. I got a few guys out on Irish wickets, but it wasn't until I went to South Africa — where wickets are like billiard tables — that I realized there was an art to making a ball turn.)

I finished school with a satisfactory leaving certificate and absolutely no idea of what to do. As Mum was very keen, and because it seemed the thing to do — and because I knew that, in Ireland, the universities breed successful players — I got admission to Trinity College, Dublin. I was to do natural science, although I had also applied for medicine. Today my grades wouldn't have got me an interview, but then it was still possible for an ordinary mortal to become a doctor.

I often wonder what would have happened if I had studied medicine. My fanaticism for rugby would probably have interfered. A guy I sat with all through school, whose grades were similar to mine, got in and did qualify. But he worked like hell and I know that I could never have matched that effort. (His name was Sebastian Delmote. Just after qualifying he dropped dead while doing voluntary work in Nepal. I was shocked at the waste of such a dedicated chap — but there you are, if your name is on the bullet, that's that.)

My name wasn't on a bullet, it was on a rugby ball. I passed time in the summer working on a fruit farm in Worcestershire with my best mate, Dermot Strong. We hitched to Worcester occasionally and watched cricket. I remember watching Mike Procter hitting a fabulous ton for Gloucester in a Gillette Cup semifinal. He was in a different league to the rest. Years later I dismissed him in a charity game in Johannesburg — but I suspect he wasn't trying as hard as he was that day in Worcester!

I came home early, trained and played pre-season rugby with the local Greystones club and prepared to become a university rugby player — oh yes, and a student as well.

3

Trinity is an unusual university. I've heard it described as the ultimate Irish joke: the foremost brains in Ireland set out to establish a collegiate university, based on Oxford and Cambridge — but they couldn't get beyond the first college, Trinity, because they couldn't count to two. Ho, flipping ho!

It's an ancient institution, right in the middle of the city. Surrounded by high green railings set on high grey walls, it's like an island amid the busiest streets in the country. When you enter, it is like going into a church; a timeless sort of world, where no one else exists except students and staff. Trinity is overcrowded nowadays, and anyone can walk through the place, but that atmosphere still prevails. It belonged to me for four mostly happy years.

I have no idea why I chose to read Natural Science, although a few of my mates were doing it and I had good marks in geology and biology. But what did I know, and what did I really care? I was a student: three or four years stretched ahead of me like Bilbo Baggins's road to the lonely mountain. And before the university term had even started, I was thrust right into rugby and right into the headlines.

To get fit I had played a number of games with the Greystones Under-19 side. They had good spirit and a very good coach, Mick Dunne. I did a lot of place-kicking practice for the first time in my life, and accuracy was there. One evening, out of the blue, I got a call from the Trinity senior captain, Dick Spring (he went on to play for Ireland, lead the Labour Party and become deputy Prime Minister in the coalition government of Garrett Fitzgerald).

Dick told me that his scrum-half was injured. Could I play for the first fifteen the following Saturday in Belfast?

So here I was, seventeen years of age and looking about fourteen, being asked to play a senior club match. I didn't know how to react. My parents were a bit worried, and Dad suggested I contact my old school teachers. Derek Cole, who had played senior rugby a few years earlier, said I should go for it and I did.

It meant a train journey to Belfast, which at that stage of my career was the equivalent of a Lions tour. I met the side on the Tuesday and trained with them. I couldn't get over how huge they were, and how old. Of course it was a typical student side, with most of the guys between nineteen and twenty-two — nowadays I would regard them as babies. Anyway, on the train I had to learn the line-out codes. This proved difficult. At school I called the signals, holding my hands on my knees, for the throw to the front; on my hips, for the back; or simply scratching my private parts, for the middle. (This last signal had been contrived to embarrass me, knowing that all the girls from the Proddie schools were at the games supporting us.)

Now it was different. But I settled down, we won a narrow victory over NIFC and I managed to kick seventeen points, including a long dropped goal. Mike Gibson (the legendary centre) did not play for them that match, much to my disappointment, but it really was a dream debut — and of course the press again made a meal of it. The train journey home was great fun, with all the Dublin sides who had travelled north that day occupying two carriages. Drinking, cards and singing were the order of the day, but in those days I sat quietly on my own sipping a Coke. I reckon all the guys thought I was a bit wet, and I suppose I was.

There was another seventeen-year-old in our side — he had no such inhibitions, and he got drunk with all the other guys and generally entered into all the fun. It sounds daft now, but I felt a bit sorry for him, succumbing to temptation so easily. Now I look back and feel sorry for *myself* — so many great nights with the lads, and I missed them by sitting quietly on my own. What is it they say? Youth is a great thing, it's just a pity it's wasted on the young.

The season was great for me. In the next match I scored nineteen points, including my first try. When the regular scrum-half returned after injury, I was kept on for my kicking and put on the right wing. I enjoyed that too, and got my colours in the annual match against University College, Dublin, where we won for the first time in years.

The Colours Match, as it is called, is really the Dublin version of England's varsity match between Oxford and Cambridge, and I can tell you it's even more keenly fought. In those days there was a lot of bad blood. Later, I was very proud that in my year as captain at Trinity we patched up a lot of differences and the players became more friendly. But in my early days a big punch-up in the first few minutes was almost compulsory.

When it happened in my first Colours Match, I ran in from the right wing and tried to get involved. I must have thought this was the thing to do in senior rugby; I waded in and grabbed the nearest blue arm that was involved in smacking a white jersey. The arm came away, attached to a lock called Kevin Mays, the largest rugby player in the country. Kevin is about six-foot-seven and — luckily for me — a real gentleman. He took one look at this teenager squaring up to him and started to laugh, very kindly; then he gently led me away from the fray.

We won, I kicked all the goals I could, and it was more of the hero stuff. But it was about this time that I began to realize that the sportwriters were not all rugby experts with an absolutely accurate eye for the game. Take the Colours Match. I played most of it on the other wing. I made a few tackles; covered well to make a catch in defence and ran a bit before passing to our right wing. I kicked four out of four goals, three of them in front of the posts; after John Boyd got injured I replaced him at scrum-half and passed about four balls to our fly-half. That was the sum total of my contribution to the game.

However, some of the writers made it out as something really special. I noticed that, when you are on the way up, you can do no wrong. After all the schoolboy heroics, Ian Burns and I were the two hottest properties in Irish rugby. I learnt that if I passed the ball, and ten passes later somebody happened to score a try, the papers would say I had 'initiated' a try-scoring move. If I made a few mistakes and threw a few bad passes, then I 'kept trying despite bad ball from the pack'.

Luckily I had Ollie Bourke close by. After every game he would phone and we'd go through it piece by piece. He was always totally objective, and he taught me to be my own harshest critic. To have a mentor like that was so fortunate: it stopped me believing all the overboard publicity. In fact, I may even have become far too critical of myself. After I had played well but not brilliantly, I would go into a depression for a day or two.

Mum realized this, and she always tried to get me back to reality — but it must have been hard. Of course, I was also growing up. I was a late developer; with my life depending on rugby, any setback affected everything.

Ollie Bourke was coaching the Leinster Under-19 side, the provincial team, and although I was a year younger than the rest I was made captain. We beat the London schoolboys on the eve of an England-Ireland game, and Ulster in Belfast.

The trip to England was really a laugh. For some reason we went on a Thursday, played on the Friday, saw the international and returned on the Sunday. This was a real tour! After thumping the English at the London Irish ground, we had only one instruction: don't get arrested. Well, although I was an outsider in most of the fun, the boys went to town. Rooms were wrecked, ice buckets were emptied over the side of the hotel onto the crowded streets of London, pints of stout were drained copiously. To cap it all, Ireland beat England in a spectacular high-scoring game.

After the game we went to Harlequins ground. Being just across the road from Twickenham, it was packed solid. There was a very officious uniformed guy on the door, and he only allowed people in on production of a club membership form. We were about to leave when Michael Hickey, our full-back, suddenly announced that we were personal guests of Bob Hiller (the former England full-back who played for the Quins). It was a real piece of cheek, and we got terribly worried when the guy informed us that Mr Hiller was actually present: so Mick was led in to verify the story. I thought we should make a run for it, but next minute Mick was back with Bob Hiller who loudly welcomed us and asked us where the hell we had been.

I never forgot that generosity. He'd sized up the situation in an instant, and with no explanation from Mick had taken control. So we spent a great evening partying at Harlequins. But I was totally shocked on the plane next day when I learned that two of our players had sneaked into the Harlequin dressing rooms and pinched a few jerseys. To me that just wasn't on — but I suppose that stealing jerseys is as old as the game itself. Anyway, it was a memorable weekend, and I found that international away games are about a hell of a lot more than just the rugby match. In those days I was interested in playing and then talking about it afterwards — boring little boy I must have been.

My first year in university was very strange. Academically I was OK: the first year of Natural Science offered a wide number of basic subjects, like chemistry, maths and geology. The classes were huge and I had plenty of friends from Dublin High School: I'm ashamed to say I did very little work. Of course I had no career at all in mind. I had convinced myself that I was a budding geologist, but my main aspirations were on the rugby field.

All of us High School boys were cocky. I suppose that we'd had a year as total heroes at school, and we sort of assumed we were above all the other students. We were loud, often caused a bit of rumpus in lectures, and generally acted pretty much as we pleased. Serious students must have considered us total idiots: to have infantile rugby players at the back playing the fool was annoying.

One class in particular was a real joke. It was compulsory to do a statistics course. The trouble was that the lecturer was only a statistic himself — a mouse of a man, a real boffin, and he had little interest in the students. He used to potter around the blackboard setting and solving obscure little problems, with one of those droning voices that invite mockery and sleep. For two hours a week we had to endure this. One day a particular student, right at the back of this huge amphitheatre, built and launched a paper aeroplane.

It was a magnificent effort. The design enabled it to float slowly downwards in ever decreasing circles until it came to a perfect landing on the lecturer's desk. There was silence for a moment; then everyone burst into spontaneous applause. The lecturer had no idea what had happened. Well, that was it. From then on each of his lectures was like one great manufacturing plant for aeroplanes. It would go on for two hours against a constant downpour of paper planes. At the end the floor was covered with them, and on the hour the poor lecturer would stop, pick up his bag and leave without a word. There were attempts to introduce water pistols, but nothing equalled the effect of that one plane.

But our little lecturer got his own back. At the end of the year he set the most savage exam paper in living memory. Although it was only a minor subject, the rules provided that a grade of less than thirty percent in statistics would mean failing the whole year.

The exam was on a Wednesday afternoon. I went in early to try and swot. A problem was that I had no notes whatsoever, and of course the text book was unfathomable.

Then something remarkable happened. I found I wasn't alone in the small lecture room where I'd decided to try to study. One of the swots was there. I'd never spoken to him. He came from the south of Ireland, right in the country, and I only recognized him because he always sat right in the front in lectures; being very tall, he was always a natural target for our aeroplanes.

Somehow we got chatting that Wednesday, and I blurted out that I was on panic stations. To my amazement, in one of the greatest acts of charity I have ever witnessed, let alone experienced, he proceeded to take me through about half a dozen of exercises that might come up in the exam. One thing that I have is a great instinct for self-preservation. My brain was in a state of acute awareness — mainly through fear. What he did made sense, and I managed to get four of the questions correct

30

and so pass the exam. Had I not met that guy I would have failed a whole university year. Instead I got through, with a real fright. From then on I always managed to do enough, followed by a final cramming binge, to get through. My grades steadily improved. In the end I graduated with an upper second Honours degree — and seeing that, in my subjects, only two first class honours were awarded in fifteen years, I reckoned that was all right.

Although rugby was the core of my life, I also discovered that right at the top of the Junior Common Room building lay a siren for weak undergraduate ships. This was the snooker room. It was a smoky, dark place, and it was love at first sight. One of the key men here was a chap from school who had gone to Trinity a year previously. He was, unusually, a Scot by the name of Billy Hunter. Despite fears that he would end up a criminal because he used to be involved in all the illegal school gambling behind the bicycle sheds, Billy had turned out OK. He was a good snooker player, and he seemed quite glad to take me under his wing. If I had a quid for every lecture I skipped because I was snookered behind the green ball, I'd be reasonably rich. And I reckon my rugby fitness was greatly helped by sprinting up the three or four flights of stairs about four times a day to get a table.

And that was my first year at university. Rugby was first and foremost by a mile; then it was snooker; and finally, just at the end of the year, a brief scare over exams. It seems mad, looking back. My parents made many sacrifices to get me to university, but this never even occurred to me. Having grown up with totally supportive parents, I just assumed that that was the way things were.

My brother Dave was a year ahead of me at Trinity, reading history and political science, and he was far more studious. But he didn't share my rather puritanical views on life, and I think he got a hell of a lot more fun out of university. It's funny how my rather confused principles centred mostly on *Thou Shalt Not* (drink, smoke and poke), rather than on *Thou Must* (behave and work harder). But I was still a mixed-up kid inside: it was only because of rugby that everyone assumed I was in control and was simply a highly disciplined young man.

Did I realize that I was different? I don't think so. You see, my whole life was rugby. Any worries about my career, the future or adulthood were always cast aside in preparation, physical and mental, for the next game.

After the first year at Trinity my mate Dermot Strong came up with the idea that we should try and work in the United States for the summer. Dermot was in the rival University College, studying for a B.Comm, but we were firm friends. He was great fun, a natural comedian and a bit of a rascal. But his parents were missionary doctors, which put him into an angelic box as far as parents and other authorities were concerned, and he could get away with murder. (He had returned from India for his final years of schooling, also lived in Greystones and went to High School. We became good mates.) I should explain that in Ireland one of the big attractions of a university education is the chance to use the long summer vacations to work — either to help with fees for the following year, or just to travel. Jobs in Ireland are hard to come by at the best of times, and most of the students go to the UK.

I had already worked on a fruit farm in Worcestershire, and would also spend two summers working at Smedleys canning factory in Cambridgeshire. It really was slave labour, but they had a tradition of Irish students, and they'd even appointed an Irish liaison officer to organize the tide of Paddies who arrived each summer. I believe that at one time they had used English students, but the place had been 'blacked' in an effort to cripple the company and force them to improve student conditions. Smedleys, no doubt a bit peeved by the British student action, responded by getting Irish students over. They also added salt to the British student wound by improving conditions. We worked an 80-hour week, starting by pushing brooms or sorting out leaves from a conveyor belt of peas, or some other soul-destroying task that no sane person other than a student would do.

I was on a broom when they asked for a volunteer to work at what was reckoned to be the worst job in the factory: operating the slide. This meant lifting heavy hooks onto an overhead rail, and then catching the huge metal baskets full of cans after a crane had lifted them from the pressure kettles. It was physical, hot, dirty and quite risky work, but to my mind much better than sitting next to a conveyor belt, so I volunteered. I also realized that to do that for a summer would be the equivalent of a weight-lifting course, and with a rugby season ahead that swung it. I was also paid more and allowed to wear black jeans and T-shirt provided, which was a lot better than the ridiculous baggy overalls and 'snood' caps that were standard and compulsory student attire. Some weeks I earned up to £130, which seemed like a fortune. Dave also worked there that summer; a couple of years after that, so did my younger brother Peter. I think the Robbie family had a lot to thank Smedleys for — and I hope vice versa, as we certainly canned a lot of peas and carrots and strawberries.

32

It's interesting how status symbols work, isn't it? To Irish students, your grades or subject of study were outweighed by where you worked during the summer — never mind the amount of money earned. The fact I had worked on the ovens gave me a higher place in the pecking order, but this fell well below building site work in London. Perhaps working on an oil rig in the North Sea has now taken over in status. But when I was at Trinity, to come back from London with a blue donkey-jacket, displaying that luminous yellow strip proudly proclaiming McAlpine or Wimpey or some other patron saint of Irish labour, was indeed a high prize. It set you above most of your mates for the coming year.

But even that paled into insignificance beside the most prized scalp of all. That was to arrive in college for the start of a new winter term with a 'guess where I've been' jacket. This was the term for a North American lumber jacket — it indicated that you had worked the summer in the United States. This was the ultimate adventure. You had to get a visa, and then travel to and hold down a job on the other side of the Atlantic — it guaranteed you royal status.

Why was it that we all wanted to set ourselves up as heroes of the working classes? After all, many of us were studying for the professions and would end up fairly wealthy. Even the most liberal arts degree meant that a future of manual labour would be out. I suppose it was a bit of a guilt complex. Perhaps we all felt a bit too privileged in our academic halls, while Irishmen had through the years been forced by famine, strife and unemployment to emigrate and do the jobs that no one else would stoop to. I think we wanted to show that we, too, could identify with this part of our heritage before gaily resuming our path to a totally different world.

Anyway, my mate Dermot had got it into his head that we were going to the States after our first year. A lot went into the arrangements, and as we had to start a long time before the summer, I was happy enough in my snooker and rugby world to let him do all the work.

Dermot is a remarkable guy when he puts his mind to something. With no rugby background, he set himself targets and actually made the Greystones Under-19 side that year. He went to study agriculture, but decided his future lay in business and changed to a B.Comm. He has since graduated, sailed through chartered accountancy, worked part-time as a disk jockey; and he's now married, very successful and living in Vancouver. Although we have lost touch a bit, I know that one day we'll meet, and — just as with all real friends — nothing will have changed.

To a man like this, getting to the States was not a problem. I should explain here that to get a temporary visa to work in the States is like getting somebody to say the rosary for you on the Shankhill Road. Every year the American government issued a limited number of student visas to Ireland, and of course there was always a mad rush to get them. I don't know how he fixed it, but we were on the list. The next step was getting a job. He managed to get a letter from his uncle, a rich Boston doctor, stating that he would back us in times of disaster. We were among the lucky hundred or so, and that summer we spent about two-and-a-half months working stateside, came back with our jackets and a lot of mixed memories.

The plan was that we would go to Boston, and try and get work while staying with Dermot's relations. We stayed a night in New York, and went for a walk downtown into all sorts of sleazy areas, with a couple of dollars 'mugger's money' in our pockets and thé rest in our shoes. This is how we thought the locals got about. We got a bus to Boston the next day. We were excited, but I can remember noting how very different New York was to the the image that is put over. A lot of poverty was evident, and much of it on racial grounds — that was revealing.

We were met by Dermot's relations, who were absolutely loaded. He was a top surgeon and they lived in an area called Newton Centre, about as affluent as could be imagined. We were very nicely welcomed and they helped us to find jobs — although this was a lot harder than we'd imagined. First of all, Boston is the student centre of America and it was very much first come, first served. For a few days we were not served at all.

Then we got in with a sort of labour agency that was frequented by people who were stoned out of their heads most of the day. Everyone seemed to smoke there, and when it was offered to us and we declined, the great joke was laughed at for weeks. Every time we arrived for work, all the 'heads' started to laugh all over again. We made quite a hit with our fellow workers.

But the people who ran the place seemed to realize that at last they had two reasonably keen youngsters on their books, and we got work almost straight away in a warehouse. While Dermot made boxes I had to fill pallets, using a little scooter to get around and also a fork-lift truck. A non-driver like me was in heaven. Most of the men who worked there, the full-time staff, were quite old; a number were of Irish descent, and we were adopted by them. They used to bring us food and always included us in anything going on. I corresponded with one of them for years.

Then we had a bit of a disaster. Dermot's relations kicked us out in the street. It was all very calamitous. They were nice, wealthy, ultra-conservative Americans, with two kids about our age and we got on well. It was weekend trips to Cape Cod to their beach house and we had fun. But the parents were absolutely terrified of freaks, as they called long-haired youngsters. The real fear was drugs, and I don't think a night went by without the conversation turning to their pet subject. We began to think that they were a bit paranoid.

At the time in Ireland, long hair was very much in. Although we were not particularly hairy by our standards, our hair was long in our hosts' eyes. And I suppose we outstayed our welcome. Both Dermot and I came from homes where the doors were always open; we always had people staying. Now I realize that visitors are like fish — they go off after a few days. And we were a bit cocky.

One night I returned after a late shift to find Dermot most upset, telling me we had to leave in the morning. At dinner he'd disagreed with his uncle, and words had followed and then an ultimatum.

Now we were in a bind. We were on the street with limited funds. We tossed a coin: I went to work while Dermot set about finding accommodation. We ended up in a sort of a doss-house for down-and-outs. When we moved into our room it was being fumigated; the best thing about it was the iron door. We laughed at this — until during our second night we were wakened by sounds of a huge row going on down the passage, followed by loud crashes and bangs. In the morning the police were there, and there was a lot of blood all over the passage.

We changed jobs a few days later and got work as carpeters at a high-quality place that manufactured stereo equipment. We had to make little trollies covered in lush carpeting. We lied our way into the job, saying we had previous experience. When the foreman saw I was battling to use a screwdriver he knew we were lying, but being of Irish descent he said that we could have a trial. We learnt quickly, and were known soon as the best workers in the factory. We needed money so badly that we were afraid to give anything less than our best and that was enough. We spent some happy days in that carpeter's shop.

One day we passed a security firm called Action Detective. Earlier I referred to the status symbols of vacation work, and the highest accolades of all were reserved for those who worked as security guards in the States. Dermot and I decided to go in for a laugh. Inside we met the fattest guy I have ever seen; he was festooned with guns, and we used to say that he resembled a Christmas tree. He was an Italian and very pleasant.

Dermot looked about seventeen in those days; with shorts on, which I had at the time, I could easily have passed for about fifteen. I can just imagine what this Rambo type must have been thinking when we turned up looking for work. But we had the visas and that proved we were over eighteen, so he took our details and gave us a 'Don't call us' message. At least we had tried.

A couple of days later we got a call from the guy saying that one of his men had got shot and that he needed guards for the weekend — urgently. We jumped at it and so achieved our dream. We had uniforms and night sticks, and of course took photos to prove it. We worked anywhere, any time, and even guarded a jewellery building one Saturday night. It was right in the middle of Boston's combat zone, which also houses the red light district.

At eighteen you do things that at a later stage you wouldn't dare take on for a fortune. Still, it was all good fun. Between jobs we took time off to travel up to the White Mountains in New Jersey. By coincidence we met a guy called David Woods, who had left High School a few years before us on a Rotary exchange to the States. He had stayed on, and was at Harvard. We dossed with him for a while, and even attended a few history tutorials where we were given the stage and asked questions on Ireland. I, of course, knew very little about the economics and politics, and they weren't interested in rugby. Luckily Dermot was there and we bluffed it well.

One of David's mates was an Australian Olympic swimmer. Because of this we were able to swim in the Harvard pool whenever we wanted. It was crazy: most Harvard students couldn't use it all day, and here we were treating it as our own, as well as attending history lectures, staying on campus and having a ball. We just acted as though we owned the place. I've used this tactic many times since and, you know, it always works.

After that it was back to New York and back home to Ireland, resplendent in our 'guess where I've been jackets' and full of tales, suitably embellished, of what working men's lives consisted of in the States.

4

My second year at Trinity was relatively quiet. By now the massive first-year classes had shrunk to manageable proportions; in second year there were fewer subjects, but each was studied in far greater depth. I had dropped chemistry, maths, biology and the dreaded statistics. My choices were now geography and geology. Funnily enough, I became good friends with one of the senior geography lecturers, Dr James Killen, and as a result was keen to take his course. Believe it or not, it was statistical applications, and because he was a brilliant lecturer with a genuine desire to help his students in every way, I actually passed the year with an honours grade.

It brought home just how important the role of the teacher is. So many people have possible careers cut off for ever because of one bad teacher during an important year. I think of maths in particular: a good teacher can bring the subject down to the understanding of almost every pupil. At school I achieved an honours grade in higher chemistry, solely because of an excellent teacher. Jennie and I are determined that we shall take a real interest in the progress of our children, making sure that at every stage they have a teacher willing to battle with them.

I had a relatively quiet rugby season. The senior scrum-half from the previous year was elected captain of the university; as they had an excellent kicker, I played for and captained the second fifteen. I was only eighteen, but thanks to the grounding I had received from Ollie Bourke I made a good job of it. We only lost once in the dozen or so games in which I was skipper, and the side contained many very useful youngsters.

My style of captaincy was totally authoritarian, because I knew that I had more knowledge of the game than anyone else and I was totally committed. I know that sounds arrogant, but I don't think this was the case. All the players, I'm sure, regarded me as a bit odd. But I was friendly, always critical — even over-critical — of my own game, and so wrapped up in rugby that somehow they accepted it. I also captained the Leinster Under-19 side again under Ollie Bourke. Despite losing to Connaught, traditionally the weakest province in the country, we had huge wins against Ulster and also Llanelli Youth, the Welsh champions.

Of all the sides I have played for, this one played the best rugby of all. It was due to Ollie's coaching and a really good spirit. I learnt the importance of basic rules in rugby, with each player having the right to make overriding decisions and the rest of the side then backing him to the hilt.

We had great fun as well: in typical Irish fashion, the side had many characters. One of them was a genuine skinhead, which in those days of flowing locks made him really stick out. He was as rough as hell, but played his heart out every time. His name was John Nolan, and after that year I only saw him once again. It was in my first international, in the first few minutes when the sheer occasion, crowd and noise were still overpowering me. At the first line-out of the game, my eyes looked for a minute at the packed terrace and I saw the face of John. Our eyes met — at least a 1000-1 chance — and he gave me a huge thumbs-up.

Years after I heard that John had died in a road accident, not long after I saw him that day. I hardly knew the guy, but such is the camaraderie of all rugby sides that I confess I shed a quiet tear.

I was a very emotional person in those days. I think I still am, but Jennie says I'm not. I don't cry at funerals, and I really don't make a meal of goodbyes. I get cross easily, but it's only out of frustration. But in those far-off Trinity days, when I suppose I was going through a sort of delayed adolescence, I could be very emotional indeed.

Round about that time there was a big scandal in Greystones. An old lady was murdered: in those days that sort of thing was absolutely unheard of in our lives. It turned out that a mental patient had done it. However, the old lady's grand-nephew was a friend of mine, not close but a guy I had grown up with. To cut a long story short, a guy in Trinity, somewhere along the line, had got it wrong: he told me that my mate had been arrested. In fact he had been questioned, but only as part of the investigative routine; but in typical Irish gossip fashion, it got out that my mate was guilty. I was shattered, and worked myself into a hell of a state. We had a vital match that afternoon, and I actually broke down before it — although I somehow played the game, and played well.

I look back now and cannot believe that I played. At that moment I thought that a friend of mine was a murderer, and yet I could still put it all behind me for rugby. It just shows the effect rugby had on me: it wasn't a game, but a disease.

Thanks to my academic mentor at this stage, my grades improved and I passed the year. I went to work in England at the canning factory in Wisbech with brother Dave. It was the first time in my life that I had earned real money.

One little incident that I remember was quite enlightening. It was in the canteen. As usual I was sitting on the fringes of quite a big group of students. One of them was holding forth about rugby and the Irish side; naturally I listened with interest, and was really embarrassed when he turned to me and predicted loudly that I would get an Irish cap the next year. I told him not to be so stupid, but he insisted that it would happen and he even revealed that he had a sizeable bet on it.

Now I always had dreamed that I would make it. I suppose, as a believer to a degree in predestination (at odds, I suppose, with my rather backtracking Christian beliefs at that stage), I was confident about it. But that was the first time anyone had actually expressed the view that the great day wasn't far away. I didn't agree — I thought about five years would be the time — but the remarks remained in my memory. As it turned out, he won his bet.

To my total surprise I was elected captain of the Dublin University Football Club for the next season. I had been asked to stand, and I did so with no real confidence or ambition — and was staggered when I won quite easily. At nineteen I was the youngest captain in the history of the second oldest rugby club in the world. After the shock wore off, I decided that I would give it a real go. The previous year's captaincy experience had given confidence. I also knew that I was a very good judge of a player, in terms of ability and character. All along the ups and downs of my career, I have learnt to trust my instincts in this regard, and I have rarely been wrong.

I think the same applies to most walks of life. If you have a real love of something, and if you have the basic knowledge, then your gut feeling about a decision will usually be correct. Well, I was a walking rugby encyclopaedia at that stage.

At Trinity, the university club is run by the captain, with the help of his elected secretary and a committee consisting of players and old boys. I was very lucky to have a good secretary, steeped in the club's tradition, so I could concentrate almost entirely on the playing side. There we were lucky as well: our coach was Roly Meates, who had also just been named as Irish coach of the season. Technically he was the best in the business, but he needed a strong skipper with him — in those days, I provided that. To say that I was a tartar is incorrect, but I had such commitment and such a belief in my own ideas that it must have seemed like that to many.

Anyway, the methods worked, and we had the most successful year the club had known since the heady days of the 1920s. We won the Colours Match, beat all the Irish universities to win the championship, and defeated Oxford, Cambridge and the visiting Sydney University side. We lost only a handful of games, and we won the club knockout Cup for only the second time since 1926. It was a fantastic year, and when I tell you that in the replay of our drawn final we beat a Blackrock club side that included Fergus Slattery, Willie Duggan, Ray McLoughlin and Ned Byrne, all seasoned internationals or future caps, then I think you'll appreciate the achievement. We also had great players, though, and a number — then all bona fide students — went on to great things. Mike Gibson (the number eight), Mick Fitzpatrick, Donal Spring and I all played for Ireland.

However, by the time that final was played, I had already been capped. How that happened is out of the realms of dream and fantasy.

Thanks to our great success during the year, after years of struggle, I was again the darling of the press. 'The shy, clean-cut, academic little general' — this was the sort of garbage that was being churned out but, with the exception of 'academic', I suppose that's the way it was. There's no doubt that I played my slightly unusual reputation to the hilt. In true Irish fashion, it was rousing team talks and heavy motivational stuff all round (and my dramatic training from Mum came in handy). I was also playing well, behind a very good pack, and as a result was picked on the bench for the senior Leinster provincial side.

Johnnie Moloney was the scrum-half. Only two years earlier he had been on the victorious 1974 Lions side in South Africa, as deputy to Gareth Edwards, so I was happy just to be there. But Leinster did badly, and for the last interprovincial wholesale changes were made. Johnnie Moloney and Mick Quinn were dropped, and at half-back were named John Robbie and a certain Ollie Campbell. I was absolutely terrified, but things went well. We won a good victory against Ulster; I threw out huge passes (with quite a few that missed Ollie), and a few lucky bounces made my speculative kicks look good. Ollie was brilliant: he never missed a kick, and with that outrageous dummy of his scored a clever try near the end. But the papers gave me equal billing and I had moved up a rung on the ladder.

40   I particularly remember the comments which appeared the following

Monday in the evening press, in the Con Houlihan column. This is one of the most entertaining sports columns that I've encountered anywhere, and the writer is one of those unkempt geniuses that one occasionally meets in Ireland. He wrote about the game under the heading of 'Robbie's Edwardian performance' — a favourable comparison with Gareth Edwards. The article is still a source of great pride.

Later on, though, the same Con Houlihan seemed to take a dislike to me and I never again got such a write-up. It was nice while it lasted.

Ireland were to play the Aussies in January 1976, and I looked forward to watching the game. The trial teams were announced, with a scrum-half for each side and two others in the pool of reserves. I was not one of them, and not at all worried or surprised. After the trial, a squad of thirty would be picked to train the next day; then, after dinner, the selectors would go back in and pick the fifteen to play the Aussies.

I went to the trial, paid my money and watched the senior side play well. Ollie was outstanding and Robbie McGrath played well at scrum-half, I thought, scoring a late try. For me, that was that. On the way home we all picked our teams, and McGrath was scrum-half in all of them.

After tea at home, the phone rang. It was Roly Meates, in his capacity as Irish coach; in a curious arrangement, he sat in at selection meetings but had no vote. He told me not to ask any questions, but just to turn up at the squad practice the next day. He wouldn't tell me any more, rang off, and I was left to wonder. I had just begun to think that, in a rush of blood, they might have picked me as reserve, when the squad was announced on TV. Four scrum-halves were named and I wasn't among them. Robbie McGrath, Johnnie Moloney, Donal Caniffe and Willie Oakes were the guys to turn up the next day; I then realized that one of them probably had a minor injury, and they wanted me to cover for him.

I was very happy; in fact, I was elated. I'd be training with the big boys, and maybe I'd even get a tracksuit. No, that would be out of the question. I went down to the pub with my friends to have an orange juice and wait for Match of the Day (soccer) on the telly. The 'local', the Burnaby, is only two hundred metres from home and we walked down. As soon as we settled in, a phone message came: I had to go home immediately. I got home, and Mum and Dad told me that Roly had rung, and would ring again in ten minutes.

I guessed that they had changed their minds, and that Roly wanted to break it to me gently that my services at the squad session would no longer be required. Roly rang again: I was not to say a word to anyone, to pretend that I knew nothing when the next call came, and never to say that he had called. I asked him what the hell was going on, and then he told me I had been picked to play scrum-half for Ireland against Australia.

I was totally dumbstruck. Roly rang off. I told my parents, who could hardly believe it. Then the phone started. The first call was from Ned van Esbeck, the *Irish Times* correspondent and very much the senior rugby writer. Although Ned and I have had our differences over the years, in those days we had a good relationship: in fact, the guys used to joke that he was my uncle, because of a number of good write-ups he had given me. Anyway, he told me of my selection.

Then I realized that Roly had actually jumped the gun. I'm sure he did it out of friendship and excitement, and to cover for him, in case he really had overstepped the mark, I gave the greatest performance of my life. I think to this day Ned van Esbeck thinks that he broke the news of my first cap to me. But his call at least convinced me that it was not just a dream..

I was a couple of months past my twentieth birthday, I looked about seventeen, shaved twice a week if I was lucky, was still very scared playing against good club teams. And here I was, selected out of the blue for my country and fulfilling my life's ambition.

The fuss was incredible. For two days I sat by the phone taking calls. The letter box was full every day. The papers were full of it, and my life was no longer my own. Funnily enough, it was Dad who, amidst all the excitement, seemed to be the only one who spared a thought for Robbie McGrath — the man who must have felt he was in for his first cap. Dad even met him at a dinner a few days later, where the master of ceremonies, on learning that John Robbie's dad was there, made a real meal of it — until he realized that Robbie McGrath was also present.

The really crazy thing is that I also had a feeling of deep disappointment. I couldn't get rid of it. The reason was that all this had not happened to plan. My dreams had always had me sitting on the fringes; fighting for recognition; and finally getting the call at the height of my playing prowess. In fact, it had all come too easily.

Ireland lost by running out of steam to the tour-hardened Aussies. Ollie Campbell was excellent but, amazingly, he missed a number of kicks. Finally the skipper, centre Mike Gibson, gave the ball to me and said have a go. I kicked a good goal, and one more easy one. I had a tidy game and looked confident (or so I reckoned when I watched the video later). I was too shy to go to the big dance afterwards, having no girlfriend, and so I went out for a quiet meal with Ollie Bourke and Ollie Campbell.

The next day Ireland were slated but generally I was praised — except for one writer who criticized me for something or other. This was significant: in all the years since junior rugby, it was the first word of criticism I had ever received in the papers. Again, I was to learn a painful lesson. I was now up to be knocked and soon the tide would turn — but not for a bit.

I did all right, there's no doubt about that, even though we lost to Australia, but looking back I know that the selection decision was wrong. I was not ready to play international rugby. I think you have to be outstanding and confident, at the level below international, even to be considered. But I had played one competent interprovincial and that was it. I still don't know what happened: they picked the squad without me, then included me in the side itself, leap-frogging me over four experienced, good scrum-halves. I still cannot believe it. Perhaps they had good wine at dinner.

I kept my place for the French game in Paris, where we were annihilated 26-3. I got another penalty, but I think it was the best game I played in a green jersey. I tackled as never before, and came off, although disappointed, feeling great. But the papers were very muted, and I was dropped for the game with Wales. I was phoned by the chairman of selectors and told that they were worried about the Irish pack; against the Welsh forwards, he said, they were afraid for my safety. It was the most gentle down-to-earth bump in the history of the game. Just as I had felt a strange disappointment, along with all the euphoria, at being picked, I now had a feeling of relief at being dropped: the pressure was off. And no matter what happened now, I had my cap.

I suddenly started playing really well for Trinity, and led them to all the success imaginable. Then at the end of the season a touring party was picked to go on Ireland's first-ever tour to New Zealand. At scrum-half, there it was, JC Robbie — I was back.

The whole episode of my first cap was really like a dream. The two weeks from selection until the game were filled with nerves. I trained like hell, and I remember that two days before the game I got the worst migraine headache I have ever had — I must have been suffering real stress. After the Aussie game, I played for Trinity against Sydney University, on a really mucky day. We won, but only just, and I can remember nearly hitting a friend of mine after the game at the party.

Now I didn't drink, or very rarely in those days, so it wasn't booze, and in fact I have never hit anyone in anger in my adult life. So why did I nearly do it? Billy Stickland was and is a good mate of mine, and at the dinner he made some reference to the way the press treated me. I don't remember the details, but I saw red and nearly took a swing at him. I don't think he even noticed — but big Mike Gibson did. Mike took me home to his family's house that night, where his mum gave us a meal and I slept well.

It must have been a sort of delayed reaction to realizing that, at twenty, I had achieved my only ambition — and there was nothing to replace it. This all happened a week after the Aussie game, and after all the excitement had died down, I couldn't handle the emptiness that was left. A minor incident, perhaps, but I think it shows what a hold the game had on me. Perhaps the realization that there must be something more to life was just beginning to nag at my subconscious. Of course, during the season, it never nagged for long, because there was always next week's game to occupy my mind. Although I was very young in those days, that attitude has stayed with me. Whenever there has been any doubt at all about my career, emigration, choice of where to live — in fact, almost anything — I have always been able to put the doubt behind me either until the next season, or even until the next big game.

It's only now that I have retired, when I can describe myself as having a 'great rugby future behind me', that the decisions that have to be made assume their real importance. Maybe there will always be some other substitute that will enable me to say, 'I'll really get down to it after so-and-so.' Perhaps that is just the way I am made.

It's funny. I had always had total contempt for people who believe in astrology. All the guff about star signs being significant always left me cold. In fact, I had a standard dinner-party joke that, whenever anyone asked me my sign, I would reply that I was 'Pyrex' — explaining that I was a test-tube baby. But just recently I heard on the radio a discussion about my star sign, which is Scorpio. It was quite uncanny: the Scorpion keeps adopting some project or other, follows it fanatically before realizing that it doesn't quite fulfill him, then moves to another, masters it and then moves on again. I have a feeling that this is indeed how I am built. Rugby has been everything, I was a disciple and did well at it; but now I've realized that there is more. Rugby hasn't fulfilled me, much as I still like it; now I'm searching for something else to get stuck into. (I hope it will result in making loads of cash — somehow I doubt it.)

The Irish tour to New Zealand was a marvellous experience. I was the youngest in the party and looked it. On one boat trip during the tour, around the Bay of Islands in North Auckland, some New Zealander glanced at me and remarked in all seriousness that it was nice of the New Zealand rugby union to allow the Irish manager to bring his son along on tour.

Of course, after a bad domestic season, the press had written us off. One Irish writer suggested that the Irish team should go, not to New Zealand, but to Galway, as that would be the only way that we might win a match. Remarks like that stung the team; under Tom Grace's inspiring captaincy, we did much better than anyone imagined. In the provincial games we were only wallopped once, by the mighty Canterbury side; in the Test match in Wellington, we missed a number of kicks and still only lost 11-3 — not too bad at all!

It's interesting to look at the tour because in many ways I again got caught up, especially at the beginning, in the whole image thing. In the first match we played South Canterbury, the strongest of the second division sides, and they were motivated as hell. But we scored good tries and beat them easily. Somewhere in the first half they took a drop-out, the ball was palmed badly to me and I had to spring forward to control it. Without knowing it, and fuelled by 93-octane fear, I shot straight through their pack. I side-stepped a defender, threw a couple of dummies, looked desperately for a green jersey and finally managed to pick up Willie Duggan, galloping on my left in support. I passed, he caught, and it was a try. That, with no false modesty, is as I remember the play.

However, on trotting back, centre Mike Gibson (one of my heroes) came over and said: 'John, that was magic.' It was the greatest praise I had ever received. That night I watched the try on the news, and I couldn't believe how fantastic it looked. It seemed I had spotted a gap, consciously exploded through it, done a bit on the ball to suck in the defence, and put Willie in for the try. It was voted *Try of the Month* and of course now, even in New Zealand, I was the next superstar. This lasted for about half the tour, then things settled down. I suppose a realistic appraisal would have said, 'promising, but a lot to learn'.

For a rugby player, touring is the greatest thing there is — and for a long time South African players have missed out. Okay, they have the advantage that their domestic rugby is played at an intensity that is frightening, with enormous publicity and with facilities that the average

45

provincial player in Europe can only guess at. But most of them have missed out on the best fun of all.

On that tour I was very naive, meaning that I was only interested in the rugby side of things. I looked forward to training, which under Roly Meates meant a lot of hard running. The big donkeys dreaded it, but I enjoyed getting to a level of fitness that in an amateur sport can only be achieved on a tour. Of course I was scared stiff during the matches, but I suppose I was not alone. We expected all New Zealand sides to be on a level with Five Nations teams, and the fact that some of them weren't was a pleasant surprise.

Tom Grace, Gibson, Stewart McKinney and the late Shay Deering were fantastic — these guys were like fathers, and they seemed to exude so much confidence that I thought perhaps it was just my tender years that had me so scared. Before the first game, I arrived back in the changing rooms, having visited the lavatory for the umpteenth time, when Tom asked me if I was all right. I said I was scared stiff. As we walked out into the tunnel, he turned to me and confessed that he felt the same. For a moment I wanted to run back inside: realizing that we were all in the same boat almost put me over the edge. But learning that a senior player was shit-scared was important; in later years, I always tried to give the impression that everything was OK, just in case any of the youngsters felt as I did.

There is no doubt I was lucky to be on tour with those senior men. Years later, I read a article on cricket by Brian Close. He wrote about the misery of his first tour with England: he was eighteen, and got absolutely no help or encouragement from anyone. To cap it all, he was injured in one of the earlier games, but played in a Test and then broke down. He was made to feel like an outcast, and he confesses that at one time he contemplated suicide. I suppose I thought that such help was the norm — now I realize it was exceptional.

As I've said before, in all Irish sides emotional build-ups are very much the order of the day, and I could be as dramatic as the best of them. Once, during a team talk the night before the Colours match in my year of captaincy, I made a conscious effort to start weeping. It sounds so daft, but it worked beautifully. We were hot favourites, and I felt that a bit of over-confidence had set in. There was joking and messing about, and in those days I felt that was wrong. (Nowadays I would be the main comedian.) So, in keeping with my image as the guy who lived for rugby and rugby alone, I timed my entrance and immediately started with a real gut-wrenching speech. As I got to the part about how none of us would ever forgive ourselves if we lost, I started to cry. Well, the effect was electric: total concentration, and the atmosphere changed dramatically. It stayed that way, and the next day we beat UCD fairly easily.

I often used acting to my team's advantage. The next day, when I went to toss with the UCD captain, I had to walk past their dressing-room. They were in a huddle, arms linked, engaging in some heavy psyching up. I popped my head in, and in a very cheerful, matter-of-fact way wished them all a good game and lots of luck. I think it was a bit of a deflation for them.

New Zealand was very interesting. The people were most friendly, although all they wanted to talk about was the game itself. In those days that suited me fine. For most of the tour I turned in early, drank only milk and lived for the training. I took lots of photos, of course — mainly of the stadiums where we played. (I was fascinated by sports grounds, and during university lectures used to doodle all the time, designing magnificent 200 000-seater grounds where in my imagination I would play — brilliantly of course.) Later in the tour I started to relax a bit; some of the senior players tried to lead me astray, as I was in danger of getting stale. After the second game, the other scrum-half broke his leg in training, and I ended up playing most of the games.

As on all tours, there were funny incidents, high-jinks and the odd argument — and, I'm sure, lots of other activities from the over-18 section.

After the first game, it was such a relief to win that celebrations were long and hard. I stayed in the hotel, in the main street of Timaru, and watched TV with Mike Gibson (he was also fairly puritanical by nature). We must have seemed like an odd pair — the oldest player, about thirty-four and looking about forty, and me, who looked and acted about fifteen.

Anyway, fairly late, a car skidded and ploughed its way through the front window of the hotel. Inside was a very drunk local guy, a Maori. He was unhurt and seemed totally out of it. Of course, the press made hay — 'Irish team in dice with death', etc, etc. The next day one of the senior players told me that an Irish player had also been in the car, but had the presence of mind to get out and gap it down the street. Of course that part of it was hushed up — but I had to laugh when, about ten years later, I learnt that there were two Irish players in the car: the one I knew, and the senior player who had told me all about it.

On the way home we stopped in Fiji for a few days. This was good fun, although the Test was hard and played in difficult conditions. Luckily I was on the bench, and I remember being delighted when our two reserves had to go on and I could relax. I watched small green frogs scampering out of each muddy patch when a player landed in it; at the end there was a sort of slime on all the jerseys. It was a never-to-be-repeated sight.

We travelled throughout the island in an old bus with no windows. By now I had loosened up a bit, and had even got a bit drunk in Auckland. I had told the team about the current craze of 'lobbing moons' — pulling one's trousers down, bending over and displaying the bare backside to all and sundry. The trick was to choose the time and the place with the most care to get the greatest effect. The Fijian bus without windows was too much of a temptation, and so I lobbed a moon out at a village through which we were passing. The locals were totally amazed, and we all had a great laugh until I couldn't find my wallet. It looked like I had lobbed all my travellers cheques out the window. In the end we discovered that they had just fallen down the side of the seat — but it was a close call.

We returned home, not quite as heroes but certainly having done better than anyone had expected, and with the makings of a useful side. The management and coaching had been excellent — far better in New Zealand than it was a few years later on the Irish tour to South Africa, but perhaps others would disagree. Overall, I had done well. Despite having an unexciting sort of Test, except for one really great catch under fierce pressure near my own line, the verdict was that I was one of the successes.

I had mixed feelings, though. Sure, I had been part of the only Irish side to have played in New Zealand, and we held our own in nearly all the games. It was also a big thing amongst my friends at home just to have been a rugby tourist, and to invoke the 'no stories from the tour' rule — all done with a knowing wink, as though I had now joined the ranks of the men about town (nudge nudge, wink wink, and so on). However, there were a number of things worrying me.

I knew that I was not running enough as a scrum-half. I was certainly fit enough, and when I was pushed into situations where there was no alternative, then I usually performed well. It was taking a conscious decision to run, and then seeing the breakthrough, that was the problem.

In every break there is that split-second where you commit yourself, after which you can no longer pass or kick — the point of no return. It is also the point where you leave yourself open to being tackled hard,

48

often by someone you can't see. At this stage I would get away from the side of the scrum or ruck, and then — when I could have gone for the gap — I would angle in, draw the cover and give a pass to a man in support. Mind you, this was often the right thing to do; but there are times when a scrum-half (and indeed any back) has to evidence himself as a threat, make them tackle him, and I wasn't doing this. Looking back, I realize that I never really got over it. Sure, I learnt to conceal it well, and to recognize when there was a break on that did not involve that terrible second when the tackler makes his move. And by working with a good number eight, I made many good breaks where not a hand was laid on me.

It was the other kind of break I could never make, and the only conclusion is that I have always been scared. In fact, in those days I was often very scared on the field. Once, in our game against Canterbury, I displayed real cowardice. The very name 'Canterbury' meant dirty play to me. This was a result of the 1971 Lions tour to New Zealand, when there was a lot of thuggery. Although things had changed by 1976, I (being steeped in the game) had a subconscious terror of the province. Their pack was magnificent the day we played them. ,

At one stage, a few yards from our line, a scrappy ball was knocked back to me from a line-out. I had to make an instant decision: go forward, kill the ball and back into our pack; or stay back and hope it bounced to me. I chose the latter out of fear. One of their forwards came through, claimed the ball and his pack drove him over for a try.

After the game most people felt that it was in no way my fault: I had decided to wait for the bounce, and had been unlucky. I think I half-believed them. It was only later, when Mike Gibson and I were sharing a soft drink alone in the bar, that I really admitted the cowardice to myself. Quite matter-of-factly, Gibbo asked me if I had stayed back because I was scared. I lied to him, saying that it had been a calculated decision to wait for the bounce, and so on. He said nothing — but I think he knew.

I felt awful, like someone who has been caught stealing by his parents, or cheating by his favourite teacher. But I suppose it wasn't a crime. After all, I was only twenty, weighed about eleven stone and was playing against motivated provincial sides in New Zealand. If I was evaluating another player, I would have said 'Well done, a great tour'. But I had to evaluate myself; thanks to Ollie Bourke, that was one thing I never fooled myself about.

I suppose the motto 'To thine own self be true' is one that I have

49

always tried to live by — even if fooling others can almost become a way of life.

I returned home, didn't stop training (which was stupid), took my exams which Trinity had kindly let me write late, and looked forward to the new season. There was a Lions tour at the end of it, and I wanted a crack at that. Little did I know that when the Lions would be battling their way through an unsuccessful and difficult tour, I would be picking up the pieces of what seemed to be my shattered life.

5

My last year at Trinity went by quickly. I actually did quite a bit of work, and even got the rugby club to help me with my dissertation for my degree. It entailed some statistical work, with some sort of a survey; then the results would be analysed and the findings presented. In typical Robbie fashion, I managed to do mine with the least amount of work, as I had about thirty pairs of legs belonging to rugby colleagues. I got a good final degree, an upper second.

Despite all the success of the previous year, and attempts to get me to stand again for captain, I declined. I believed before I was in charge that a year was enough, and I stuck by that. On the day of my successor's election I got drunk. It was a long-standing ambition of my team to get me drunk, and at each stage in the Cup campaign, as I drank my orange juice, I told them that if we won the cup I would oblige.

So we had a celebration in the pavilion bar, and I joined in at last. It all went a bit far; at one stage I even threw the trophy, worth thousands and made of silver, at another guy across the room. He ducked — I think he was too jarred to catch it — and it hit the wall. The priceless Leinster club trophy was hammered back into shape in the next few days by a jeweller (a relative of one of our players), but to this day the small silver figurine on the lid, if you look closely, has only one foot. The other was lost in the soldering process when we desperately tried to repair it. I was reminded of it last year when a couple of Scots and English players were severely reprimanded for trying to play soccer with the Calcutta Cup. The secret is, boys, not to get caught.

The first international of the 1977 season was in Cardiff against Wales. In those days Wales were probably the best side in the world. Ireland, having built up a great spirit during the New Zealand tour, were then dealt a bad blow when the selectors picked five new caps. I was on the bench, Robbie McGrath deservedly got his first cap, and they had put in a few real youngsters. (Note the way I considered myself experienced — I was twenty-one!) After Willie Duggan and Welshman Geoff Wheel

51

were sent off, Wales got on top and won well.

Willie Duggan is a strange bloke. He was as hard as nails, and undoubtedly a key player for Ireland for nearly a decade. I had always got on very well with him, and after moving to South Africa was delighted to hear that he was to tour with an international side in 1983. After the game in Cape Town we had a discussion which turned into an argument and ended in a major row. It was silly drunken stuff, but I was most upset. I can't even remember what the original discussion was about. Luckily Willie and I met a year later when I was on a trip home and the incident was forgotten. Although he was a bit careless, I loved playing with Willie — he was one of the hardest players I ever encountered. He was in the opposition the day Trinity won the cup. Apparently in the final, near the end, one of his team-mates — a notorious thug — aimed a kick at one of our players. I didn't see it, but have been told that Willie informed his colleague that if he did that again, Willie would fill him in. It's a nice story, and I believe it.

England then won at Lansdowne Road in the mud, and I was recalled for the Scots game at Murrayfield. I was delighted — being left out was tough to bear. I also had started playing well again, and was very fit. We narrowly lost to the Scots, but I had a good game. I was told that I had outplayed Dougie Morgan, the Scottish scrum-half — although I didn't think so — and that I was in the running for a place on the Lions tour.

Gareth Edwards was unavailable for the tour, and we all knew that the Welsh understudy, Brynmor Williams, would get the nod as number one. That, it was reckoned, left Dougie Morgan and me. There was a month to go before the final game, against France in Dublin, and I trained like mad. Ireland had lost all three Five Nations games so far, and we were determined to give the French a good go, and to stop them winning the Grand Slam.

We started well, and I got two good passes away under pressure; I was feeling great. I then had a snap drop attempt which missed, and then I tried a break from a scrum. I got going, and then slipped on the greasy surface — there had been rain before the match after a few days dry spell. As I fell, two French players — I saw on the video later that it was Rives and Screla — dived over my body. There was a sort of a crack in my leg, and as the ruck broke up I thought I had really hurt myself. The game was a couple of minutes old.

Fergus Slattery, with about as much medical knowledge as I had, told me that I was all right. I told him I had broken my leg. I can still remember him telling me I was OK as I was carried off. My leg hurt — but the tears in my eyes were because I knew that my Lions dream was ended. I only realized as I went off that my whole motivation had been to get on that Lions side. I had never told anyone or even admitted it to myself — until I understood that I couldn't go.

Ireland went down gallantly; I had a spiral fracture in my right leg. I was able to go to the dinner pumped up on painkillers — just as well, as I had invited a young lady, the first time I had taken her out, and it would have been a bit rough on her if I hadn't showed up. All the French guys were most sympathetic, which made me feel really important, but I was quite shattered. As it turned out, Dougie had a brilliant game for Scotland and he and Brynmor went to New Zealand. In retrospect, I don't think I would have gone even if I had finished the game. But I believe I would have been the replacement, and perhaps made it in the end, as I did three years later in 1980.

I got a letter from Mike Gibson (senior) during the summer, telling me what a dreadful tour it was. I am glad, now, that I missed the tour and, funnily enough, I'm also glad I broke my leg.

In the hotel before the French game, I had been approached by Ian Robertson, the Cambridge university coach. He spoke about me going up to Cambridge for a couple of years. This was a surprise: I had managed to get through at Trinity, but Cambridge? Surely that was only for rich geniuses. But Ian convinced me otherwise, and I phoned my parents who thought it was worth pursuing.

When my leg went snap, I thought that all this would fall away. Also, of course, there was the rest of the winter without rugby. This had never happened to me before. Suddenly I had nothing much to do.

I did make a bit of an effort, though. I started to visit the various societies at Trinity, and became aware that there was life beyond rugby. However, far from making me keen and interested, it filled me with despair. As I've said before, I was beginning to realize that perhaps I had neglected something in life, and now the truth of it hit me with a hell of a clout: in terms of knowledge and awareness of the world, I was deeply ignorant...

One evening our class was invited to a cocktail party at one of the lecturer's houses. He and his wife were academics and obviously well-read in just about everything. There were no rugby guys present (they were all training) and so I had no one to talk to. As the conversation moved into politics, through economics and the arts, it dawned on me that not only was I not contributing, but that I was incapable of doing

53

so. I could offer no comment on any of these topics, to a group of people whom I knew quite well.

At one point the question arose of the controversial English politician Enoch Powell standing for some parliamentary seat in Ulster. I plucked up the courage to say something. It was a disaster: I got it all wrong, and even mentioned a county that was in the south as his possible constituency — it displayed my ignorance very nicely. That was the worst moment of my life; the polite titters and turned heads gave me nightmares. And I had to face it, as there was no immediate battle on the field to delay confronting the fact that my general knowledge was abysmal. I went into a real depression. Most of my friends must have thought it was just the broken leg, but it wasn't. It was my broken bubble of complacency, which had been built around an inflated idea of the importance of sport. It was a heck of a downer.

Mum was very good, and also Dad. They hadn't known what had been going on in my mind. Dad made a great suggestion. He said I should make a conscious effort to read the newspaper, a quality paper, every day. Up till then I used to buy the *Irish Times*. After a quick glance at the front page, I turned automatically to the sport, followed by the cartoons and the television page. That, for me, was reading the paper. Now I decided to go to the library each day, armed with the paper, and read it from cover to cover. At first I was totally lost, but after a while I started to get into what was going; when the subject of discussion was current affairs, I wasn't totally out of it. But I still had a long way to go.

Dad had also helped a lot regarding my career. I had never been drawn to any career, although if I had really wanted to I think I could have got into medical school. I had flirted with the idea of geology, simply because I was good at it. But on university field trips, when all the others were going wild because of some rocky outcrop or other, all I wanted to do was to get back to our bus. But at nineteen or twenty the world expects you, especially if you are a student, to have a career in mind. One of our courses was regional and town planning, and I quite liked it. So I announced to all and sundry that this was to be my career.

Suddenly all was well. I was going to change the face of Irish life by becoming a planner. I was particularly fascinated by the history of the subject, and I pictured myself tearing down the dirty parts of Dublin and, like Baron Haussmann, building up a sort of 'new Paris' in their place. It was all very fanciful, but at least I had an answer when people insisted on talking to me about careers. Inside, however, I knew it wasn't for me.

One of the great things about university was living on campus. For the first two years I lived at home and commuted, just like school; but in my third year, as rugby captain, I got one of the best sets of rooms on campus, sharing them with Dave. This was something we agreed on a few years before, when we discovered that we could actually get on quite well. The next year, because of rugby connections, I managed to pull a fast one and get rooms again. This was almost unheard of, but we weren't arguing: Ali Stewart, the first fifteen hooker, moved in with me. He was then a bigger layabout than I was, but he was a great cook. Many was the day when I came back from a lecture to find him slaving over a hot stove. We got on very well.

At weekends I always went home. I had lots of friends in Greystones, and a lot of my night life revolved around the local tennis club in summer and of course the rugby club in winter. The rugby club, I supposed, always hoped that I would join them after Trinity, and so I always was allowed into dances for free. But I had lived there for so long that I would have had many friends even without my new-found 'fame'.

Anyway, by going home at weekends, and sometimes for a night during the week, it meant that I always got a lift in with Dad the morning after. I got to know him as a friend, and one day I confessed my absolute despair about what I was going to do after graduating. He listened very sympathetically, and then told me that a number of directors from Guinness (the brewery where he was the marine engineer in charge of the ships) had expressed an interest.

So I had a few interviews and they were keen for me to join. Even when the prospect of going to Cambridge arose, they encouraged it and said to come and see them afterwards. I had no particular ambition to work for a brewery, but at least they were a respected company — and once again, to have a career in mind would enable me to get around those awkward questions about what I was going to do — apart from sport and town planning, that is. Mum and Dad were most supportive at this time, and when Dermot, my mate from Greystones, suggested that we go around Europe in the summer, they encouraged me.

Once again I got a job in the Wisbech canning plant and this time Peter, my other brother, came along. Being an old hand, I landed one of the best student jobs, working in quality control. This involved walking through the plant with a clipboard and performing various tests on the peas at various stages of the cooking and canning cycle. It had tremendous power, this job: one word from you and a whole batch of peas could be discarded and then a cleaning team would have to sterilize the whole line. God knows why students were given this job, as the grounds for mischief were vast, but there you are. I had a job that relied to a small degree on brains, and that gave great status.

Mind you, we were a fairly tame crowd. A lot of the night-shift guys who were supposed to clean the factory did the whole job spaced out of their brains on dope. So it was quite good selection by the student liaison officer: all the 'straights' got the day jobs, and all the 'heads' worked at night. That way there was no real culture clash, and as only cleaning was done at night I suppose there was less chance of an accident.

There was another canning factory in Hereford where a lot of mates of mine went to work. There things weren't as smooth, with a lot of animosity between the local supervisors and the visiting students. I heard the next term how one of the guys, on his last day, had found a dead rat on the road; he carried it into the plant, and had it canned with some choice ripe strawberries. A week later hundreds of health inspectors descended on the place, closed it down and would only allow it to open after the whole factory had been sterilized. All the students made a fortune out of overtime. It was a dreadful thing — but I must admit we laughed ourselves sick.

I made quite a lot of cash, and then I went to my Auntie Gwen's house in the Midlands where I met up with Dermot. He had arranged Interrail tickets for us, which meant that for the ridiculous sum of about £80 the bearer could have unlimited train travel all over Europe for thirty days. And if you had nowhere to sleep, you could always get on a night train somewhere, and then catch a train back to where you wanted to spend the day. We used this trick a few times, and we had a good holiday.

First we went to Paris and saw all the sights. Then we headed south and spent a week in St Tropez. My only real girlfriend at that stage, a lovely Belfast girl whom I had gone out with a few times over the years, was working there and so we had a floor to sleep on. We spent the days on the beach and the evenings walking through the village mingling with the rich and famous. I was nearly run over by Charles Aznavour one day and I dined out on that often. We also saw Ronnie Lane of the Small Faces giving a sort of impromptu concert on the harbour's edge, but in fact he was so pissed or stoned that he could hardly stand, let alone sing. We also saw many other acts, the names of which escape me, but it was the greatest free show we had ever seen.

We moved on after a week, looking like hippies with our hair getting longer and our skins browner and browner. We went via Monaco to Italy and spent some time in Rome. It was beautiful, but I found the dirt tragic. Then the train again down south to Brindisi, and across by ferry to Greece. We got to Athens and spent two nights living on the roof of a home for down-and-out seamen. God knows, just like the security job in the States, I wouldn't do it now, but then it was all great fun. Little did I know that at that very time two Greek guys, employees of a big business, were looking for us to give us the time of our lives. Apparently Dad had been involved in selling one of the Guinness tankers to their company, and when they heard that I was in Athens, they offered to take us all over the place for nothing. The snag was that they couldn't find us, so it was more railway carriages and doss-houses for us.

We decided to go to the islands then, and ended up on Mykonos. Being young Irish students, we headed for 'Paradise Beach' where there is nude bathing. We spent the first few days lying only on our fronts, such was the scenery, and I confess we were too shy to go the whole way ourselves. We spent a week there and then started the long haul home.

We were in really great shape, as our diet consisted, for economic reasons, of fruit and brown bread loaves. Every second day we splashed out and bought a pasta meal at Freddies, the restaurant on the beach. But on the ferry back to Piraeus, the port of Athens, I ate too many peaches. The effect was dreadful pains in my stomach. These passed — but then, in the middle of a packed bus in Athens, I got that dreadful groaning in my stomach, followed by a very definite feeling that the bottom was about to fall out of my world. Without saying anything I grabbed Dermot and we forced our way off the bus. I sprinted for the nearest building and with great artistic excellence, borne out of necessity, managed to explain that if I didn't get to a toilet there could be trouble for everyone. I was herded to the basement of one of those ancient dungeon-type places that are common in some parts of Europe. There was an equally ancient hag sitting guarding the door. I flung all my change at her, and just managed to get into one of the cubicles before Krakatoa erupted. Now it would have been bad enough in a normal loo, but this was one of those infernal holes in the ground, with squatting blocks for your feet. I hadn't used one of those before, and attempted the whole operation from a standing position — with disastrous results. I ended up about three stones lighter. Minus one set of clothes and after a shower, we were on the road again, forever warned about the perils involved in eating too much fruit.

We just made it onto the express from Athens to Salzburg, a trip right through Greece and Yugoslavia. We were armed with a packet of biscuits and a bar of chocolate. We didn't know that it would not stop, and that we couldn't buy anything else during the journey. For about two days, that was all we had to eat; for company, we had an ancient, black-clad Greek lady who at intervals of about five minutes stood and spat loudly out of the window. It was hardly the Orient Express, but it was an experience.

We finally got the ferry home, looking like wild animals. We had been and seen, and I would make it compulsory for all kids of that age to embark on something similar.

Now it was off to study at Cambridge University. By now I was having second thoughts, was scared out of my mind, felt totally inadequate and had a right leg that still looked like an uncooked chicken bone. It was also very sore, so there was not even the comfort of making a go of it on the rugby field. Still, it had all been decided, and I was to do a postgraduate course in something called Land Economy. What the hell was that?

My two years at Christ's College had a very important influence. Unlike going to Trinity or playing for Ireland, it had never entered my head that I might go to Cambridge. I had played against Oxford and Cambridge twice, on tour with Trinity, and like everyone else I marvelled at the beauty and atmosphere of each place. To me they spelled 'privilege', and this, coupled no doubt with a bit of jealousy, had given me a bit of a negative attitude. When they approached me, it all became different. I immediately had a mental image of JC Robbie resplendent in the blue-and-white of the university side, and I suppose that made up my mind. Mum and Dad decided not to stand in my way, and the whole exercise cost them a lot. Typically, I never considered the sacrifices they made. It's not that I was a particularly selfish person, at least I don't think I was; it's just that I had no experience of the cost of living. I suppose we had a sort of feeling that life and purchases were a right and not a privilege.

I remember, when I was very small, being chosen to do a Christmas TV advert for Raleigh bikes. A friend of Mum's was in the advertising business, and cheeky small blonde kids were always top of the shopping list. Anyway, I had to race down the stairs of a house, gaze at the presents around the tree, gasp as my eyes picked out the new bike and turn to my (very youthful and beautiful) 'parents' and utter the stunning imaginative words: 'It's a Raleigh!' The ad ended with me riding the bike around the tree. All great fun for a ten-year-old, but the trouble was that it kept reappearing each Christmas. For a gawky fourteen-year-old, about to crash into the nightmare of adolescence, the nightly appearance of the advert made me blush scarlet.

However, for doing the ad I received the princely sum of £21. This really was big bucks in those days, and I was most irate when Mum suggested that some of it went on the coal bill. I felt it was mine and mine alone, and in the end I think a compromise was reached — half of it went on coal, and the rest on a new Scalextric racing-car set for me. I cringe now, looking back at all the toys, expeditions, clothes, sports gear and so on that was given without question by Mum and Dad, and the little thanks they received. I hope that the gratitude that we as a family now have for Mum, and the great love we have for the memory of Dad is some compensation.

They footed the bill for Cambridge, then, and it was agreed that I would pay it off in years to come. The university said that with my degree from Trinity, and the reference from my professor, I had to do the post-graduate Land Economy course. I arrived a few days before term, scared stiff. I felt like a total impostor, and if I could have got out of the whole thing there and then, I would have. I was in Christ's College purely because I had been told to apply there, and that the rugby officials would do the rest, which they did. The first day I spent settling in, buying some stuff and walking around like some country bogman up in the big smoke for the first time.

Ian Robertson said he would meet me in the evening, as there was a local rugby club function on and the university players always went along. It would be a good chance for me to meet my future team-mates. We got a taxi to the club and when I got inside everyone, absolutely everyone, was blind drunk. People were literally falling all over the place. They were all nice enough, but when I asked for an orange juice, I'm afraid their interest in me waned. I felt totally out of it. The secretary was the Blues' number eight, a Welshman called Eddie Butler. I had never heard of him, but I took an instant dislike to him. He, I'm sure, had similar feelings towards me. My adventure looked like becoming a nightmare.

In the next few weeks I settled down a bit, started attending lectures and settling on my area of study. Using all my experience from Trinity, I put in a proposal to investigate 'The effect of regional policy on the Republic of Ireland'. Hell, it sounded impressive, and everyone thought this was a capital idea. Once again I had a hook on which to hang convenient answers to any questions that might arise as to what I was doing at Cambridge. It all sounded plausible. But inside I was screaming out that I was there to further my rugby career, and that I had a vague idea of a career in management — whatever that meant — with Guinness in Dublin. Oh, how I wished I was an undergraduate and just had lectures and exams to contend with. Still, I managed to do a fair bit of work — although I have learnt that unless you have a goal in mind and a real desire to study, you are in deep trouble. But that stretched out in front of me, tomorrow's problem. For now, I had to get my leg right and start playing rugby and erecting my usual barricades against decisions.

For many years Oxbridge rugby had been in the doldrums. After the 1950s or so, the Varsity match had become a bore and crowds had dwindled. Then Ian Robertson, a former Cambridge Blue, had arrived to coach his old university. He said he would only do it if there was a serious effort to recruit quality players, and if there was a real commitment to play expansive rugby, win or lose. These he got, and for a few years the Cambridge sides revolutionized English rugby. They played with a style and near-arrogance that brought the crowds flocking back to the Varsity match, and the national selectors scuttling to watch them play just about every Saturday. A few years before I got there, they had a back-line that included future England cap Alistair Hignell at fullback; ex-All Black Mike O'Callaghan and Scotland B flyer Gordon Wood on the wings; Peter Warfield of England fame in the centre, along with a young genius called James Thornton. At half-back they had Alan Wordsworth, a future England player; and Alun Lewis, a guy who I think talked himself out of any Welsh caps, but as a youngster he was brilliant. He went as a replacement on the 1977 Lions tour to New Zealand.

These guys tore the big clubs apart. They had small, fast, fit packs and they ran everything. I believe that English, and possibly British, rugby owes Ian Robertson a hell of a debt; perhaps if he were not the most cynical, sarcastic man alive he would get more credit. After a while I got to understand his sense of humour, but it was a long haul. He is now a good friend and an exceptional radio and TV sports journalist.

In my first year most of these players were gone, but we still had a good nucleus. My biggest problem was the scrum-half. I was still crocked, and he kept on turning in brilliant performances. In the end he moved to centre, still performed well, and after one game in the second fifteen I made my debut. We were to play Richmond at home.

Once again I was scared stiff and felt like a schoolboy, not a seasoned international. I was so keyed up and anxious to make an impres-

What a fat little baby boy! Me in pram.

The Robbie Kids: Dave, self, Peter and Janie

I love this picture. Robbie and Campbell enjoying training the day before we played the Boks in the final test in 1980. Ollie is my greatest rugby mate.

Me as a youngster after catching fish in Greystones.

Two years later and we beat Castleknock on the way to the schools Senior Cup victory. The high school player with his arms out is our captain Don Lewis.

Schools cup heroes in dire need of a haircut! John Robbie, Skipper Don Lewis and Ian Burns. Posing for the newspapers.

Greystones harbour with Bray Head in the distance. On an evening like that I
walked round the head on my own - aged eight.

Schools Junior Cup and we lose to Castleknock

Looking into Trinity College, Dublin today. I owned it for four years. The top left window on the brick building in the background was my room

Just back from working on a
farm in England. Sweet sixteen
with hair down my back — my
kids can't believe this photo!

Trinity in the good old days

Not bad for a *bona fide* student pack. Our front five in the final: Nick Fitzpatrick,
Ali Stewart, Ollie Waldron, Donal Spring and Simon Hughes

1976. The youngest ever skipper of Trinity and only our second cup since
1926. A few days later the little silver player on the lid lost a foot!

Above: My Big Fight. My first colours match. The arm on the right belongs to me. The arm I'm grabbing belongs to Kevin Mays, the biggest player in the country!

Left: Status symbol number one. A photo of my days as a security guard in the States — I wouldn't do it now!

Below: Security guard hard at work in Boston.

Butler to Robbie and Cambridge are on the attack against the
1978 All Blacks. One of my favourite photos — taken by Dave
Allan's brother, Peter Tynan O'Mahony.

After the All Black game 1978. Dad, Dave, self and Janie
prepare for a photo session with Jack McVitty (on the right).

My first cap against Australia. Can you believe thirteen years ago?

Auckland vs Ireland 1976. Just look at the terror on my face.
In front of me from left: Tom Feighery, Harry Steele, Moss
Keane, Roger Clegg, Emmett O' Rafferty and Willie Duggan.

1980 — opening for the Lions with Ollie Campbell. Later I stepped in a sprinkler hole and badly sprained my ankle. That night I anaesthetized it fully with alcohol!

Playing against England in 1981. I was dropped afterwards. Steve Smith has the ball. I got the nod ahead of him in the 1980 Lions but never detected any resentment.

Playing against Japan at the Olympic stadium. The headlines on this magazine cover say it all!

The smile says it all — a Lion at last. The picture doesn't show the massive hangover from Bulawayo the night before!

The Lions go mining in Johannesburg. Felgan Reece, Wardie, self, Noisey Murphy, Graeme Price, Billy, Alan Tomes, Dr Jack Matthews and Clive Williams.

Wardie watches me score for the Lions against Griquas. The touch judge doesn't share our joy!

My first game on merit for the Lions Saturday side, against W.P. Jeff Squire
(on ground), self, Colin Tucker, Graeme Price, Billy and Maurice Colclough.
What a pack to play behind.

Gary Player demonstrates his finger strength with his lead practice
driver. In awe the Lions are Peter Wheeler, self, Andy Irvine and
Clive Woodward. We couldn't get close to achieving the lift.

Tackling Pierre Berbizier in 1981, Ireland v France. He was a
very intelligent scrum-half.

Donal Spring and I in action for Ireland. Later I went on tour
to SA — on principle he stayed but we remain firm friends.

Lions vs Junior Boks 1980. Gawie Visagie has me firmly in
his sights. This was the game in which I tackled my guts out.

1980 The eight Lions called out as replacements. Wardie, self, Ian Stephens,
Gareth Williams, Paul Dodge, Phil Orr, Andy Irvine and Steve Smith.

sion that I really cocked it up at the start. I never saw the ball for about the first five minutes, and then we got a penalty just outside our twenty-five. I saw that the opposition had their backs turned, so I tapped a quick one to myself. Unfortunately, in my haste, I tapped it too far forward and fumbled it; tried to regain it and fumbled again. A dreadful knock-on. By now I was really embarrassed. Desperate to display annoyance, in an attempt to communicate to the big crowd that this did not always happen, I tried to kick the bouncing ball up the field. Even this didn't work, I sliced it terribly, and to my dismay it flew sideways off my boot, over the stand and out of the ground. There was a sort of a stunned silence at this little performance, and I felt a complete fool. But I recovered and in the end played quite well — and my leg held up. I became a permanent member of the Blues, and enjoyed facilities and privileges that I had never experienced before, and would not again until I became a provincial player in South Africa.

It was very good for me to have got out of Ireland at that time. I had been playing a role that was expected of me — the sports-mad little saint. Well, perhaps 'saint' is the wrong word, but I do have a feeling that to some people I was a sort of role model for their sons. If they had only known what was crackling around sometimes inside my head.

I was fed up with drinking orange juice. In Ireland, I didn't have the character to be able to enjoy a party or even a social gathering, as I was just too hung up and shy. If I had taken even a couple of shandies I would have loosened up considerably. The trouble was that if I simply picked up a beer — and I tried this a few times — I would be surrounded by goggling people exclaiming loudly that they thought I didn't drink. In the end it wasn't worth all the hassle. But in Cambridge no one gave a tuppenny damn if I drank neat Scotch the whole time or smoked dope or even howled at the moon at night. In short, I could sort out my head without worrying what effect this would have on the image that had been created in Ireland, an image that I was constantly battling with.

I launched myself into the non-stop round of cocktail parties that are a feature of college life in Cambridge. At first I was very reserved, and would find myself in deep conversations in corners about obscure subjects like the meaning of life. Then a couple of my team-mates took me in hand. They told me that the whole idea was to have fun, and to tell the biggest lies one could. From then on it was conversations about my course in brain surgery or bonsai tree appreciation, or whatever took my fancy. It was all a bit unreal, but it just about described life in the student part of the town. In fact, there was a famous sign painted on the common which separates the collegiate part of town from the rest. As you walked away from the university, you passed a public loo on which was daubed: 'You are now re-entering reality.'

We were hot favourites for the Varsity match that year, but, on a shocking day, lost 15-7 to a motivated Oxford side, dominated by the Welsh flyhalf Gareth Davies. I was upset, I hadn't played well, and I vowed that next year it would be different. And the rest of my life would be different from that time on: during the Christmas holidays I fell in love for the first time.

But before I get onto that, talk of my first Varsity game reminds me of a memorable meeting after it. One of our centres had a good friend, a girl from Cambridge called Jenny, and he took her to the big formal bash afterwards. (This was before I met Jennie, the girl who is now my wife.) The next day, after we had said our farewells, I had to get a plane home to Ireland — going home for Christmas. Over breakfast this came up, and as my plane was in the afternoon, Jenny invited me to her home in London to pass the time and then to have lunch before I went. It was a good idea — I was knackered after the game and also a little shattered at losing, and also a bit depressed as I had not played very well. Just before lunch, Jenny's mum said that her husband would be joining us, and I confess that I thought to myself, 'Oh God, no doubt he'll be some boring old bugger who will want to know all about the game etc etc.' The bell rang, and her daddy walked in. I recognized him immediately — and was suddenly wide awake. I had to be, just to break even in the conversation, such was his depth of knowledge and his practice of asking me my opinion. It was Enoch Powell.

For once I actually managed to do quite well, thanks to the daily read of the papers; on the plane later I got a sneak preview of a major speech he was to make a few days later at some big meeting. I had asked him for a copy and had resisted the temptation to ask him to autograph it. (I reckoned that would brand me as a souvenir hunter, and not a serious intellectual interested in what he had to say. Amazing the lengths we go to to promote our image.)

I must say that, until that lunch, I had always thought of Enoch Powell as some sort of a twisted, racist ogre; a fanatic in fact. But he was friendly, very lively and with an intellect that was frightening. He also had a great sense of humour. I particularly remember that he drew our attention to the packet from which the sausages had come: they were labelled as 'thick' Irish sausages. This is why I kept my counsel and thought carefully before I spoke. Afterwards I felt I had lunched with a great man and his very gracious wife and daughter, and that was something to relate down at the local when I got home.

It was also a coincidence: it was in a conversation about Enoch Powell a year or so earlier that I had disgraced myself, and discovered that I was hopelessly uninformed. God bless the man, he helped me to grow up — even though he knew nothing about it.

I met Jennie, my wife, at a rugby match. I suppose that was inevitable. I had long been aware of this smashing-looking girl whom I knew lived somewhere in the Greystones area, but somehow we had never really met. I think she had been to a few of the church youth club meetings when we were all quite young, and I had once seen her in a restaurant in Dublin, a trendy sort of place, when I was having a hamburger with Dermot. I told him then that I rather fancied this girl; even her name, Jennie Stanley, seemed to have a ring to it. But Dermot and I were long on talk but spectacularly short on action in matters pertaining to going out with members of the opposite sex, and so nothing really happened. But I added her name to the small list of girls that I was attracted to in those days. (She was one of three, but I didn't really think I stood a chance with any of them.)

I came home from Cambridge, and was quite shocked to hear brother Dave say a few times at the dinner table that he had got to know a girl who was really good fun — Jennie Stanley. I must have blushed, but I realized she was around town and I started seeing her — at the other end of long bars and so on. One Saturday I walked up to the rugby club to watch Greystones play. It was on a Sunday and so no gate money was taken — Holy Ireland, you know — but one of my friends on the committee saw me and, as was the practice, asked me to carry round the hat. I did, and found myself asking Jennie for a contribution. We got chatting, and seemed to get on.

Now we were standing on the small bank that runs parallel to the car park. The car park was full, but not the bank — which means, in Greystones, that a lot of spectators are watching from the bar. Anyway, it started to rain and in a very daring move I asked Jennie to go up to the bar to have a drink and watch the rest of the match. I felt a real idiot when she said that it was okay, as her dad and a friend were in a car watching the game — and the car was just behind us. The first time I tried to chat up my future wife, the whole operation was watched by my future father-in-law. I bet that hasn't been done anywhere else since Victorian times.

Anyway, we all went to the bar afterwards, had a few drinks, made friends. We started going out soon afterwards and now, all these years later, we have two kids and — most important — we're still best friends.

In fact, with family I have been extremely lucky. I've told you about the Robbie mob. There's also our dear auntie Gwen who lives not far from Birmingham. My cousins Clive and David are now living in Bristol, but they all regard Greystones as their second home. We also have Uncle Leslie living with his family in Airdrie just outside Glasgow. He is a lot older than us, and is I suppose the last link to Dad's side of the family. I was particularly pleased, and so was Dad, when Les came over for my first cap and also went to Edinburgh when I played against Scotland there.

Jennie and I getting married has also brought her mob, the Stanleys, and all the Robbies very close. As I've said, Dave really got to know them first, but since then we have all become almost a single family. I'm very lucky in that Jack, Jennie's dad, is about my best friend, and not many blokes can say that about their fathers-in-law. Jennie's mum, Pat, is great as well, and she came over to South Africa when Susan, our daughter, was born. Never has a son-in-law been so spoilt.

Jennie's youngest sister is living with us in South Africa pursuing her career as a design artist. Sandra and Phillip are still in Greystones and when we go back the first thing we try and do is have some sort of a reunion. It's funny how Jen and I both take happy families for granted. In South Africa the divorce rate is absolutely frightening, and as a result lots of kids don't get the solid family base that we had. It's sad.

I played in the Irish trial while I was at home, but only got to the bench. Johnnie Moloney was skipper, fair enough, but I knew that I was on thin ice because a young player, a bundle of energy from Ulster, was the talk of the town as a future international scrum-half. His name was Colin Patterson and my fears were well founded: for the last three Five Nations games, he sat on the bench and I was out in the cold.

My return to Cambridge was very traumatic. When I left home after the holiday, I was given a lot of money by a few friends of mine. I won't name them, but they were rugby followers and also people who knew my family well. They had obviously clubbed together and come up with a big wad of notes, and it was a gift to ease the burden of study. I was flabbergasted, and of course refused to accept it, but they insisted. The only quid pro quo they had asked for was that possibly, many years on, I might remember the deed; perhaps if I was in a position to help another youngster, then I would do so. It was a fantastic thing, done by people who were by no means wealthy, and it had nothing to do with rugby.

So I set off to the airport with this pile of notes — it came to almost a thousand pounds — bulging in my inside pocket. This terrified me. I had never seen an amount like this, let alone carried it on my person, and I had absolutely no idea of what to do. I wasn't sure about things like currency limits and exchange controls, they were just words that I heard in conversations before I rejoined them when the talk got back to sport. With this mental picture of being led away for questioning by customs officials, I had a brainwave. At the airport I opened my big suitcase and stuffed the money in among my clothes. There it would be safe, and I proceeded onto the plane and over to London.

I got my suitcase off the conveyor, and just to be certain opened it to check that the money was there. It was gone. I searched; I emptied the case onto the floor, but it was no good. My money, the gift from those wonderful friends, had been swiped. I went to the airport authorities; the police were called; of course it was all hopeless. I can only assume that the then infamous Heathrow baggage handlers (and I stress 'then') had somehow gone through my stuff, found the windfall and nicked it. I particularly remember one of the airport staff sneering slightly as he heard the story. I think it was because I was at Cambridge; immediately, I'm sure, he thought privilege, just as I had once done. I nearly hit him, and had to be taken outside for a walk to cool down. It was all so terrible, and I felt so, so stupid at what I had done.

The only hope I have is that the person who swiped the cash was able to use it well, and possibly the spirit in which the gift was given was not wasted. I sometimes have this fantasy about heaven. I imagine that the first thing that happens to you after being fitted with wings is that St Peter takes you to this great big video shop. In luxury he plays you the video of your life, except that it is multi-dimensional, with every event that took place. It's also revealed what was taking place in other people's lives at the time. If so, the first thing I shall do is fast-forward it to that day at the airport, to see just what happened to that money and how it was eventually used. I suppose after that, I'd also look at many other of the events that I've written about in this book. I often get the feeling in other books, and not just rugby books, that the author, when discussing his life in relation to a certain happening, first researches it fully and then, years after, puts his thoughts into perspective. I have tried to avoid this, even though to do it completely is perhaps impossible. I have tried to express what was inside my head at the time.

I arrived back at Cambridge in a fit of total depression. I was also away from Jennie, which made it worse. But there was work to be done: at a meeting of all the rugby Blues, to my amazement, I was elected skipper. There were two candidates, myself and Eddie Butler, the big Welsh guy who I had disliked at first sight. By now we were good friends.

During the previous term we had played a game in London with a weakened side, and in the bus on the way back, over many beers, the whole team and club was discussed. Somewhere along the line I accused Eddie of being a very selfish person, as he played the game for himself. I told him that he just didn't realize that with his ability and great character, he could in fact do much more than just play for the team. My memories are vague, but I think it was this conversation that gave me the nomination and I must say I was honoured, even though I had assumed that Eddie would be the captain.

I soon discovered that the Cambridge rugby captain carried quite a lot of status at the university. Suddenly I was on committees, getting invited to all sorts of functions and having my views sought on a lot of differing subjects. It also meant that Christ's College gave me my room again, and installed a telephone for me. It was all good fun. Just like Trinity, I had a great bunch of guys around me and I could worry about play rather than administration. That suited me just fine.

The Oxbridge system is strange. The Blues side trains and plays like hell up to the Varsity match in December, and then for the second term its importance is diminished. Some guys play for more fashionable clubs, and let younger ones play for the university. I stopped this, managed to get quite a good team together and we won most of our matches in style. The committee were delighted, and I was pleased because it built my reputation. I soon discovered that captaining Cambridge was very different from captaining an Irish side like Trinity. There was far less emotion involved.

If I had given some of my Trinity calls to arms in the dressing-room before a match at Cambridge, half the team would have started to laugh. There were men there who really played in the Corinthian spirit. Training was a bit of tactics, and then half-an-hour's hard touch-rugby. There were very few laps and press-ups, and the only running sessions done were without the ball, just before the Varsity match. But I soon found that, in a match situation, these 'amateurs' were just as committed, and played every bit as hard as the Trinity guys who ran and exercised like hell and sat through Shakespearian orations exhorting them to die for the cause.

Looking back, I think that there must be more bull involved in the so-called motivation of rugby sides than in any other sport. Now I think I would take more of an Andy Ripley approach to the game. He was a very hard player indeed, and I remember him guesting for the Irish Wolfhounds against Cardiff. I suppose he had something to prove to the Welsh that day, as they had always considered him a poor man's Mervyn Davies. With no change to his laid-back, laughing approach, he proceeded to run into everything that moved and tackle with a ferocity that I have seldom seen. This was the man who, when leading the London Counties side, asked his players to do a team whistle in training. I can imagine what a few Irish coaches would have thought of that — but he was a great player.

One of the biggest thrills I had during my season of captaincy was the visit of the 1978 All Blacks, Graeme Mourie's side. They were to play Cambridge in the first game of the tour, and this had led to a bit of controversy. There was a move to break the rather privileged position enjoyed by the Oxbridge pair in relation to games against tourists. It had been suggested that, instead of facing Oxford and Cambridge in opening games, the tourists should face a combined British universities side.

I suppose this would have been fairer to all the students of Britain — but it would have broken a long tradition; and I believe the first game against the light or dark blues was perfect for the tourists. The settings are magnificent and, all being genuine students — including land economists of note like myself — they played games that were fast, clean and not too strenuous.

In short, ideal tour openers.

However, there was also a move to make the Cambridge side a past and present selection. There were a number of Cambridge officials who were in favour, fearing that if we played the varsity side against New Zealand, we would get walloped. We even had a meeting in London with some RFU officials about it. I spoke against the change, as it would be unfair to deny some of the team a chance to play the tourists. Imagine how I would have felt later in the season, asking for a team effort against Oxford from players who had been denied the opportunity to play against the All Blacks.

It was decided to keep the varsity side, and in front of a huge crowd we went down, ever so bravely, by about thirty points to twelve. We also managed a good try — and only five tries were scored against the

All Blacks on the whole tour. After the match there was a huge dinner and disco, and most of the All Blacks had a whale of a time. Dad, Dave and Janie, and of course Jack McVitty, all came to the game, and I think they enjoyed it all. The next day we had a momentous piss-up as well. That's described elsewhere, but overall the success of the game set us up for a good season.

We got revenge in the varsity match as well. All of us had felt sick after losing the previous year. Gareth Davies had been magnificent, it's true, but all Cambridge felt we had been beaten by an inferior side. This year we would make amends.

There is a great tradition surrounding the varsity match and although a lot of it sounds a bit silly, within the university scene it's fine. Each year Oxford and Cambridge play against invitation sides just before the varsity game, which is on the first Tuesday in December. After the sides are selected, each makes a sort of pilgrimage down to Twickers and is allowed to train on the hallowed turf. When we went down, we even managed to get into a row with Bob Weighill, who then was the RFU man in charge of most of the administration.

Bob was a great guy, but was wrong on this occasion. I should explain that, due to the game being televised, they had the year before provided us with a white plastic-covered ball. We didn't like it, and the argument that the TV could pick it up in the gloom of the second half cut no ice. It had been a wet day, and when we were desperately trying to get back at Oxford, the wet ball made the game degenerate — it was just too slippery to hold.

The next year we requested to play with one of the normal leather balls, or a white one of a different make — and the ball we were prepared to accept was the official one used at the first World Cup. Bob would have none of this, and he even made a veiled threat that if we didn't stop trying to change things we would be in danger of losing Twickenham as the venue. Ian Robertson then told Bob that if that happened he would tell the world about the intransigence of the RFU and the way they had threatened us. It was all a bit silly; in the end we played with a normal leather ball and served up an open, exciting game.

I knew we were going to win. At the traditional nuts and port dinner — can you believe it, nuts and port a few days before the big game? — we toasted Oxford in the traditional way. We stood and said G.D.B.O. — God Damn Bloody Oxford — which is part and parcel of all Cambridge rugby build-ups for the varsity match. It's even been rumoured that in certain varsity matches, at half time, the Cambridge team has just stood in a circle and chanted that. All tradition, all fun — and all now a distant memory.

My injuries I can remember, though. I twisted an ankle in the big invitation game just before Twickers, and I also had a bad hand. I remember Clive Norling, the referee, being amazed when he came into our dressing room to inspect the boots and he found me in the corner being injected by about three different doctors in three places. I have always taken injections for big games, even though I believe the practice is a dangerous one.

We beat them well. We kicked for position in the first half and ran them ragged in the second. Our pack was dominant and I actually played the whole game making only one tackle. Mind you, in doing that I got a boot in the head that needed stitches afterwards. I should add that the varsity match is normally a very clean affair, far cleaner than the Colours games in Dublin. It's fast and furious, though, and with the renewed interest after the years of Robertson-inspired running rugby, there are now huge crowds. It's blue blazers and carnations, and for the fans (at least the rich ones) pheasant and champers in the car park — from the back of the Rolls.

I played well and booted over some good kicks. Then, right at the end, we won a ruck on the right-hand touch line. I saw a narrow corridor and went blind; their scrum-half tried to tackle me but went too high and I handed him off. As I went for the corner, I straightened for a moment to make the cover halt, and was able to use the bit of extra room to make the corner. I dived over and slid for about five yards on the wet turf. It was the only really big-time 'atmosphere' try I scored until I went to South Africa.

Looking at it on TV, it looks amazing. But just like the good break I made in the first tour game in New Zealand, it all happened in slow motion. I booted the conversion from the touch line, and ended with seventeen points, just two short of Alistair Hignell's record for the varsity game. In fact, we ran a penalty from in front of the posts at one stage. Had I known that I was just two off the record I would have kicked it — all a bit vain, I suppose, but there you are.

Well, after the game it was fantastic. The ghost of the previous year had been well and truly laid. I was the hero — although in real rugby terms, our pack had done the hard work — and life was good.

It was home for Christmas and then back to play in the second half of the season for Pontypool, the famous Welsh club. How the hell did I get into that? I was drinking with Eddie Butler. I remember that I had

had a few too many and was holding forth about how great it must be to play in Welsh rugby. Remember that, at the time, Wales ruled the European game and had all those superstars.

Eddie told me that after Christmas Pontypool would love me to play for them. We would travel down each weekend for the games. There was a bit of a row over this in Wales, and all sorts of allegations about buying players were made, but it was all above board. I only played about half a dozen games, as the country was in the grip of one of the worst cold spells for years.

Twice we travelled down to play against Cardiff in the Welsh cup; twice the game was put off, once after twenty minutes had been played. This was done because all morning about three thousand Pontypool volunteers worked like hell clearing the pitch. The snow was falling, we were playing with a very old leather ball, black not brown (so we could see it); in the end the game had to be stopped.

Late that night we had a snowball fight in the middle of Pontypool with about half the Welsh pack. Graeme Price, Bobby Windsor, Charlie Faulkner, Eddie and I, along with John Perkins who was later capped — all playing the fool like little kids. I stopped at one point and considered how ludicrous the situation was. I imagined how a small boy with the same fanaticism that I had for the knight-like image of international players would have viewed the scene. I think a snowball hit me in my drunken face, and that woke me up.

Pontypool's beautiful ground is owned by the local council. Now because of anti-South African council feelings, and because at the time Welsh rugby had come out in support of the Lions tour to be held in 1980, Pontypool were banned from using the ground. I remember we had to play against Newbridge at another ground. Anyway, with the big Cardiff game coming up, we still had to train.

Snow was thick on the ground, and we learnt that we were to train in the grounds of the local lunatic asylum. We arrived to find that Pontypool fans (who happened to work in the roads department) had rigged up temporary lights; it was rough and ready but it gave us some light. Up to our ankles in snow, and all wrapped in tracksuits, we went about our training under the watchful eye of coach Ray Prosser and his helpers.

I vividly remember one of the players tapping me on the shoulder and pointing toward the asylum a few hundred yards away. It was a huge bleak building, and right at the top we could see that lights were on. In the windows we could see many faces peering down at us. They must have seen an expanse of white snow leading to the trees, and the pitch-black sky above. Under these small lights on poles, held up by soaking men, they must have watched us warm up, trundling round in circles. We imagined them turning to each other, warm in their fortress, and saying, 'My God, and they tell us that we are mad ...'

6

Although I had lived in Greystones all my life, many people thought I would, on completion of my spell at university, join one of the big fashionable Dublin clubs. I imagine that Wanderers and Lansdowne, the two giants who are based at Lansdowne Road, were considered the favourites to get young Robbie. However, while Ian (the other part of the Robbie-Burns partnership) was fly-half for Wanderers, his scrum-half was international Robbie McGrath, certainly one of the most loyal club men around. Lansdowne had Donald Caniffe, also an international and almost an unofficial player-coach of his club.

I think many Greystones men had secretly hoped that I would join them, and, apart from social visits, I had guested for them a number of times. In fact I had made my mind up years before: I wanted to join Greystones. It was home, and of course I had a genuine affection — no, I think love is a better word — for the whole atmosphere of the place and a number of their main *alikadoos* (a favourite British/Irish rugby word for the officials). But for some reason I had never told them this; I'm not sure why, it certainly wasn't out of devilment, and as rugby in Ireland is (or certainly was) one hundred percent amateur, there was never a thought of 'putting up the rent'.

In South Africa it is very different. Expenses are far more, shall I say, charitably viewed than in Ireland. In South Africa, a good player coming into town would certainly wait a while before declaring his allegiance. That way a number of clubs will put up various 'deals' for him to consider, and then he'll make his choice; the following year, another club might speak to him and he would move. Of course, the official reason would be that his wife couldn't get on with the other wives, or some such nonsense. The clubs never complain, as each is as guilty as the next — at least amongst the big outfits. As a result a couple of big businessmen, or small businessmen who deal in cash, never go amiss within a club and are often to be found on committees. Bearing in mind the crowds that go to rugby in South Africa, to say nothing of the sponsorships available, it is all very small-time. But still, compared to Ireland, it is semi-professional.

The South African provincial unions cannot do anything about it, and in fact turn a blind eye. The only time there's any drama is when details get out and are picked up by the international press. For example, a few years ago Deon Viljoen, the Transvaal prop, caused a storm when he let slip that he was unhappy about not receiving his expenses after a final. There was a huge outcry and all sorts of statements were issued about the amateur nature of the South African game. They were all nonsense, of course, but the drama passed and Deon returned to play for Transvaal again.

What do you do? If the officials running another club offer better expenses, do you turn them down and pay the mortgage on the good feeling you get from sticking to the letter of the Victorian amateur code? Try telling that one to your building society.

No, as far as Greystones was concerned, I simply didn't want to commit myself too early. At one time I even considered emigrating to Japan: I captained a Cambridge side there and was amazed at the interest in the game. We were unbeaten, and in the last game beat the full Japanese side by about 40-15. Afterwards I was approached by one of the big steel companies. They wanted me to go to Japan for a minimum of three years. I would first learn the lingo, then coach the club and at the same time do a full business management course. At the end they would guarantee me a job just about anywhere in the world. I was very flattered, but turned it down. First, I never really fancied my chances of learning the language, being a total dunce in that department; second, I reckoned I had little chance of being selected for Ireland from the other side of the world. But I loved Japan: I would put it a close second behind South Africa as a place to tour. The clash between old Japan, with its temples and rituals, and the twentieth century, with all its decadence and industrial blight, is stark.

But my main memory is of the Japanese people. The politeness and genuine interest in one's happiness is staggering. One funny incident which I will relate happened late in the tour. I should mention that, on a Japanese tour, most of the contact is not with Japanese players but with *alikadoos*, who are normally big businessmen. Anyway, after one of the games when the speeches had been made and the songs sung, two of our youngest players (about nineteen) were asked by one of the businessmen if they were enjoying themselves. One of the guys said they were, but that they hadn't met any girls. I think he had tennis club

73

socials or teenage discos in mind, but the businessman immediately decided that amends must be made. The two guys arrived at breakfast the next morning each looking about ten years older; under interrogation it turned out that they'd been taken to the Ginza area of Tokyo, painted the town red around them, and finished up with a long practical geography and biology lesson in one of Tokyo's better brothels. They stopped at showing us the footprints going up their spines, but it showed that at least a couple of players went as boys but returned as men!

On the way out, at Heathrow, the Cambridge side boarded the plane but it failed to take off — engine trouble, they told us. We disembarked and waited in the terminal building. After a while it became obvious that we were in for a long wait; someone suggested we have a drink. Being in festive mood we had Carlsberg Specials, and soon we were roaring drunk. Suddenly there was a scream — a young lady was very upset and threatening to call the police and generally going wild. One of our players, a particularly tough Welshman by the name of O'Callaghan (of all things) had decided that he was now a dog. He had been growling and barking a bit, and when this woman walked past he decided to bite her: he just leaned over and clamped his jaw around her arm — and he drew a bit of blood. Now bearing in mind that this was at Heathrow Airport in the afternoon, you can imagine the shock she got, standing one minute and then being bitten in the arm by some growling, slobbering idiot. The tour was nearly off because of that, but somehow our management got us away with it and we had a public warning. It was a shocking thing to do, but even looking back after ten years I find myself laughing — grown men behaving like animals must appeal to me.

One of my very best friends is Jack McVitty. He is my son's godfather and to a lot of rugby people in Ireland he is 'Mr Rugby', one of the real enthusiasts. Like all great people, he sets greater store on a person's character than on their playing ability. I had really got to know Jack when he was the chairman of the Leinster Under-19 selectors and I was captain. He often gave me lifts home after training sessions. He played for Greystones in the 1950s and 1960s when it was a junior club; he was a front row forward and a good one.

He subsequently moved to Lansdowne and played for the first side there, before emigrating to Northern Rhodesia where he played rugby and also, in his spare time, worked as a copper miner. Since coming to South Africa I have occasionally come across guys who worked on the Copper Belt; at the mention of McVitty, they always hold up their hands and proceed to tell me that he was the greatest rugby fanatic they'd ever met. One former mine-captain told me that once they were looking for Jack, couldn't raise him, and had to send guys down the mine to look for him. Long before they found him they heard murmured voices, occasionally dropping and then becoming high-pitched. The guy described the scene as they neared to where Jack and his mates were sitting around a lamp. Before they even came into view, all the men in the search party were well versed in the argument as to who was the greatest fly-half of all time, Jackie Kyle of Ireland or Cliff Morgan of Wales. Apparently Jack and his mate, presumably a Welshman, had spent their shift and long after in deep argument over this hugely important issue. Had they not found Jack, so intense was the discussion that they would probably be still there today.

Jack is a big man, a typical prop, and just about the whole rugby world breathed a sigh of relief when he survived a serious heart attack a few years ago. (Mind you, if he had passed away it would have been hugely appropriate — it happened in the bar at Lansdowne Road.)

When I captained Cambridge against the All Blacks on the first game of their tour in 1978, Jack arranged a whole load of guys to come over and see the match. It was a great occasion, a huge crowd and a good game. Celebrations went on long and hard, and Jack and I arranged to meet to do a bit of sightseeing the next day. Dave, Janie and Dad had also come to the game but only Dave stayed on for the next day.

I had planned trips to colleges, churches, museums and so on; as we set off, I was a bit disappointed when Jack said that he would first just like to see the inside of a real English pub. Well, I was taken in completely. At about half past eleven we entered the Eagle public house in Cambridge; at about half past eleven that night we staggered out.

A truly memorable day, it has gone down as the 'Day of the Little Boards' — a reference to a story that was told about McVitty that day. The teller was one Peter Tynan-O'Mahony, a great rugby friend, first-rate writer and the younger brother of Dave Allen, the famous comedian.

Now, to understand the story you really have to understand that Jack McVitty was the ultimate rugby fanatic, a man for whom rugby memorabilia have the status of religious relics. Anyway, at Lansdowne Road, before they built the new bottom section of the West stand, the players used to get changed in the old Lansdowne pavilion. To run onto the field, each player had to run through the gate and step over an old wooden board — more accurately, a lattice-type arrangement of slats, held together by a few crossbeams. This was known as the 'little boards'.

75

Now to the average person it was a muddy, wooden, worn square — but to Jack it was holy. As he saw it, every mark and every scratch had been caused, possibly, by a famous foot running on to play an international, and therefore the Little Boards represented a history of the game in Ireland.

I'm sure you can imagine the importance of this to all fellow fanatics, especially after a good few pints of stout. Anyway, one evening, during the building of the new stand, Jack was winding his way from the Lansdowne bar to the car park, when he saw to his horror that the little boards had been taken up, replaced by tarmac and cast aside as builder's rubble.

It was as if the Shroud of Turin had been used to clean somebody's windscreen — sacrilege! Quick as a flash, Jack picked them up and carried them to his car and deposited them in the boot. For once he did not stop at Jim Doyle's in Bray, the watering hole of all Greystones men. Instead he hot-footed it to his beautiful home in Delgany, a few miles south of the town. Now Margaret, Jack's charming wife, is well used to him. She nodded gravely when he told her of the desecration that had occurred; she agreed that something had to be done. She even summoned up a bit of feigned enthusiasm when she learned of the theft to preserve the sacred relic. But she finally flipped her lid when Jack asked her on which wall of the living room she would like the Little Boards hung. As far as I know, to this day the boards are to be found in all their glory in the garage of Jack McVitty in Delgany, that little village just outside Greystones in County Wicklow. In fact, the greatest secret society in the world, a group that makes the Freemasons or the Broederbond look like an open street-corner meeting, is the Brotherhood of the Little Boards. Each member carries a splinter of the boards in his wallet, can you believe it.

Of course the whole thing was great fun, and told in such a manner that day in Cambridge that the whole pub was spellbound. The day has been commemorated with special scrolls which were hand-printed and hung in honour in the homes of all those who were present. The day, the fun and the real rugby friendship remain one of my most treasured memories.

Later that year, the same Peter Tynan-O'Mahony wrote to me and said that his brother Dave (the comedian) had two sons, and that the three of them would be going to the Varsity match. I got them tickets and arranged for them to come to the dressing-room afterwards. We made a bit of a fuss of them, and of course the team was delighted to meet one of Britain's best-known comedians. It was a small thing to do, and it made two little boys happy. Well, first Dave Allen invited me and two of my mates down to London to see his one-man show. It was great, and we met him afterwards. Then, about a year later when he was performing in Dublin, he invited my whole family and a few friends to the show; afterwards we went down to the dressing-room where he had laid on champagne and food. It was a fantastic gesture, the mark of a real star — and it taught me just how important saying 'Thank you' is. If you take the trouble to phone or drop a line after someone has been kind, the warmth it engenders is terrific. As one who calmly breezed through life accepting everything almost as a matter of course, it was a good lesson.

I suppose, in some ways, this book is meant as a 'thank you' to all those who showed me great kindness along the way, starting right off with Mum and Dad, but who perhaps never got the thanks they deserved. Another story which demonstrates that concerns the great Tony O'Reilly, a man I have never met but whom I have worshipped from afar.

The first time I heard his name, I must have been about seven or eight, 'my' team Bective Rangers had beaten Old Belvedere. Grandpa told me that it would have been different if O'Reilly had played. For some reason the memory stuck. Over the years I discovered that he was a great player and became an even greater businessman. Anyway, a few years ago, when Greystones were to tour overseas, Jack McVitty wrote to Tony in Pittsburgh and asked him to write a piece for the tour brochure. This he did, and true to form it was the best contribution of the lot. Jack wrote thanking Tony and sent him a copy of the finished booklet. That was surely the end of it, but no — a few weeks later Jack received another letter from Tony, thanking him for the brochure and commenting that he had particularly enjoyed one of the other articles.

To return to my joining of Greystones. One day I was somewhere with Jack McVitty; someone in the bar happened to refer to the next season, and almost without thinking I said that I was looking forward to playing for Stones. That was it. In the car home Jack asked me if he had heard correctly, I said yes, and he was delighted. The next day he asked me if I was prepared to stand for captain — I wasn't even a member of the club yet! I said I would, provided that it caused no rows.

I was being a bit devious. First, I knew that I had this reputation as a bit of a 'header' — but also that I was regarded as some sort of magician — look at Trinity, look at Cambridge. I also knew that Greystones had a potentially great back line, and that the overall standard of club rugby was not great. In a nutshell, I knew how to galvanize the club and build its reputation, and also have a lot of fun. I think we achieved that in no uncertain terms, though we narrowly failed to win a trophy.

I was also made captain of the full Leinster team. This came right out of the blue. Ollie Campbell had been captain for the game against Ulster, and we had won narrowly. Mick Doyle was the new coach, and I'm afraid we didn't think much of him. Like a lot of Irish coaches — mind you, it also applies to coaches everywhere — he was not organized; one thing that players hate is training sessions that do not seem well planned. (Roly Meates could give a session of forty-five minutes, including a warm-up that made everyone work hard, covered all areas of the game, never involved any hanging around listening to waffle and was also very enjoyable.)

We had a Wednesday evening Leinster practice two weeks or so before our annual game against Llanelli. It was raining, and after our bad game against Ulster we weren't looking forward to a long aimless session. As we arrived in dribs and drabs, the chairman of the selectors (wealthy meat baron and race-horse owner Mick Cuddy) drew me aside, punched me in the arm and said: 'We've made you captain, get the lads going.'

I lost my temper. Looking back, I cannot imagine why. The team, including a number of very senior players, some of them British Lions (or as the Irish insist, British and Irish Lions), was starting to get changed when I stormed in. I told them that there would be a delay and that I would be chatting to the brace of Michaels, Cuddy and Doyle, for a while. We went into the adjoining room and I told them I was pissed off. First of all, I would not be told in that manner of my captaincy; I expected to be asked. Second, before accepting I wanted an assurance that I would not just be there to toss the coin, but that I would have a major say in the running of the side. Third, I felt that a philosophy for the side had to be agreed upon by the players — otherwise it would be the same old rubbish of the interprovincial side being used solely as a stepping board to the final Irish trial. I don't know what the coach, a former Lion himself, and the chairman thought of this, but it was the start of two fantastic years. That night the team never did get changed. We talked it out, and agreed on our strengths and just what we were going to do.

On the Saturday we took Llanelli apart and won something like 21-0, and they had guys like Derek Quinnell, Ray Gravell and JJ Williams. It was a good start. Apart from a game lost on tour in Romania, where

78

I admit to getting complacent for once, we lost no other game in two years. We won the provincial championship twice, once beating Ulster by thirty points in Belfast; wins over Llanelli (twice), South of Scotland, Italy and — the best of the lot — Romania, who had beaten Munster heavily and also drawn with Ireland. It was a great side, and I must say that eventually Mick Doyle won the respect of the players. He was that rare breed of coach who allowed the players a major say, but could always give us a valuable overview of how things stood. The side was really run by Ollie and myself, and my fellow Greystones centre Paul McNaughton. Also in that Leinster side were Fergus Slattery, Phil Orr, Johnny Moloney (mostly on the wing at that stage), so to be captain, and a successful one, was quite an achievement. But I didn't even pause to consider it at the time: I was so wrapped up, and so confident in my methods, that what I said was generally done. What might have been said behind my back I don't know, but as success followed success it really didn't matter.

There was a beautiful story from this time that is always told by Roly Meates. It concerns a great Dublin character by the name of 'Tojo' Byrne. Tojo was a very good prop who played a number of games for Leinster. However, he was small, and one of those guys who for many years was always at the trials as a sub or on the B team. He is a Dublin butcher and has a marvellous sense of humour.

It was a shocking day, and a shocking Leinster trial. Near the end the A side number eight went off injured. Tojo was asked to go on as a replacement, even though it meant playing out of position. As he shuffled on, a packet of cigarettes fell out of his pocket. Then, as he took his place in the line-out, he looked at his opposite number. Tojo, at five-eight, was standing against Nicky Sweetman, six-foot-seven. Tojo is supposed to have turned to Irish scrum-half Johnny Moloney and asked him, in a loud voice, if he wanted it off the top, or caught and driven.

I happen to figure in another Tojo story that was told by none other than the great Willie John in a radio programme — and it's true. In my first season with Greystones, we reached the final of the League and played against St Mary's (for whom Tojo played). We had a very small pack, but it was mobile and extremely fast; we had developed a rucking style and it worked well. When a breakdown occurred, I made the decision for the pack to drive over the top. I used to call 'aeroplanes' and the forwards chasing after the ball would then raise their arms sideways and this enabled the nearest player to link and so the players arrived and drove in pairs, rather than on their own.

79

This is the secret to effective rucking. It worked well and we were in this final. Sure enough, the first opportunity presented itself just under the grandstand early in the game. 'Aeroplanes, aeroplanes,' I shouted, whereupon Tojo fell on the loose ball shouting 'Mayday, Mayday!' The final had to be stopped for a minute to enable us to stop laughing.

Colin Patterson had a fine season as Irish scrum-half and I sat on the bench. The nearest I came to a game was against France, when our wing was injured and Noel Murphy sent me to warm up. I was waiting on the side line to run on when the wing decided to carry on — and so it was another capless season. But if I had been picking the side, I would have picked Colin. He had weaknesses, sure, we all do, but the great thing he had was an unbelievable belief in his own ability; I suppose it was a cockiness, even an arrogance. I wish that, in a rugby sense, I had it in those days. It was only later in South Africa that I developed it — and I'm convinced it's a vital part of the make-up of nearly all successful players.

Before the game against France, coach Noel Murphy called me aside. He said that the way I had acted as a reserve over the two seasons filled him with admiration; the fact that I hadn't bitched or backstabbed Colin was praiseworthy. I was staggered; I had never even considered it, as I felt that Colin was the man for the job. But receiving that from Noel made me feel like a hero. Again, another important lesson: it's easy to forget the guys who are out of the limelight. After that, as a captain, I always tried to include the reserves and other squad guys in everything that was going on.

A lot of players were critical of Noel's rather disorganized approach, but I don't think anyone could ever question his commitment. He made me feel great, and I was thrilled for him when he was picked to coach the 1980 Lions in South Africa. The team was chosen after the last Five Nations internationals, and for a number of Irish players it was a bit of a false start — all very embarrassing.

What happened was that the Lions squad was announced on a Sunday. Now a relative of one of the Trinity players was listening to the radio. She heard the tail-end of some discussion on the *possible* makeup of the party. And she'd tuned in when possible reserves were being named — and thought it was the Lions squad announcement. A number of Irish names were there, including mine. Of course, she got onto the phone straight away with the news that we had been selected. At the time I was training with Greystones. The champagne was out immediately and half the town was there celebrating my selection. However,

I knew in my heart that a mistake had been made. I knew that Terry Holmes, the Welsh star, and Colin Patterson were the best scrum-halves, and both were available.

Then at about 5.30 pm the real side was announced: none of the names we'd heard were in. It's funny that, as it turned out, most of them eventually went as replacements — but my mate, the big Irish number eight Mike Gibson, didn't get the nod. Apparently he had also been celebrating his selection when the news broke.

I wasn't really disappointed, as I had never expected to go, and I was thrilled to be on the Barbarians Easter tour to Wales. That was fun, as a lot of youngsters went. We beat Cardiff in the big game, and I played well in partnership with John Horton, the English fly-half. As a special tribute to Cardiff, Billy Beaumont (the newly named Lions captain) led the Baa Baas. I was shocked when we ran out and the crowd, who had wanted a Welshman to lead the Lions, booed him onto the field. After the tour, to Billy's great credit, even the most died-in-the-wool Welshman agreed that he did a superb job as Lions skipper. But more of that later.

The Lions departed, and I led Leinster on the short tour to Romania. It was tough, but the fun we had with a happy, united side made up for it. Going behind the Iron Curtain for the first time was also an experience. The poor food, lack of service and delays everywhere couldn't spoil it for us, though, and the friendliness of the people was tremendous. As a special treat on the way back, we were invited as guests to watch the Romania vs Soviet Union match in Bucharest. This was an eye-opener: here were two sides that none of us really considered as part of the rugby world serving up a hard-fought, skilful game. I remember being particularly impressed with the way that the home side changed their tactics midstream, and in the end won well. I asked myself if I could have done that with my side in similar circumstances.

They say that people are the same the world over. Well, I'm not sure about that — but one thing I am certain of is that rugby players are all the same. Leinster, Romania and the Soviets were all staying at the same hotel in the middle of Bucharest. At first it was all a bit forced. At the cocktail party the Soviet players all drank orange juice and stayed at one side. We had got to know a few of the locals, a couple of them spoke English and so we made small talk. After the party ended, on the dot at eight, someone suggested that we adjourn to one of the player's rooms and continue. To our surprise the Russians and Romanians also came, and gradually the bottles got emptier and we got fuller. Suddenly the language problem melted away. Track suits were swapped, souvenirs for the coming Moscow Olympics were given, jeans were taken out and traded and then the singing started. It was a night to remember, and one that absolutely epitomized what the traditionalists mean when they talk about the rugby spirit of old. The night ended with us toasting Khrushchev (quite why we weren't toasting Brehznev, I can't remember). The Romanians were toasting De Valera and the Russians, Ceausescu. Somehow I don't think the players of tomorrow will see that sort of thing repeated too often. Perhaps I'm also getting old and more conscious of the status quo, but despite the inevitable rewards of a more professional game in the future, I'm glad I played in the last of the amateur days. Hell, soon I'll be talking about bringing back public floggings.

Then there was our cruise up the Danube. This came after our second game against a Southern Romanian side in Constantia, on the delta of the Danube. It involved a long bus journey, followed by a cruise and then a big meal at a restaurant somewhere beside the river. At this stage most of the players, especially the big donkey forwards, were pretty fed up with the food. There wasn't much of it, and it was very tough and usually cold. On the bus journey the two big jokers in the side, Paul McNaughton and Freddie McLennon (now living in Cape Town), walked up the bus with a list taking the lunch orders. We were told we could choose between T-bone steak or grilled chicken, and we had to say if we wanted chips, baked or sauteed potatoes, and select from a choice of vegetables — and it all had to be ordered in advance. Everyone got quite excited, and great care was taken over the menu. The cruise was fun; finally, all starving, we arrived at this impressive looking restaurant for the big meal.

There was a buzz of expectancy — which turned into a stunned silence when the food arrived. Each dish was the same: a big bowl of clear, greasy soup and in it, staring at the diner, was a huge fish head complete with eyes. That was that: nothing was eaten, and McNaughton and McLennon had to be led out to the boat — they were laughing so much they couldn't walk.

When I got home from Romania another surprise awaited me: an invitation to go to Rhodesia for a week or so to play for the Goshawks — a side like the Baa Baas or Irish Wolfhounds — along with Mike Biggar, the Scottish captain. Jennie was very good and said that it was an opportunity that couldn't be missed. Ian Robertson had put my name forward, and I felt very honoured. I also reflected that, although I would never go on a Lions tour, at least I would set foot in Africa. I kissed Jennie goodbye at Dublin airport, saying that I would see her the following Friday, would start work on the garden and generally spend time with her after the long season.

Well, the next time I saw her was about two-and-a-half months later, when I returned as a British Lions international. Somebody up above must have taken an interest in me; perhaps it was my late grandfather.

I travelled to Salisbury with Mike Biggar. I found him a good guy: we discussed the season, the Lions' chances and life in general. We finally got to Bulawayo for the Goshawks game against the Quaggas from South Africa. At the last minute a number of our better players pulled out and were replaced with club players. The general feeling was that we would be murdered. We were in the dressing room warming up, when a head was stuck round the door asking for me. It was a local journalist. He told me that Syd Millar, the Lions manager, had just phoned — and that Terry Holmes had been injured. I was to play the game and then fly to South Africa to join the Lions the next day.

I couldn't believe it. At first I thought it was a sick joke, or a misunderstanding like the one that had already occurred over selection. They had to almost hold me down and spell it out on the Bible that it was true. Well, if in the past people had criticized me for a reluctance to make physical contact while playing rugby, they should have seen me that day. I don't think I made one tackle; I never once attempted a break; and the only time I showed any emotion was when the final whistle went and I was still uninjured. We lost by a mile but I didn't give a damn: I was going to be a Lion.

The same sort of mixed emotions descended, just as they had done when I learnt of my first cap for Ireland. It's very difficult to explain it properly. Here was I, aged twenty-four, already an Irish player, and now going on to become a Lion. I had dreamt about this for years and years. I had almost tasted the ecstasy so many times that when it arrived it seemed such a letdown. Still, if I had reservations, none of the other Goshawks did. It was John Robbie Day and the whole place went bananas. I was now an adopted Rhodie, and even if the stupid Bok selectors decided to ignore Ray Mordt and David Smith, at least they had one player involved — me. This was the sort of sentiment that was being discussed that night; we were all jarred out of our minds and as a result I had a sore head the next day when I flew to Cape Town via Johannesburg.

The Lions were to play that day in Stellenbosch; if I was on time,

83

I would sit on the bench. I had a blazer, my Irish one, a couple of pounds in cash and enough clothes for a five-day trip. I never gave a thought to Guinness, despite only having leave for a week; and I confess that I never even considered Jennie. She learned of the developments on the TV news. She was torn between being overjoyed for me, and bitterly disappointed at the long separation that now was on the cards.

We arrived in Cape Town, and I was driven to Stellenbosch where Billy Beaumont and Syd Millar were waiting. I was welcomed and then we went straight to the dressing-rooms where the side was changing. There was no time for introductions, just a quick nod to a few of the Irish guys, into my Lions red jersey and then onto the bench, trying to learn the line-out signals. Syd told me that even if I never played a game on tour, for the rest of my life I would be a fully fledged British Lion. That was typical of Syd, to set a man's mind at rest right from the start.

I have called the side the British Lions. Now I know that will be taken as an affront by some Irishmen who insist that the team is the 'British and Irish' Lions. I used to feel strongly about it, but now I find it cumbersome; and I feel that, as the rugby world with the exception of the Irish Republic calls them the British Lions — at least on all occasions other than when Irish people are present — then it doesn't really matter a damn. If anyone is offended, then I'm sorry: no offence intended.

7

I was horrified a while ago to read that some top Welsh official had said that the day of the Lions tour was over, and that future touring sides should only be from the individual countries.

What a load of nonsense. Ask any player from the Five Nations what the ultimate rugby honour is and he will tell you straightaway — it's to tour with the Lions.

For the first few weeks of my tour I could hardly believe it. When my mum was on her first visit to Africa recently, she said she kept getting a sort of a glow inside, a feeling that was unreal because she was actually in Africa after all these years of reading and dreaming about it. I know what she was talking about, because I experienced the same with the Lions.

In many ways, the manner in which I got onto the tour as an early replacement was ideal. I was as much of a Lion as the great Willie-John McBride; Syd Millar had assured me that all Lions are equal and that took all the pressure off. I could sit back, play my best and not worry — it was all a bonus.

I made an early decision to do and see everything. I used to get up in the morning at about 7.30, have breakfast and then just go for a walk. I walked the streets of every town we visited, and when in Durban I walked on the beach. I chatted to the fishermen, guys who had been up all night, at Umhlanga; policemen in Johannesburg; coloured dustmen in Cape Town. I was fascinated by life, South Africa, and I wanted to see it all.

Once on the tour, the whole Lions party was invited to fly for a couple of days up to the Caprivi strip, right on the northern border of South West Africa/Namibia, to spend time as guests of the famous unit that is known as the Bushman Regiment. The trip is unique, there's nothing in the world like it, and the evenings are spent singing with and watching the locals dancing.

So I discovered later — I was horrified when the team decided to decline the offer and instead spend a few more days in Durban by the sea. Ollie Campbell, Tony Ward and I asked if we could go north on our own, but we were told we couldn't, we had to go with the side. General Jannie Geldenhuys, the Chief of the SADF, heard about my disappointment and this year I finally made the trip. It was an experience that everyone on that Lions tour would have remembered as a highlight.

I must just mention here that I have enjoyed getting to know General Geldenhuys. When you consider the responsibility he has and the decisions he has had to take, it's strange that he is always such a friendly, relaxed gentleman. He is a big rugby fan, and indeed we always used to have a chat after the Transvaal/Northerns games at Loftus. For a number of years, each time I met him, he used to remember that he had promised to send me on the trip to the Border. He would take out a bit of paper and make a note to himself — but still the trip never came. Then, about two years ago after a Northerns game, I was leaving Loftus after a few beers. As the lift opened, out walked the General with his attendants. All the others present snapped to attention and there was saluting all over the place; I, being a bit jarred, said something like: 'You bastard, I'm still waiting.' No one could believe their ears and after a few words the general moved on. I saw the looks of horror, and explained that we were friends and that Geldenhuys had promised me a trip to Namibia. One of the guys told me that if I talked to the General like that again I'd get my trip all right — for two years and with a short haircut!

Other Lions memories include going to a Bill Haley concert in the now demolished Colosseum in Johannesburg. Ollie, Tony and I went, and I remember being tempted when the guy next to us lit up a few joints and passed them over to us. In the end we declined, but still we had a great time. Bill Haley died soon afterwards, and that made our trip to see him seem even more important.

Another good night was at our hotel, a luxury job just north of Durban. Staying and performing there was Matt Munro, the famous singer. He turned out to be quite a rugby fan, and in fact became a big buddy of Dr Jack Matthews, the great Welsh centre of the 1950s who was our team medic. One night Matt got so jarred with Jack that he fell off his bar stool and tore a rib cartilage. The next night a few of us went to his show and he winced every time he hit a high note. The audience thought it was emotion, but we knew. He was a nice guy, and I'm sure a few rugby players who got to know him had a lump in their throats when we learnt of his death a few years ago.

Playing a charity cricket match in Jo'burg was also fun. Although it was winter, there wasn't a cloud in the sky as a Lions Eleven, strengthened by the great Graeme Pollock, met a South African side in a friendly. Ollie and I opened the batting for our team and we put on nearly fifty. However, when fielding, I nearly ended my tour by stepping in a sprinkler hole and badly spraining my ankle. It swelled up something awful and turned black and blue. I confess that I adopted Plan B and got absolutely mouldy drunk that night. When I meet Graeme Pollock these days, I sometimes think he has a twinkle in his eye as if to say: 'Robbie, I remember the way we first met and you had to be carried home.' Maybe I'm imagining things.

Syd Miller was a truly great manager. Of course, he knew South African rugby, having toured as a player and later as coach to the legendary 1974 Lions side. When I arrived he immediately organized clothes, money, anything I needed. He was scrupulously fair as well, and at times could impose discipline with only a word when it was needed. He was no mug, either. We called him 'Mallet Head'. It sounds unkind, but I assure you it was good-natured affection. We all loved him. But once during the tour the South African camp made some accusations about the Lions' dirty play and Syd was furious. He was diplomatic, but he made it quite clear that the Lions would not be messed around. In the end Morne du Plessis, the excellent Springbok skipper, defused the whole situation and all was well. But Syd had made his point. Unfortunately it would appear that tour managers of his calibre are few and far between.

Noel Murphy was the coach and I think at first a few of the non-Irish players were a bit disappointed in Noel, or 'Noisey' as he is always known. Noel was a world-class flanker and a great Lion himself. As a coach, he was always a bit disorganized. He was great fun but sometimes he addressed the troops in a very roundabout way that is typical of natives of the city of Cork. But as the tour went on I think the players began to figure that under all the rambling was a very committed man who put the players first. He would have died for us, and at the end we would have done the same for him. Unlike some Lions coaches, he showed no favouritism to the players from his country, and when Tests are being lost that is crucial. His style of coaching was, I believe, too conservative for the collective talents of the team. But with a bit of luck the series could easily have been drawn, and for any side to do that in South Africa is an achievement.

Sometimes Noel, a non-drinker, would really cut loose — not with drink, except on one famous occasion when Billy Beaumont and a few of the others laced Noel's drink with neat vodka. What I mean is that on occasions Noel could put aside the pressures of coaching and become a naughty schoolboy again. I remember one day we were at a party in the house of our liaison officer, Oom Choet Visser in Bloemfontein. All the songs had been sung when Noel announced that he was going to hypnotize a few players. He chose Billy Beaumont and Alan Martin, the Welsh lock. I was immediately interested, as I've always been interested in being hypnotized (it's never happened but I live in hope).

Anyway, Noel laid them down in the middle of the big crowd of players, pressmen and hangers on, and proceeded to walk around them making the usual noises, getting them to relax, 'heavy eyelids' and so on. As he walked around the spreadeagled pair he would catch hold of their trouser legs and gently shake them. He did the same with their shirtsleeves. At the end he pronounced that they were in a trance and commanded them to try and get up. They strained a bit and couldn't move. He clapped his hands and they awoke scratching their heads. It was all very impressive, and for a few minutes Billy and Alan could be seen sitting quietly, wiping their brows, deep in thought.

After a few minutes someone else asked Noel to do it again. He pretended to protest but then asked for volunteers. I was up like a shot, along with a few other of the youngsters. Of course this was the 'sting', and we were the unknowing suckers. I lay on the ground with my eyes shut, desperately willing myself into a trance and aware of my legs being gently shaken by Noel; the fact that this opened up a sort of trouser-tunnel from my ankles right up to my groin did not occur to me. The next moment Noel produced a pint glass of frozen water and this was hurled right up my leg. I cannot describe just how wet you get when the trick is done. Apparently Noel has been catching people with this party trick for years, and despite doing it hundreds of times he still cries with laughter each time another mug gets caught.

Billy Beaumont was the captain and I have no praise high enough for him as a leader, a person and a player. Of course he knew that a lot of Welshmen wanted a Welsh captain; the Welsh nation felt they had been cheated that year when Paul Ringer was sent off against England. This must have put Billy under a lot of pressure, especially at the beginning of the tour. But he just played it straight down the middle. He was always available for a chat, was good fun and obviously decided never to ask any of his players to do anything he wasn't prepared to do himself. I was amazed, at training sessions, at the way he ran. I had grown up at Irish squad sessions where the backs ran on and the donkeys trundled far, far behind. I expected that all sides allowed their forwards to jog along à la Moss Keane, Phil Orr, and Willie Duggan. Not so. Billy set a standard and big guys like Maurice Colclough, Alan Tomes and Graham Price were more than happy to match his efforts.

Billy was an excellent player as well. I sometimes think that he gets a lot of praise for his captaincy, but that history has neglected to give him credit for his playing ability. He isn't tall for a modern lock, but with timing and clever variation managed to win a lot of line-out ball. He was also very mobile and drove very hard; he had great guts and despite an injured knee on tour gave everything with no complaint. I was worried early on that, as a youngster, and especially as a replacement from the Irish bench (as opposed to a current international) Billy and some of the other Englishmen might have resented that I got the nod over Steve Smith, the English scrum-half. If so they never showed it, and right from the start I was made very welcome.

I was lucky in that I played well. The conditions suited me — very dry, big crowds and lots of interest (like a lot of sportsmen I always find it easier to play in front of big crowds rather than one man and his dog). And of course I felt under no pressure. I got all my passes away well, kicked at the right time and even made a few breaks. And my tackling for some reason improved enormously. In Ireland I had always been very much a covering scrum-half, almost a second fullback; here, with so many good players, I tended to stay a bit closer to the ball and I was so determined to be worth my place that I got stuck in. I felt great when Ollie Campbell told me that he couldn't believe how many tackles I was making — just as when Mike Gibson had complimented me four years before in New Zealand, praise from Ollie was not shallow. I was thrilled.

I also remember the second game I played on the tour. It was at the Wanderers against the Junior Boks — the game in which Rodney O'Donnell broke his neck. For a long time we were under fierce pressure, and I made about half a dozen tackles in the space of about five minutes. One of them was on their strong wing Darius Botha, right in front of our bench. I heard Billy (who wasn't playing) shouting 'Well done', and once again I felt really good. Praise like that is very motivational — its value is often underestimated.

Incidentally, as well as being a very brave full-back, Rod will also go down as being the most superstitious player ever to represent his

89

country. All his various practices to ward off evil luck would almost fill a book on their own. The Lions had great fun with this. When Friday the 13th fell, Rod woke up and came out of his room: there was a ladder over his door, salt along the corridor and taped lines all across the carpet — Rod's big fear was stepping on lines. There was also an eerie message written on the door.

Ray Gravell got the blame, but let me now confess: Ollie Campbell and I got up at 4.30 that morning and set all the traps. We thought it a great laugh — until, soon after, Rodney broke his neck. Ollie and I actually wondered if Rodney had a point after all — but then we learnt that, far from being unlucky, he was actually very fortunate to still have the use of his limbs. If Dr John O'Driscoll hadn't been playing and shouted to the ambulance men when Rod went down not to move him, then he could have died or been paralysed. And the fact that John was even playing against the Junior Boks that day was because Colm Tucker had sprained his ankle. More luck for Rodney.

Billy was also an impressive captain off the field. The spirit of the party was excellent, but inevitably there were minor personality clashes and the odd bit of friction. For some reason a couple of the Welsh guys seemed to enjoy niggling me — perhaps it was because I had been to Cambridge. Also, I have always been a collector of useless information and tend to think that others are as interested in it as I am. Perhaps that made me sound like a bit of a know-all. Alan Philips, the Welsh hooker, who I have since met and enjoyed talking to, seemed to delight in rubbing me up the wrong way. There was once a discussion on photography, and I made a comment about how photographs appear to put weight onto the person being snapped, hence the reason for models being thin. I think I had heard details from Jennie who had done a photographic course at art school. It was a harmless remark, but Alan turned and asked me if I thought I was David Bailey. I got a bit cross — he said it in a really snide way — but there was no incident.

A few days later the team had a trip to a sports store. Afterwards I was to visit a hospital: Roger Young, the former Irish scrum-half who lives in Cape Town, had asked me to go and I had requested the players in one of the minibuses to wait outside the hotel for a minute while I got the address.

When I came down the bus had gone and I was stuck. Afterwards one of the guys told me that Alan had told them not to wait and off they had gone. I was upset — I had told Roger I would be there. Suddenly Billy walked out of the hotel, asked what was wrong and then said, not to worry, he would go with me. He organized a taxi in no time — Lions captains are good at that sort of thing — and we went along and had a sobering but very interesting day at this hospital for kids who suffer from tragic handicaps. In his book, Billy says it was one of the most moving experiences he had on tour. I agree with him. Here we were, young men in the prime of health undertaking a tour which involved fun galore, suddenly confronted with small kids living and coping with dreadful handicaps. It brought us back to earth.

In general it was a trouble-free tour, and that was mainly due to Billy, Syd, Noel and Jack Matthews — an exceptional management team. With all the interest and, of course, money in South Africa, we were treated like kings. I remember we met some British footballers, including Steve Heighway and Viv Anderson along with top manager Dave Sexton, who were on a coaching scheme. We were being swamped at hotels by autograph hunters while they were ignored. As someone who was used to the opposite treatment when professional footballers in Britain were around, it was a big ego trip and good fun.

Actually the meeting of famous people on a major tour was one of the fun parts. I had not realized that so many people were interested in Bill Haley, Matt Munro, Christiaan Barnard and other personalities: whenever our paths crossed we were always introduced. Also, of course, many famous players from bygone days were there following the tour. I remember meeting Bleddyn Williams, the Welsh centre; I also became friendly with the late Carwyn James, and what a gentleman he was.

Jean Pierre Rives, the French flanker, was there as well at the end of the tour. I was in Pretoria with Noel at some function or other, and we got a lift back with some bloke in a sports car who was taking Jean Pierre back to Johannesburg. We got hopelessly lost, and I recall that as we sped at breakneck speed down a back road we could see a fork ahead. 'Go left,' said Noel to the driver. 'Please go right,' said I. 'Please go fuckeeng slower!' screamed Rives, who could speak little English, from the back seat. The driver, a South African, was laughing so much he nearly crashed.

But the funniest moment, I think, came after the third Test in Port Elizabeth. The Lions had gone into the game two down, and so it was the decider. In shocking weather we lost 12-10, and thereby the series. The Lions were very disappointed — it was a game that had been won everywhere but on the scoreboard. Still, there was no sulking. In best tradition the Lions decided to bury their sorrows and so a monumental piss-up was held. A few equally drunk South African fans had got into the hotel's off-limits area, and a bit of a skirmish had developed. At one stage Syd, Noel, I think Billy, and Jack Matthews had chucked a couple of the intruders down the stairs from our floor. Jack looked down and saw a gold watch on the floor. He picked it up and hurled it down after the guys, with a cry of 'And take your blasted watch with you!' Then he saw his bare wrist: in the excitement he'd flung his own watch down the stairs.

Another extraordinary thing happened during the game. I was on the bench for the Lions with, amongst others, Tony Ward, the Irish fly-half. Now with the weather being really bad — driving rain and sleet — the crowd had pushed its way right under the big stand at Boet Erasmus, the Test ground in Port Elizabeth. Many fans had decided to walk back into town to watch the game on TV. As a result there was total chaos inside and outside the stadium. Anyway, as we were changing, Tony realized to his horror that he had forgotten his boots. He was very upset — he has tiny feet, and couldn't borrow a pair from anyone else. It was impossible to send back to the hotel because of the crush outside, so I told him just to say nothing and sit on the bench in his socks.

A few minutes before the kick off, we substitutes went to sit in the stand. But because of the crowd we had to walk out the back and around the front of the stand. This took us about five minutes, and by the time we arrived around the front the game had started. We heard a shout, and saw that Ollie Campbell, the Lions fly-half, was down injured. He had a wound in his head that was pumping blood. Noel immediately told Tony to warm up.

Wardie asked me what the hell he should do now. I said, 'Pray as hard as you can.' It must have worked, because Ollie somehow continued, and to this day I don't think Noel knows how close he was to learning that his replacement fly-half and goal-kicker in a series decider between the Lions and the Boks had arrived with no boots. I don't think Noel's heart would have survived.

To stop the Lions tours would be a tragedy. Who cares if the odd series is lost? The same officials and journalists decrying the recent results are the ones claiming that 'the game's the thing,' and that the result is secondary to the fun and camaraderie off the field. Well, the Lions lost the 1980 series 3-1. The Boks deserved to win, because they had a team geared to play to its strengths. We lost because we had a magnificent pack of forwards, quite the best I have ever played behind, but a tactical unawareness of how to win the series. I believe that a desire to win all the provincial games, and a lack of courage to allow the team to make early tour mistakes in order to develop a more expansive style, cost us the series. I have read books on the tour where the backline is blamed, but I blame the decision-makers who framed our tactics. The Lions had backs of the calibre of Colin Patterson, Ollie Campbell, Dai Richards, Ray Gravell, John Carleton, Clive Woodward and Andy Irvine at full-back. To say that with the amount of ball being won by the pack that this backline, or one with a few of the other players, was incapable of using it is nonsense. Instead of moving all balls early in the tour, thus developing a pattern of movement and support, the team kicked for position and drove excessively with the pack. It was good enough against the provinces, but in the Tests it was different.

One day, I think it was before the third Test, we were training in Port Elizabeth. The Lions side was practising winning the ball from a set phase, moving it to first centre where it was then hoofed up in the air. This was a main tactic to draw up the defending line and then turn them. I noticed that sitting on the grandstand deep in conversation were Carwyn James, Chalkie White and Ian Robertson. They were three of the best backline coaches ever produced by British rugby, watching the cream of the current players practising booting the ball up in the air. I must say I felt a little ashamed.

One of the problems, I think, was that all the heavies on the tour were donkeys. Syd, Noel and Billy were forwards; the senior players were Graham Price, Peter Wheeler, Geoff Squire and Derek Quinnell. Where was the backline representation? One of the great constants in rugby, I believe, is that forwards don't really understand backline play. All they know is that for them to work hard and win ball, have it passed backwards and then watch as the next breakdown is behind the advantage line, is depressing. They would far rather have the ball hoofed up the field as it means that they go forward. Often a side has to make mistake after mistake in a backline, until finally the pattern emerges and then the alignment, timing, backing up and — above all — confidence means that the breaks start to come.

In this regard I must confess that I was a little disappointed in Andy Irvine. Andy became a good mate on tour, and of course he was a brilliant attacking full-back. When he arrived as a replacement, I felt that at least we had a man with sufficient standing as a player to really influence our pattern of play. (Remember that Ollie and I and Clive Woodward and Dai Richards were all really youngsters, and did not have the clout to influence the pattern. Gareth Davies and Terry Holmes were injured, and it's difficult for an injured player to have an impact.) In

93

private conversation Andy was very forceful and he fully supported the backline view that the ball should be released quicker and that it should be moved more — but in team meetings he was much less forceful, and so our rather pedestrian tactics continued. Things only changed in the last Test, and by then it was too late.

We won the last one, our only victory in the series. Perhaps I'm being a bit hard on the donkeys. Perhaps they knew that our big weakness was the lack of a real back row flyer to match Rob Louw to the breakdown. I do know that as a unit they were fabulous. At times I stood behind them and wanted to applaud as they toyed with some province or other. It was a great pity that a side good enough to win the series came short.

What of the Boks? Well, they were very motivated and they played to their strengths. Before the Tests we had heard a lot about Naas Botha. We were told that he was the big danger man, and we even practised defensive patterns to try and curb him. In reality, though, he was not a real factor in the series win. He played OK, sure, and in the first Test his tactical kicking was good — but he was not one of the stars. The guys who gave us headaches were Rob Louw on the flank and Gysie Pienaar at full-back. Everything that they did turned to gold in the Tests, and with Gerrie Germishuys in deadly finishing form on the wing they were the key men. Morne du Plessis was an outstanding skipper, and at all times he was diplomacy personified. We did not rate him as highly as South Africans do as a player, but as a skipper he had the Lions' respect.

After one of the Tests, the Lions had lost again and it was time to let off steam. The officials had laid on a mammoth spread at the hotel. The chefs had done a super job, and in particular the cakes, pastries and souffles were magnificent. We were all hanging around waiting for the Boks to arrive; of course by now we had been sipping beers for a good while. It all started off so quietly. Someone flicked a bit of cream at someone else. Well, when the Boks arrived with their wives the place looked like that scene in *The Great Race* where Tony Curtis is walking through the cake fight. Morne looked in amazement and had the sense to just ignore it. Billy later told us that he was talking to some South African official about quite a serious matter when he suddenly realized that the guy was staring at his head. On top of Billy's head was perched a complete Black Forest gateau. We let off steam all right, but it was fun, nothing was broken and we were popular.

94

One of the real features on a Lions tour is the effect that the posse of touring journalists has on the side. Because it was South Africa, the 1980 press corps consisted of rugby scribes and also a fair number who were there to comment on a far wider range of things. It was apparent that there was friction between the two sets of journalists, and this was borne out when the first reports that they had written started to filter back in letters from home. It was as though there were three different tours. First, there was the one seen by the rugby journalists ('all is well'); then the political one ('the players are unhappy'); and finally there was the real tour seen through the players' eyes.

All the press clippings that started to come back to us on tour must have had an effect on the tour management. At one stage, quite near the end, we were all called into a special meeting. Syd addressed us and asked if we were unhappy, as he had read reports to that effect. We all said we were having a whale of a time. He then asked us if we would all return to tour South Africa if selected. Ironically enough, I was the only player who indicated that I would have to think about it; everyone else said they would. In fact Peter Morgan, the young Welsh utility player who had played in only a few games on the tour, brought the house down by saying that he'd love to come back again as next time they might let him have a game!

I suppose I was being a bit hypocritical when I displayed my uncertainty. Most visitors to South Africa say on arrival just how different it is to what they had imagined. From media reports one expects to see blatant hatred between all the races, and also one assumes that all white South Africans are going to be Nazis — or at least thoroughly unlikeable people. The fact that my overall impression of the place was very different worried me. I knew that in many ways we had seen South Africa from a very privileged viewpoint. We had been treated like superstars, and anyone who had annoyed us would have been removed from our vicinity.

In fact, once we arrived at our hotel in Cape Town and there was a black soccer team also booking in. One of their players spoke to Billy and said they were all very disappointed in the Lions. Billy assumed he was talking about the defeats in the first two Tests, but the guy went on to explain that he thought we should have refused the invitation to tour. He was a little bit rude and must have been overheard. Anyway, when we came back from training the soccer side had been moved to another hotel.

We went to townships, and nobody can hide the overcrowding and lack of facilities. No, I knew there was a lot of injustice in the country, 95 but there was also so much goodwill in the place — and so many people, English and Afrikaans, were prepared to concede that dreadful errors had been made and that reforms were needed. It was almost as though I felt that John Robbie, wonderboy and patron saint of Irish youth, must automatically be seen to be against contact with this system that everyone condemns out of hand. That I could see willingness to change, and so much good being done in sport, actually caused me to have doubts about which way to commit myself on future sporting visits. But more of that later.

I had a marvellous time with the Lions, played well, made hundreds of friends and saw more of South Africa than most South Africans have seen. Having originally gone to Zimbabwe-Rhodesia for a week, I arrived home months later. I was also in a bit of trouble at work.

During a Lions year, all players selected for their national trials get asked about availability for the tour. I was therefore sounded out and so asked my boss what the story was from the company's side. He checked with Guinness and indicated that there would be no problem. But I had used up most of my leave in Romania, and with the week in Zimbabwe. After I got the Lions call, I didn't give Guinness a thought until near the end of the tour. I was so wrapped up in the whole thing, living my dreams, that work seemed a world away. Then I started to realize that I had set off for a week, and had simply not come back; I hadn't phoned or written or anything. At the time I was working in the Guinness Traffic Department as part of a small, disciplined team; if one of the team was away it meant that the others' lives were that much harder — and I never even gave this a thought. With a few weeks to go, I suddenly got the message that I had been very irresponsible. I tried to phone my boss, but couldn't get him. I then sat down and wrote a long letter outlining what had happened.

Just before I posted it, Rodney O'Donnell, the Irish full-back, rejoined the team. He had broken his neck in the game against the Junior Springboks, and had undergone an operation in Johannesburg. He was with us for a few days before flying back to Dublin. I asked Rodney to do me a favour and drop the letter in to Guinness. But it turned out that Rodney's op had not been a success, and on arrival home he had to be rushed in for a second operation. As a result my boss got a call from Rodney's mum asking him to pick up my letter at her house.

My boss could easily have lost his temper. For the way in which he reacted, recognizing youthful exuberance, I will be forever grateful — but once again I had put the game ahead of a good career with one of the best employers in the country.

On arrival home I was once more a star. No, that's an exaggeration — but at least I came back as the Lions Test scrum-half, whereas I had left as an Irish reserve. The tour had been a success even though the series had been lost, and in all the assessments I had come out well. I had certainly played well, and in many ways the games I had on tour were the playing highlights of my career. I had for once got picked above Colin Patterson — although in fairness he damaged his leg in the penultimate game, playing for the weaker Wednesday side. When I made the side for the final Test on the Saturday he was officially 'not available' — but a week before I had been picked against the strong Western Province side; we beat them by thirty points, so I think I was in anyway (and Noel Murphy told me so).

I had started as a temporary replacement, and ended up playing in eight games, including those against the Junior Boks, Northern Transvaal, Western Province, the Barbarians and South Africa in the final Test. I had passed well, kicked and tackled competently, and made a few breaks at the right time. My confidence was sky-high. There was a time on tour when I even got a bit cocky. The 'fifth Test' was always going to be the game against Northern Transvaal, traditionally the strongest province. From the moment the Lions arrived, players and management had been led to believe that Northerns were even stronger than the Boks.

The day we arrived in Pretoria for the game, we were met by a bunch of vintage cars and we drove in style through the city. Thousands of people came out to watch, and at the head of the procession they even had a real live lion in a cage on the back of a lorry — and alongside it a huge bull (Northerns are known as the Blue Bulls). Anyway, on the morning of the game Colin got a flu bug and I got a very late call to play. This was the Test side, and we were all very nervous. (In the dressing-room just before we went out, centre Ray Gravell — that Welsh lunatic with a heart as big as himself — lost his gum-shield. He was in such a state that when the ref came in to check our boots, the whole side was crawling around trying to locate Ray's bloody gum-shield. The legend goes that Ray discovered that, in fact, it was in his mouth, but that's an exaggeration — it was in his bag.)

We played Northerns in front of almost 70 000 people, and we really drilled them up front. We were 16-0 up at half-time, and although the final score was 16-9, we all knew that the better side had won — and they conceded this at the reception. I had a good game, and at one stage

97

made a clean break down the left; I was straight through, with just their full-back to beat. Normally, in a situation like that, if I couldn't draw him and put another player in, I tended to kick (fancy footwork not being my strongest point). But the Northerns full-back was a guy called Pierre Edwards, and for the Lions he had become something of a joke. He looked so awkward, well over six feet and spindly: with his balding head he reminded us of a praying mantis, and we couldn't take him seriously.

So I decided I would take Edwards on. I feinted right and went left, and was just imagining the headline announcing the score when his tackle cut me in half. Never in my career was I hit so hard, and I certainly learned a lesson — don't judge a book by its cover. Later I played against him at provincial level, and he really was one of the safest fullbacks I have ever encountered. I never was one-on-one to him again — but if it had happened, I would have chipped ahead and chased.

It was unreal to think that, just as I had once followed every minute of every Lions game since I was a little kid, learning every detail about the players, now there were hundreds of kids doing the same about us. Reading the books about the tour and hunting eagerly for pictures or references to oneself was also exciting; so was the knowledge that I had moved up the pecking order of those who had ever played the game. Many great players never played for the Lions, often through cruel luck or injury or bad selection or whatever. I was lucky: when I look back, I still get a buzz, and sense that same disbelief I felt at the time. When I consider the number of good British players at club, county, provincial and international level, then the thought that I made it to the top three or four, at that time, is quite awesome.

The memories are mostly good, but just like a school or a university, there is a dimension of fleetingness. When I walk into Trinity I get this feeling that it has moved on, it no longer belongs to me; when I meet my old tour mates, there is sometimes an element of that. A few years after I moved to South Africa to live, I met a few of the Welsh boys who were out on tour. Sure, we chatted — but it wasn't the same: they were more involved in their current tour, with its own in-jokes, fun, scandal, playing patterns and so on. Mind you, last year there was an international touch rugby tournament at Sun City, and I met Peter Wheeler, who had been hooker for the 1980 Lions. Even though he was a senior player on the tour and I was a baby, it was just like old times. We went and had a few jars and discussed players and friends: it was as though the years had disappeared, and we were on the tour again. Perhaps it was the beer.

The South African dimension troubled me a lot. I almost felt guilty at enjoying the tour so much. I kept saying that there were things that really upset me, and that I wasn't sure if Ireland should go the following year — but once more I was playing a role. I have often heard it said that to turn down a chance to tour South Africa must be a very difficult decision: I now believe that to go on tour is even more difficult.

To say 'no' is easy. Everyone says, 'What a moral thing to do,' and of course no one would dare to criticize you. But to stand up and be counted as tourist means you are there to be knocked, especially if you go a second time. A first trip can easily be justified on the grounds of wanting to see the place for yourself; to go again leaves you wide open. On the one hand you have all this information about the evil of South Africa, much of it very true; on the other, there is this feeling that perhaps there is another side. Maybe there are aspects of the country that need encouragement; possibly the isolationist argument is not the best one.

I had all these feelings spinning around my head for most of the year following the Lions tour. But the bit of hassle over the Lions was nothing compared to the rows and ructions that happened before Ireland went in 1981.

8

Feeling a bit sheepish, I started work again at Guinness and really got stuck in. I even remember pulling out of an early season trial for Leinster due to pressure of work. I was accused of ducking the trial through over-confidence, but that wasn't true. I genuinely made an effort to try to achieve the same buzz in my job that I did when I was involved in rugby. But it didn't work.

I had a good season. Leinster had great spirit, were well managed, and developed a feeling that winning was almost a right — something that is common to all successful sides, as long as it doesn't become confused with complacency. It didn't with us: we took the championship again, and in the last game hammered Ulster by thirty points in Belfast. We scored lots of tries, ran everything and were being talked about as one of the best Irish provincial sides ever. I was very much the boss, although Ollie Campbell and Paul McNaughton were able lieutenants. Funnily enough, Fergus Slattery, Willie Duggan and Phil Orr — although valuable members of the side — weren't really 'executive members of the management', if I can put it that way. Then, before the trial, the leading Irish rugby journalist, Edmund van Esbeck of *The Irish Times*, asked for an interview.

This was a mistake for me. Ned was very fair, but again I was being put on the spot over South Africa. I was torn between saying, yes, I think the tour should go ahead and that the efforts of the South African rugby administrators to put their house in order should be supported with visits; or living up to the image of the Irish saint. Although I now support passionately all the moves that have been made to ensure meaningful improvements for all races, in those days I felt obliged to say that I hadn't made up my mind whether to tour (if selected). Inside I was feeling that I wanted to go, for many reasons — but should John Robbie be seen to support the tour? I was afraid to stand up for my convictions.

The article came out and, although I thought it read well and I still had my options open, many people told me that I had talked myself out of the Irish captaincy for the 1981 season. I had never really considered this, as Fergus Slattery was the skipper and had done a good job. But I was Leinster captain ahead of him, and I did have this reputation for getting the best out of sides, and also for playing an expansive type of rugby. I don't know whether I was in with a real shout, but I made the Irish side easily, Slats was skipper and we had a good team. However, we blew a half-time lead over France, Ollie Campbell was moved to centre and Tony Ward came back at fly-half. I believe this affected the side badly, and we lost 9-8 to Wales at Cardiff, despite scoring two tries to nil. Wardie was absolutely brilliant in that game, but I still believe that Ollie at fly-half in that particular Irish side was better.

That game in Wales was, for me, the most difficult ever. I had done something to my back against France, and should never have played at Cardiff. I remember in training doing a lot of sit-ups. Nowadays I know that the exercise should never even be attempted with straight legs, such is the pressure it puts on the lower back — but in those days we were uninformed. Two days after the French game I woke up and I couldn't straighten; even breathing was terribly sore. I ignored it, but it didn't improve: still, no problems, the Welsh game was two weeks away.

A week later I was still in trouble, and I told the selectors that I was doubtful, but the team had been announced and I was in. Still I treated the back, and still it was sore. The selectors told me to travel and leave it to the last moment. The night before the game I was in agony. I bumped into Phil Bennett, the Welsh fly-half who was then in broadcasting, in the hotel and he refused to believe that I was going to play. X-rays had revealed nothing, but I felt I must pull out. Then Pat Whelan, the Irish hooker, took me aside. When I said I was going to pull out, he advised me to reconsider.

Now I had never played against Wales before, and with my Welsh blood it had always been an ambition to do so. Also, of course, I knew there were replacements. Pat said that if I could trot onto the field, his advice was to play. Anyway I faked the fitness test, passed it, and stood in the middle of Cardiff Arms Park, listening to 60 000 people singing the anthems, knowing that I couldn't actually stand straight. Somehow I managed to finish the game, although I did little of note, and I kept my place for the next game. In fact, my place was in doubt — but I suppose as I had played in real pain, for the honour of my country and all that, they could hardly drop me.

101

It's funny how often that question about playing with an injury crops up, isn't it? I must confess that although I don't agree with the practice, I once played a Varsity match with so many injections in my ankle and shoulder that I felt at half-time that the juice from the orange might start squirting from my skin. I also played for Transvaal once with a broken bone in my foot, and that cost me about eight weeks of the season as a result of the damage done.

But by far the worst was that game against Wales. If Pat Whelan hadn't spoken to me, I would never have played. Mind you, there is a lock who used to play in Ireland called Emmett O'Rafferty. I always rated him as a hard, aggressive lock, although he was not good in the line-out. After many years, he was finally picked for his first Irish cap, against France in Paris. At the last training run, the day before, he pulled a muscle. The Irish coach knew he was hiding something, but couldn't pin him down. The story goes that the coach appealed to his love of Ireland and guaranteed that if he withdrew from the French game, come hell or high water he would get selected against Wales.

Armed with his guarantee, Emmett admitted his sore muscle and pulled out. His replacement, Harry Steel, a retreaded number eight, played, performed brilliantly and — you guessed it — Emmett never got his international cap for Ireland. I know bloody well what Emmett would do if he had the same choice again. The lesson is clear: 'Never turn down the chance of a piss' — and don't believe promises made under pressure.

Of course, I should be saying that Emmett made a noble decision for the good of his country. Although I would have been very cross with a guy who played for me hiding an injury, in this day and age of replacements, and seeing it was his first cap, who would have blamed him for taking a chance?

My back cleared up with intensive physiotherapy and carefully programmed exercise, although even today, after a game of tennis or if I have to stand for a long time, it gets sore. Acupuncture has proved the best treatment for it over the years; luckily the Transvaal physio during our good years was a practitioner of the art.

So I kept my place for the English game, but again we lost (10-6), and I was slated for taking on the back row too much. I don't quite know why I did it — except I felt that by passing back to Wardie running across the field, as he always used to do then, we weren't going to get anywhere. Perhaps I overdid it. In the last few minutes I broke right and scissored with our right wing. It worked perfectly, drew the

·defence and opened a clear path to the line. Unfortunately, Frank Quinn dropped the ball and the chance of victory was gone. We'd lost and I was dropped. I was furious. Although I hadn't set the stage alight, I had always been tidy and felt that one missed pass by Frank (also dropped) was being used to make us scapegoats.

The next day at work I got a call from Paddy Madigan, the chairman of selectors. I can see now that it was a very decent thing to phone me for a chat, but at the time I blew up. I effed him and blinded him from a height, and ended by slamming the phone down. I only regretted it on the Saturday before the Scottish game when Robbie McGrath — who replaced me — dislocated his shoulder in a club game. When I heard that I got a hell of a shock. Luckily Paddy Madigan has a sense of humour, didn't hold the outburst against me, and I was back in the side.

We played Scotland at Murrayfield in the worst rain I have ever played in. We lost 10-9, Bruce Hay intercepting a terrible pass from Tony Ward. I played well, at least I thought so, and I was thanked after the game by the selectors for my efforts. But my record for Ireland was — believe it or not — played nine, lost nine. Forget that in almost all the games the margin of defeat was very small: it is a hell of a record. I actually became the answer to a quiz question that started to do the rounds: 'Which British Lion who never played on a losing Lions side had a record of played nine, lost nine for his country?' I was very upset about it for ages, but the Lions' Test win — at the time of writing it's still their last — was some comfort.

The most amusing angle on this happened a year or so after I went to live in South Africa. Having lost so often for Ireland, I was very interested to see that Ireland then won her first Triple Crown for nearly forty years. Ollie Campbell's kicking was a major factor, but full marks to all involved. Of course the publicity was fantastic, and by chance I was in Dublin when a Test was to be played a while after. I was naturally very keen to see the new Irish approach that had received so much attention — the fitness, the flair and most of all the will to win. But against Wales that day Ireland were well beaten. After the game the crowd dispersed; as I was walking slowly down from the West stand at Lansdowne Road, a loud voice came from the seats high above me: 'Hey, Robbie,' it roared, 'you're some good luck charm!' I laughed, the crowd laughed, and it was nice to be remembered.

Anyway, the losing 1981 season was over. There was now the tour of South Africa to look forward to, if it ever took place. The Lions tour had not caused too many problems in terms of demonstrations against

103

rugby or the players; at least we in Ireland weren't too aware of it. (I know John Carleton, the English wing, resigned his job; he was a teacher with a Labour-controlled council and he was not given permission to go.) Because the Lions are selected from Britain and from Ireland, and because the rugby authorities were united, it went ahead. Afterwards I was aware of little trouble, and the only interest seemed to be purely of a rugby nature.

Now it was Ireland on her own, and opinion was really split. The rugby authorities were adamant that the tour should go ahead: South Africa had been part of the international rugby family for almost a century, and her attempts to integrate rugby — despite apartheid laws — had to be supported. That was the view of most of the players. However, South Africa was and is the most hated nation on earth. Many people equate white South Africans with the Nazis, and until the regime in Pretoria is overthrown, to have any contact with the place is seen to be unacceptable. That was the other view, and I suppose there was a scale of intensity of feeling between these two extremes.

I examined my conscience. I am reminded now of a meeting with a former team-mate of mine who had become very involved with Amnesty International. He gave me a lecture on the evils of apartheid for about two hours in his flat in Dublin. It was very upsetting, but he was unable to give me any real solutions to the country's problems — at least, solutions that I thought would be realistic. (He had never been to South Africa.) He believed in one-man one-vote, and nothing else. The fact that virtually all of Africa did not have democratic systems, and that so many Irish organizations were involved in relief work (made necessary by mismanagement), cut no ice with him. The main thrust of his argument was that because, in rugby terms, I had a high profile in Ireland, my pulling out of the tour on moral grounds would have a big influence on whether or not the tour went ahead.

I believe now that this was nonsense: even if the IRFU had to send twenty-five third fifteen players they were not going to cancel. But my friend had the right approach. He had appealed to the image that I had of myself — or believed I had. Would Sir Galahad do something unpopular? I was very near to pulling out of the tour after that chat, even though inside I was in favour. At that time I was being dishonest with myself and now I look back with sorrow at my lack of guts. However, I later made the decision to go and I can live with that.

A number of players did pull out. The government did not support the tour, and all government or semi-state employees couldn't go or had to resign. Moss Keane, Paul McNaughton and Cieran Fitzgerald were among them. Hugo Macneil and Tony Ward pulled out on moral grounds, and I respect them for it (although Tony has since told me that, had he been able to choose again, he would have gone). Donal Spring was another who withdrew, and despite lots of people saying it was a political decision because his older brother had parliamentary aspirations, I also respect him for it.

One day I had a real row in a bar in Dublin. At the time I was on shift work at Guinness and used to get a bus home to Greystones in the afternoon. I missed my bus from College Green in Dublin by a whisker, and that meant an hour's wait for the next one. It started to rain, and so I went across the road to the College Mooney, a big ale-house in Dublin. I bought an evening paper and was just about to read it over a quiet half-pint of Guinness when I heard my name called. It was Sean Kilfeather, the Gaelic Football correspondent from *The Irish Times*. I knew of him, and was quite flattered that he came over.

We had a chat. It was all very civilized, and he told me that in fact he was being joined by Eamonn Dunphy, the soccer player-turned-journalist. I was delighted, as I had admired the book that Dunphy had written exposing many of the myths about British soccer, and looked forward to meeting him. He arrived a few minutes later and Frank introduced us. Eamonn looked at me and suddenly announced that, in his mind, rugby had done more to harm Ireland than anything else in history, including the crown of England. I was a bit stunned and said nothing. Eamonn was like an opened tap and went on to give his views about the tour, interspersed with his own hatred of rugby as an elitist sport.

Now, the Irish soccer team had recently played in Argentina, and this had coincided with a lot of articles about human rights abuses there. I asked him his views on this, and the question seemed to throw him a bit. He didn't answer, and then launched an attack on me because as a university graduate I was automatically a member of the oppressing upper classes, etc, etc. I started to get annoyed, and I thought Eamonn was a stupid little chip-shouldered troublemaker. I told him that my father had started his working life labouring in a coal-yard after the Great Depression and through his hard work at sea, his after-hours study and later his work as a marine engineer, he had made enough for his kids to have the chance of a university education. I told him, that far from feeling guilty about this, I was extremely proud.

Then I realized that Eamonn had a few drinks on board, and he disappeared somewhere. I still read Eamonn's articles and enjoy them, but he takes himself extremely seriously. Apparently he once really lost his temper when some TV people did a hilarious impersonation of him on a World Cup panel, and he spoilt it all by taking umbrage. At least he is not boring, and I suppose that's something.

However, our meeting must have done something, because the next weekend he wrote a rambling article castigating everything to do with rugby — but not a mention about the soccer links with Argentina and the Soviet Union. I felt quite proud of myself, but didn't get mentioned in despatches in the article.

Mike Gibson, the Irish number eight and my former Trinity team-mate, also worked at Guinness. We decided to approach the company just to clarify the position regarding the tour (this was months before it took place). The Guinness position was that, although they were privately delighted at the possibility of our selections, the government was against the tour and therefore they couldn't give us special paid leave — which would have been the normal arrangement for an international tour. However — and this was the important part — if we had leave available it was company policy never to interfere with how or where that was taken. In other words, we could go with their blessing but had to take annual leave. A statement to this effect was issued, and so we were in the clear.

This was crucial, as by then I had now decided to go if selected. I had been very confused until a rugby official collared me one day. He asked me if I thought there were any countries in the world that were clear of all injustice. I said, of course not.

He asked me if I would therefore refuse to tour anywhere with a rugby side. I said, don't be silly. He then asked where I drew the line between a country that was acceptable to visit, and one that wasn't. He asked me how I justified playing in the north of Ireland, a province that to many southerners is an occupied part of their country. I replied that because rugby is always above politics, it wasn't a factor. He asked me how I could justify playing against Romania the year before, when politically it fell under the Soviet bloc with all its documented violations of civil rights.

Then he asked how the hell could I consider not going to South Africa, especially now when at least the rugby people were attempting to throw off the shackles of segregation (those were his words) and now, more than ever, needed encouragement and support. That was it. I decided there and then to go on the tour. More than anything else, what swung it was the question of how to draw the line between the acceptable and

106

the unacceptable.

The answer, of course, is that public opinion draws that line — and public opinion is largely decided by the media. But I had been to South Africa; I had been amazed at the inaccuracy of the picture painted. Therefore my dividing line was going to be determined by my conscience and nothing else, and my conscience cried out for me to go. It was a relief, and many people told me I had made the right decision. Many didn't, though — we received a number of anonymous calls and letters, and I was actually scared by the intensity of the feelings expressed. But I was also disgusted that people who felt that way hadn't the guts to name themselves and stand up and be counted. At least I had done that — and it taught me it's better to nail the colours to the mast than sit on the fence (mixed metaphor and all).

Once the decision was made, things were easier. The weight had been lifted, and I just had to concentrate on getting picked. The feeling was that Robbie McGrath and I were certainties. (I was asked to go to Bermuda on a short tour but I turned it down — after all, I couldn't afford to waste my precious leave.) Eventually the team was picked. Gibson and I were in, and all the waiting, worrying and soul-searching seemed worth it. As usual I had a rugby mission ahead, and as usual all other problems now paled into insignificance. But that same morning I was called into the big boss's office. He told me that Guinness had changed its mind — I was not allowed to go.

I really couldn't speak. I had spent so much time and energy on the decision. I had, for once, gone through all the correct channels; now Guinness, almost my family company, had broken their word. I was furious. My boss, now a director and incidently a former scrum-half himself, asked me who my replacement would be. I remember telling him that perhaps there wouldn't be a replacement.

After I had cooled down I phoned Jennie. I told her what had happened, and she asked me if I had told them to piss off — my wife is sometimes quite direct. She said she knew that I could never work properly for them again, and that I had her permission to tell them to get lost. And so I did. Well, not really — I told them I was resigning and would go on the tour.

All hell broke loose. The papers from all over the world descended and I prepared a statement and let them take over. I was very keen to leave Guinness on a good note, because Dave also worked there and also because I would be looking for a job in Dublin and didn't want any bad blood behind my name. However, I often wonder what would have happened if I hadn't resigned, if I had forced them to fire me and then sued for wrongful dismissal (remember that they had put out a high-profile statement about not influencing an employee's leave arrangements).

But I went quietly, and I was encouraged by the support I received. I was also touched by the presentations given to me by my colleagues. One from the staff — what they call the white-collar section — and even more by the beautiful tray and crystal glasses presented to me by the Guinness lorry drivers. I had got to know a lot of these guys, and always thought they were a fantastic bunch who did a lot more for the company, in terms of public image, than they were given credit for.

I learnt afterwards that there had been quite a hullabaloo over the whole issue. Ironically, a guy I was at school with caused most of it. He was now a journalist and has become well known. His name is Peter Murtagh. It seems — this is as I was told it happened — that he stirred up the whole controversy. He knew Gibbo and I, and also knew that Guinness have extensive interests in West Africa. Even after the breweries were nationalized, they still imported a lot of concentrate from Dublin. They have to use this in the brewing process to be able to use the Guinness name on their product; this concentrate export is worth a great deal of money to Guinness in Ireland.

Apparently this guy approached the Nigerian Embassy in Dublin and told them that two Guinness employees might be on the Irish tour, and what were they going to do about it? The Nigerians were in a corner, and said they might have to take steps. Then he went to the Guinness board and told them that the Nigerians were considering action, and what were Guinness going to do? The whole thing then escalated, and there was much discussion between the board of Guinness Ireland and the head office in London. I suppose Peter was in fact getting a good story. But at the time I was furious, as he was affecting the lives of my family as well as my own.

I believe Guinness should have stood behind their original statement. After all, it embodied freedom of choice, surely a central issue in the whole anti-South African issue. I can appreciate the difficulty they were in, but what I cannot understand is how they never told Gibbo and I what was going on. Here we were, graduate trainees and apparently bright young men in the company, and yet we were being treated like kids and kept in the dark. Jennie was right: I don't think I could ever have worked happily for Guinness again. Now I'm grateful for the whole incident, and also to Peter Murtagh. Without them, I would never have made the decision that changed our lives, to go to live in South Africa.

Incidentally, in my first few months working in Johannesburg, I came across an article in a bank magazine: an Irish company was looking to go into a joint venture with a South African partner. The Irish company was — you've guessed it — Arthur Guinness, Son and Company! At first I was furious, and was about to send the article to the papers in Dublin; in fact, I was going to send it to Peter Murtagh. Can you imagine the story? Guinness, who wouldn't let amateur sportsmen Mike Gibson and John Robbie play games in South Africa, were actively looking to invest there! I nearly did it, but decided it wasn't worth the bother. After all, my brother Dave was still there; also, I believe I left with a bit of dignity, and I didn't want to spoil that. But the article in the banking journal showed how hypocritical the world of business can be.

I was out and on the dole. I felt ashamed: to my knowledge the Robbie family had never had someone in this position. Gibbo decided not to tour and to stay with Guinness. I felt sorry for him, as he had suffered a lot from injury, had missed many caps and had never toured with Ireland. Two years earlier, he had been picked to go to Australia but had to cry off; he had also been one of the victims of the false alarm over the Lions selection. I think the Irish tour was going to be the great panacea for all his problems. But he stayed, has done well in Guinness — and I was delighted that he made it back into the Irish side as recently as last year. Hell, he's even older than I am!

Being on the dole was very interesting. Every Friday I had to drive into Bray and queue with hundreds of others for welfare. I was staggered. I think for the first time in my life the term 'unemployed' took on meaning. I recognized many of the people; I didn't know them well but they were guys with families, men I assumed worked like the rest of us, and to see them unemployed was a sobering thought. Again I had mixed feelings: I was ashamed to be out of work, yet I also felt quite grown-up. It was a daft emotion for a twenty-five year old married man with a child, but there you are. Like the status that we afforded men on building sites in England, to be on the dole gave one some sort of status amongst friends.

The money I got wasn't much. Then, in my second week, the bloke behind the window told me to sign a form. I asked him what it was, but he said not to worry, just to sign. He said he felt I had been a victim of circumstance, and he wanted to help. I still have no idea what I signed, but the next week and from then on I got double money. It was needed as well, although my family and Jennie's parents helped us a lot. I should have been very worried, but I wasn't; I had this overriding feeling that this was all part of some plan or other. (At least, that's what I thought I was thinking.)

I trained like hell and was really fit as the tour departure drew near. I also was able for the first time to watch the cricket Test matches from England, ball by ball for five days, and that had always been an ambition. I watched Ian Botham's two great knocks that won the 1981 Ashes, and marvelled at Bob Willis and his demonic bowling feats. It was funny how word got around, because during those two Tests, when anything of note happened, I had to phone about a dozen people all over Dublin with the latest. Perhaps I should have charged a fee.

The great departure day arrived, and then we learnt about the cloak-and-dagger methods that we were going to use to get to South Africa. I suppose it was necessary, and we were quite worried about running the gauntlet at Dublin airport, as we'd heard that a massive demonstration had been planned. I recall playing a trick on one of the Irish guys. I phoned our winger, Terry Kennedy, known to all as 'The Rat' (rugby imaginations at work again!). He ran a clothing business, and I decided to ring him to arrange a present for Jennie. As I dialled a scheme came into my mind. He picked up the phone, and in my best Peter Sellers Indian accent I told him that I was Kadir Asmal, the high-profile leader of the Irish anti-apartheid movement, and could I talk to him? Terry was very worried, totally taken in; when I asked him to confirm some secret arrangements for our departure, I could almost see the beads of sweat pouring from his brow. He was gibbering like an idiot and nearly collapsed in relief when I told him it was me. I got a real laugh telling the boys about it at training.

It had been decided that the team would assemble in London. We were split into small groups, and each had a different escape route. Phil Orr, Freddie McLennon, Slats and myself were to fly from Belfast. I had to pick up a hired car the day before and collect the tickets; we had all been given false names, I was 'Jim Roberts' or something like that. The four of us were to fly from Belfast as it was reckoned we were the best-known players, or so I was told, and that made me feel quite important. I had got my driving license only a few months before the tour, and was awfully proud to be the driver up to Belfast. It's amazing how little pleasures mean a lot when you're young. Other players went by boat from Dublin, others flew early.

We arrived in London and met the rest of the boys, and indeed did all the things a touring team does at the beginning — like getting kitted

110

out. We trained (naturally enough) at the London Irish ground, and were amused to hear that apparently our departure from the country had not been picked up. We were actually a bit cross when the IRFU announced that we were in England. The thought of thousands of demonstrators trekking to Dublin airport to protest against the Irish tour, and then discovering that the birds had flown, appealed to our senses of humour. In retrospect I think the IRFU was correct. They were unpopular enough with a large portion of the public, and deliberate concealing of our location in London would have made it even worse.

Eventually we left Heathrow full of anticipation — and a few of us without jobs. I was super-fit because of my extra training when I was on the dole; remembering how I had played with the Lions, I was confident that I would play the best rugby of my life. As things turned out, it was a disaster. I got sick and only played a game and a half in the month or so that we were away. However, by the time I returned to Ireland I would have decided along with Jennie that we were off to live in South Africa, a decision that would have seemed ridiculous three months earlier.

Memories of the tour are not as vivid as of the Lions tour. The management wasn't as good — not meant to be a major criticism, but I suppose that, because the tour was such a personal disaster, my feelings are negative. I felt that Slats, Paddy Madigan and Tommy Kiernan — the captain, manager and coach — were not well organized; they also kept a lot to themselves. There was also a problem with the medical officer, Dr Malcolm Little, who had narrowly lost in the vote for manager. He had done a first-class job with the Irish universities, as manager, in New Zealand the year before; I had hoped that he would be brought into the management team. But he was left out of a lot of things, and became disillusioned and perhaps went off the boil a bit.

Mind you, I must have been a bit of a pain at times. I picked up a really odd sickness. I was selected for the opening game against the South African Gazelles, the Under-23 side, at Loftus. It was a hard game; most of the South Africans developed into top Springboks or close to it, so our loss by three points wasn't at all bad. Ireland was missing a number of top players, too, and had not played since the end of the season.

But the day before the game I noticed that my left arm was feeling very weak. I suddenly had difficulty moving it. I assumed that I had bumped it and numbed a nerve, but because I couldn't remember any incident I had a nagging fear at the back of my mind. Anyway, the doc

111

felt that a good rub before the game with hot stuff would clear it. But it didn't: I played the first half and, when I tried to tackle a player late in the half, couldn't clasp with my left arm and he broke and set up a try. I realized I was a liability, went off and was replaced. We lost, got drunk and I was a worried man.

It turned out that I had contracted a fairly unusual virus called *neuralgia amytrophica* which had weakened the deltoid muscle of my shoulder. I had to stay in Johannesburg for tests while the team moved on, and this was where the decision to stay in South Africa was made.

I had to report to a gym in Johannesburg each morning before going for my tests, and became friendly with the owner (whom I had met the year before with the Lions). On the Saturday he asked me if I would go to a braai (barbecue) the following day. It was at the house of a former Transvaal player, Coke Bayvel, and we had a good day. Over a few drinks I told Coke about losing my job, and he asked if I had ever considered coming to South Africa to live. I remembered a piece of advice my Dad had given me, which was to hear every offer, so I told him that would depend on what job I could get. It turned out that he was high up in a big engineering supply firm, National Trading Company, and he invited me in the following day to see the place.

I liked the people I met and NTC made me an attractive offer: a good salary, a position at head office as Market Research Officer, and a company car. All my expenses incurred in the move would be paid if I stayed with the firm for two years. I was excited by the offer. I also knew that provincial rugby in South Africa was of a high standard, and that few Irishmen had ever experienced it. Jennie had been very upset by the hassles leading up to the tour; in particular, the cowardly letters and phone calls were very worrying. I hadn't a job in Dublin — and I admit to a bit of pig-headedness concerning my decision.

When I left Guinness I had actually mentioned that I might give South Africa a try. I don't really know why I said it, as it wasn't true at the time. However, the statement was met with disbelief and the general feeling seemed to be that I couldn't make it away from Ireland and my own little niche. I must add that, up to the tour, it was probably true. I was a favourite son to many, and I did tend to see the world through green-tinted glasses. The abuse that was received over the decision to tour was all very new to me, and it was quite a shock: I realized that many Irish people were very small and narrow-minded. They had a sanctimony about issues thousands of miles away that could be conveniently ignored with regard to local problems. Many Irish people were experts on South Africa: it was the Nazis against the Cosby family; yet those same people were most indignant when some American politician pronounced on the problems of Ireland.

I felt that if I went to South Africa for a year or so, it would be fun; we could live in one of the world's most focused-on countries. It would also surprise a few people who thought I would never have the guts to go. And last, and by no means least, it would be a good rugby challenge. If I returned, on the other hand, I would still be young enough to pick up the pieces of an Irish rugby career.

Those were the reasons that I had for giving thought to such a move. However, as with so many decisions I have made, it really just seemed the right thing to do at the time. I think I've said before that I believe in a degree of predetermination; when a major decision has to be made I consider all the options and then always get a strong gut feeling about the way to go. As I'll tell you later, I met Murray Mexted, the All Blacks number eight, in Johannesburg and we became good friends. He has a saying that life is not a rehearsal — and that sums it up. I'm not pretending there haven't been moments of self-doubt, but overall there are not many decisions that I would change if I had a second chance. I hope at the end of my life I can still say that.

There's not much else to say about the 1981 Irish tour. The two Tests were lost, as were a few other tour matches. We didn't play against provinces, which was a pity; in order to give more black players a chance, we played selections. The Irish side was not very strong. We were murdered in the line-outs but scrummed well.

I was really an observer and the role frustrated me. I had gone from being a key player and successful provincial captain to an outsider, and I'm ashamed to say that I reacted by criticizing. Tom Kiernan, the coach, has a marvellous rugby brain, and I had always been a fan of his. Tommy once succeeded in getting the best out of Andy Ripley in a competition, and that was a rare feat. It was after a game for the Irish Wolfhounds and we were all on the drink. Somewhere along the line Tom had bet that he could mix a drink that would finish Andy. Andy said he couldn't, so the game was on. Tommy produced a vile, green, evil-looking mixture from behind the bar and Andy was to drink it. Andy, built like a Greek god, knocked it back with no effect; Tom conceded defeat and that was that. About five minutes later we heard a loud crash: Andy had fallen over and had to be carried out feet first. Just like his cousin, Noel Murphy, Tom was laughing like a schoolboy: he had won in the end.

113

Also like Noel, though, Tom had that Cork ability to organize in a disorganized way. I used to get irritated, and must have said something. I was an autocratic little general, and despite no official role, other than player, on the tour I had always assumed a role as a sort of adviser. I think Tom could have got very cross, and justifiably, but I think he recognized my frustration at being sidelined and let it pass. For that I will always be grateful.

I played only one more game on tour and I was made captain for the day. I was very honoured, and as the team really responded and won in style, at least I had contributed something. We played a country districts selection in Oudtshoorn: I got two tries and a drop goal. But my arm wasn't right, and even if it had been I knew that Robbie McGrath, who had played very well in the first Test, would get the nod for the second.

At least I was on the bench, and watched Ireland lose a game they should have won. Ireland played with great fire in the Tests, and Fergus Slattery was outstanding. I had never really rated him as a player; I thought he was loose and to a certain extent unreliable. Hell, how I changed my mind after the Irish tour. I realized why he is such a god in South Africa. His speed was frightening over the hard ground, and he caused havoc among the Springbok backs. He also devised a master spoiling plan for the line-outs; that, coupled with great spirit in both Tests, made the Irish a difficult side to play and the series could, with a bit of luck, have been drawn.

I don't think the achievements of 1981 got enough praise at home. A couple of years later England toured South Africa. I believe they had more talent than the Irish side, but they were absolutely destroyed. Their tails went down straightaway, whereas the Irish fought to the end. I was proud to be a part of that Irish tour, even if I had a minor role.

The most important thing was that I find out where my immediate future lay. Jennie was keen to give it a go in Johannesburg. I had a job offer with a good company, my arm was clearing up. So I returned to break the news and get ready for the great adventure of our lives. In a year I had gone from having real doubts about touring South Africa, to deciding to emigrate there for a minimum of two years. Seven years later, we are still here with absolutely no plans to leave. A lot has happened in that time.

9

Before I left South Africa after the Irish tour, a man phoned me in the team hotel in Durban on the morning of the last Test. He said he was in business, and he had a proposition for me. I was nervous and in no mood to discuss anything, and put him off. However, he insisted that he would get in touch at Jan Smuts Airport in Johannesburg. I promptly forgot all about it, continued with my packing and sat on the bench for the Test. We lost, had our farewell party and got fairly drunk. (One of our players, prop Ginger McGloughlin, got very drunk and phoned his wife late at night. The story goes that he actually fell asleep while on the phone, and lots of other players sort of popped in for a chat with his wife while he slept, all very friendly. Anyway, the next morning he wakened with a hell of a head and a bill for R600 for his troubles; I think it was all settled out of court.)

At Jan Smuts Airport I was accosted by this man in the transit lounge. He said he wanted me to work for him in Johannesburg. I was a bit hassled, but he insisted that he was going to Ireland the following week and that he would contact me. I left it at that. On my arrival home I received another call: he'd changed his mind about coming to Ireland, but wanted me to return immediately to South Africa to see his set-up. I was now convinced that he was very serious, and Jen and I agreed that after a two-week break I would go back. I even phoned NTC, the company whose offer I had not yet formally accepted; they agreed that I should see this guy, and if it didn't work out I would still be very welcome with them. When I announced the trip to South Africa, to review this second offer, the cat was out of the bag. People knew we were serious. Our families had mixed feelings, the distance being so great, but most people thought it was an exciting move.

I went for two weeks to South Africa, and was looked after very well and shown this man's operation — but I decided it was not for me and that I would take up the NTC offer. I was so sure I did not want to work there that I told him before he had even dicussed money. He was

115

a bit upset, and even tried to insist that if I subsequently took up an offer with another South African company, they would be liable for the expenses of the trip to see him. As the only precondition for the trip had been an undertaking that I had not already signed another job offer, I felt this was nonsense and I told him so. I left to go home a bit saddened at his attitude; about three years later he even took me to court over the matter. I was amazed, as he was loaded and didn't have a case, legally or morally: it was thrown out and I got all costs, but the experience wasn't pleasant. I can only assume his motivation was to save face with some of his partners, big businessmen to whom I'm sure he'd told that I was going to accept.

One of the most touching things to happen was the farewell night that Greystones rugby club gave for Jennie and me. They had done something similar for Paul McNaughton, who went to work in the United States earlier in the year; for us they spared no effort. We were allowed to invite a lot of personal friends, there was a hell of a dinner with videos and cabaret, and then they presented us with a huge set of Waterford crystal, about a hundred pieces with a beautiful ship's decanter as the centre-piece. It must have cost a fortune. Although I had lived in the village all my life, I had only played for the club for two years (albeit as skipper) and the gesture was fantastic. About the only time I had any second thoughts about emigrating was during that night; however, I think deep down I believed that in two years I would be back in Greystones.

Before we announced our plans to go, many rugby people and other businessmen did phone to offer assistance with a job in Ireland. They realized that although I had left my job in a blaze of publicity to tour, such gestures don't pay the mortgage. In fact, I had arrived back from the South African tour fairly well off, certainly with more money in my pocket than when I had left. At almost every centre, South Africans dropped in envelopes of cash for those who had lost their jobs. A few years earlier I would have turned down the money, but I was beginning to learn that rugby doesn't pay bills. Come to think of it, I had become more pragmatic about a lot of things in the year or so since the Lions tour, and a couple of incidents illustrate this.

Almost all the Lions were sponsored with kit from their local agents of a major footwear firm, the Irish players as well as those from Britain. Well, we heard that the British guys had actually received some cash as well. It now seems a very small amount — £300 each, I think. The Irish convened a meeting one evening in one of the player's rooms.

We were all there: Ollie Campbell, Tony Ward, Colin Patterson, Phil Orr, Rodney O'Donnell, Colm Tucker, John O'Driscoll and myself. The meeting was to decide whether we would contact the firm and insist on our cash. Despite two players wanting to do so, the rest of us felt that this would infringe our amateur status, and so the motion carried was to say nothing. We actually threw away £300!

Another time, Ollie and I were approached by a sports firm in South Africa; they offered us a four-figure rands fee if we would wear their make of boots in a game for the Lions. We explained that we were amateurs — but as a favour we wore their boots in many practices. Can you believe it! The tour was generating millions; the players were making money on the normal team pool arrangement, against the amateur laws but as much a part of major touring as team courts or duty boys, and here we were chucking it away.

I was also approached by a senior Lions player, a Scot, who said that the boot firm sponsoring him wanted me to sign for them the following season. He started talking cash that I couldn't believe, and I said no. Although I had never received a penny for wearing kit, I was very grateful to my sponsors who always gave me free boots. I can still remember the look of disbelief on his face and he told me that one day I would look back and laugh at my attitude. He was wrong — I now look back and cry.

Nevertheless, I still don't think that rugby should go fully professional. Much of the fun would go out of the game if guys could make their living out of appearance and win bonuses. But there is so much cash in the game that a relaxation of the amateur laws is necessary and inevitable. The problem is that, under the current laws, backhanders and under-the-table payments are taking place all the time. Okay, not in Ireland and parts of England where games are played in front of two men and their dogs — but in countries where big crowds watch, and where a total commitment is required. In South Africa, France, Italy (where company sponsorship rather than gate money provides the means) and also in Wales, the thought of playing big rugby with no compensation is laughed at, and quite rightly. This nonsense about banning players for writing books and taking the payment should go, and I believe that is on the cards: recently Billy Beaumont and Fran Cotton were reinstated as amateurs.

I once met Gordon Brown, the great Lions lock, at a function at Sun City, a few hours north of Johannesburg. He told me that to help out his local district side at an evening training session, he had to mount an operation resembling something out of a John le Carre novel to avoid detection by the guardians of the amateur faith — all because he'd written a book.

In South Africa the payment of expenses is far more sensible. Despite the rumours, very few players make really big money. But for a provincial player's commitment, which is usually five days a week, the going rate is currently about R600. Remember that in South Africa we spend a rand as a Brit spends a pound, so we are talking about a Leinster, Llanelli, South of Scotland or Lancashire player getting £600 per week. Mind you, not many of those British players train up to four nights a week with their sides, but that's the situation. It's all worked out on some formula taking into account distances, petrol, use of car and time. It's officially for expenses and nothing to do with pay-for-play. Does all of this affect the spirit of the game as played by the provinces? Well, perhaps the players and wives are a bit happier.

So, a bit older and wiser, I accepted all the gifts gratefully. I had agreed with NTC to start work in October 1981 — but I ran into problems when I applied to the South African Embassy in London for a permanent residence visa. I was horrified to hear that it could take months and months. Very worried, I thought the whole trip would have to be put back. Then I got a call from someone who wouldn't identify himself: he just said he was 'a friend of South Africa'. He asked about my visa problems and I told him, but he wouldn't say where he'd heard that I was in a spot of bother. He told me to send my application to a box number in London, which I did; it came back approved, stamped and all in order only four days later. I have no idea who looked after it. I did get a call from a Mr de Villiers at the Embassy in London; he told me that all was OK, and he finished by saying that if I ever played against Western Province to take it easy.

I often have wondered who that Mr de Villiers is: people say it was probably Dawie de Villiers, the ambassador at the time. He is now a government minister, and was one of the great Western Province and Springbok scrum-halves and captains. I'm certainly not going to ask, though, and I only mention this to illustrate the power that rugby can have in South Africa. Just about everyone is mad on the game. Even people who have never played and who never go are passionate supporters of one of the provinces. But at the time I didn't know this, despite having toured there. I was just happy to have cleared things up.

After fond farewells and quite a few tears we set off for the sun. Mind you, we weren't sure if sun would greet us. One of the things everyone envied us for was the weather we were going to encounter. We heard the stories about cloudless skies and the beautiful dry heat in Johannesburg. Imagine our shock when one day, about three weeks before we left, we saw a bulletin from Johannesburg on the ITN news. The reporter was standing saying his piece while heavy snow fell all around. Everyone in the room started to laugh, and Jen and I looked at each other: this shouldn't be happening! (Indeed it shouldn't — it was the first snowfall in Johannesburg for over twenty years, it lasted a day and we've never seen it since.) Still, it gave us a fright, and I suppose it made us ask ourselves if we were in for any more surprises.

We flew from Dublin on 18 October 1981. We stopped at Nairobi where the flight was joined by a large number of South African Moslems, returning from a pilgrimage to Mecca; a number sat near us, and they were extremely friendly. They gave a lot of Arabian coins to Johnnie, our two-year-old son. Again, here were South Africans, 'non-whites', who seemed to be very friendly to white fellow-passengers on their way to holiday or live in their country. It all seemed so normal, and backed up the impressions I had gained on the tours. It was also reassuring to Jennie — she'd never been to South Africa before.

We were met at the airport by a director of NTC, and also by the secretary of the Transvaal Rugby Football Union, Johan Walters. He had invited us to stay in his house until we got settled, and to Johan and his wife Bonnie we will always be very grateful: they looked after us splendidly.

We could not get over the heat of the place, it was a hot summer and at first it almost felt too hot. The most impressive aspect of the weather, though, were the massive storms that occurred each evening, regular as clockwork. The violence of these was incredible. The typical day was hot, getting hotter towards late afternoon, and then hazy. This haze gradually builds until it gets dark, and then changes to an evil black. Suddenly there is much jagged lightning, a roar of thunder and torrential rain for about half an hour. This clears and then it's perfect for sitting out on the stoep (as the South Africans call a porch) and having the evening meal. We couldn't get over how regular this all is. In Ireland the weather report was always an educated guess, or so it seemed to us, and the uncertainty of rain or sunshine was infuriating. In South Africa you can ask someone round for a braai the Thursday after next and be ninety-nine percent sure that the weather will be perfect. You get used to that very quickly.

The next obvious thing that struck us was the friendliness of just about everyone we met. OK, I suppose the fact that I was a Lion and an Irish player gave me a bit of interest value, but the hospitality seemed very genuine and was much appreciated. We are still good friends with many of the people we met in those days, which now seem so long ago.

I started work the day after arriving in the country, nervous but very excited. I was to take over from someone who had been promoted, and to continue market investigation projects that he was engaged on. I had no idea of the South African market, and my business experience consisted of a few years in the various sections of an Irish brewery. But I soon got the hang of it and was determined to prove myself.

Mind you, the second day I was there I crashed a company car, and that gave my entry into the firm quite a bit of publicity. Part of my deal had been a company car, and I had assumed this would be a second-hand Ford Escort or something. I was surprised when the accountant told me I had a new car coming, and he gave me the models I could get. I was staggered: they were better than cars an MD in Ireland would drive. I settled for a big Audi 2,2 litre job, out of the box, and decided that the first thing I would do was send a photo of it home. But until this arrived I was given a beautiful pool car to drive. The second day I had to attend a meeting at a company we were considering buying into, and very proudly I drove out there. I was stopped at a traffic light ('robot' in South Africa) when a large truck in front of me started to roll backwards. I hooted but it was too late — there was a crash and the front of my car was pushed in. I was mortified the next day when I arrived for work, but all my new colleagues found the whole incident hugely funny and the great joke about the new Irish driver soon spread far and wide.

I enjoyed work and was pleased when the directors signed me up for a year's business management course at Damelin, one of the better South African business schools. I had been there a week and already it seemed that the company had plans for me. It would involve hard work — but for the first time I felt motivated for something that wasn't to do with the sports field.

It was midsummer, but I soon got involved in sport. Someone invited me to a function at the Wanderers rugby club; it was actually a meeting after the team photographs, and of course there were a few beers. Everyone had told me that Wanderers was the club to join, as it was the best of the clubs which were mainly English speaking, and so I decided to go along. I couldn't believe how chuffed they all seemed to be: I recognized a few guys I'd played against with the Lions, but I couldn't believe the fuss they made over me.

Now I look back and realize that they weren't sure that I was going to join. In Johannesburg the player new to the city can play the field. He'll visit a number of the big clubs, just to get a general impression — and often to see if certain perks are forthcoming. If he is a top player then the competition for his signature is fierce. It's actually changed a bit now, because with the huge increase in the number of provincial games the top players hardly wear their club jerseys at all. For example, the Springbok wing Carel du Plessis came to Johannesburg to work, and joined Wanderers (much to our delight); he was injured for a few games at the beginning of the year, it's true, but he played only one game for his club the whole season. In the same season I played only five games for Wanderers; the rest were for Transvaal.

Therefore the club game is suffering dreadfully. In Ireland it is really believed that rugby means the clubs first and foremost, but in South Africa, and the Transvaal in particular, the clubs are almost a necessary evil, there simply to feed the provincial side. At the time I arrived I didn't know this, and assumed that club rugby would be well organized and draw crowds.

I was determined to make my mark, and I started training immediately, even though it was the middle of the cricket season. I was lucky: the Springbok wing Ray Mordt was then with the club, and I have never met a player so dedicated to fitness. He ended his career with Wigan in Rugby League and so can no longer play Union, but even today he trains harder than any player and he still puts the fear of God into me every time I see him running. Anyway, I started training with him on the track at Wanderers and pretty soon I got fit. The altitude took a while to get used to, but I'd been warned, took it easy, and acclimatized quickly.

Others weren't so lucky. My former Irish team-mate Frank Quinn arrived shortly afterwards, also to work in Johannesburg. Now Frank has never suffered from a lack of self-confidence or an underestimation of his own ability. He arrived determined to make his mark; not having trained or played for ages, he joined Ray and I at the Wanderers. In those days we did a long warm-up, extensive stretching, run-throughs and then a series of high-quality sprints — maybe ten 100 metre dashes flat out, with three minutes rest between each. It was all based on athletics training, and was very new to me; but I had been training for a month and was well into it when Frank arrived. He ignored our calls for him to take it easy and work in gently — not our Frank. The first sprint we did Frank took the gold; the second, the silver. The third he was out of the medals, and on the fourth he never made it to the finish. He almost collapsed and we had to help him to the dressing-room where he suffered violent illness at both ends. After that he eased up on the intensity and played good rugby; he also got his Transvaal colours that season.

Transvaal rugby had been in the doldrums for years. It had been one of the show-piece unions. I had read about it being the world's richest amateur sporting body, and it was based at Ellis Park in Johannesburg. I had always remembered an old photograph of the great Tony O'Reilly crashing over for a try against Transvaal on the 1955 Lions tour. For some reason the Transvaal jerseys — white, with a red bar across the middle — had always appealed to me and I was determined to wear one. But in recent years the general feeling was that there had been a lot of mismanagement of the union. It was not popular in South Africa or overseas. One of the last pieces of advice I had been given before emigrating was to beware of Transvaal and, mysteriously enough, never to accept any gifts from them — quite what that meant I didn't know.

However, there had been a change of coach and I detected an optimism. A number of players were new to the province and it was hoped that the coming season would herald a new era. With this in mind I prepared for the first club game of the season. Wanderers have an annual friendly against the Harlequin club from Pretoria, and for as long as anyone could remember Wanderers had lost. I made my debut and played well in a 21-21 draw: I dropped a goal near the end that put us back in the game, and made the break that led to Ray Mordt scoring our try. I had done well, saved the day and was pencilled in for Transvaal.

My memories of that first game are limited, but what struck me was the whole build-up to it. In South Africa on match day, it's club against club. In Ireland, the first team might be at home against one club, the seconds would be away to another and the thirds over on the other side of town. But in South Africa the games start at lunchtime: the fourths play, then the thirds, then the Under-20s and then the seconds. These games are all at the same club. Finally, when it's getting cool and all the other games are finished, the First Fifteen runs on in front of all the spectators and players from both clubs. The atmosphere is intense and each game seems to be fiercer than the last. It's a great system — but in Ireland, no pitches could stand more then one game per day because of the weather.

On the other hand, I was amazed at how low-key the dressing room preparation was. I was used to stirring team talks and impassioned calls to arms. There was none of that at all. At half-time in the seconds game, forty minutes before kick off, the players go in and get changed. There's a lot of laughing and joking and everyone is relaxed. Just before kick-off the coach comes in, the captain says a very few words and that's it. I could hardly believe it, but I've come to love it. There's no acting. Hell, I can remember guys in Ireland bashing their heads against the wall in a big production designed to show how built up they were; invariably all this aggression was left in the dressing room and during the game the same player was often like a lamb.

In South Africa there is no acting. You are in the side to do a job. A couple of years later I was invited over to Twickenham with five of the Springboks to take part in the seventy-fifth anniversary of the Twickenham ground. It was England against a World Fifteen and I was on the bench. David Leslie captained the side, and of course he gave a real Celtic build-up to the game. Afterwards Rob Louw in particular was amazed at the performance. He told me that Leslie had actually punched him in the dressing-room. Poor old Rob had got a hell of a shock — and hadn't been sure whether he was expected to punch back.

On that trip to England we had a lot of laughs. The South African contingent was Rob, myself, Danie Gerber, Errol Tobias, Avril Williams and Rudi Visagie, the giant lock from the Free State. He played in Bloemfontein, a very conservative town. There are jokes in South Africa that in Bloemfontein even the hippies wear safari suits, and they also claim that if you ask for an escort agency in Bloemfontein someone will take you to the nearest Ford dealer. Anyway, 'Vleis' Visagie (*vleis* is Afrikaans for meat) was overseas for the first time and I think quite nervous about his lack of travelling experience. I laughed like hell when we got off our bus in London and the first thing we saw was a punk rocker and his girl. Both were dressed only in black binliners and their heads were shaved, apart from an orange cockscomb of hair. Well, Vleis stared as these for a moment, and uttered the classic line that he didn't think that it would catch on in Bloemfontein. We agreed with him.

I also played in the annual Raikes Memorial game that year, traditionally the first game of the season in the Transvaal: Witwatersrand University take on an invitation side. I was chuffed to be asked, and delighted when I saw that our skipper was to be Murray Mexted, the All Black number eight. I had long admired him — and was shocked when I met him. He seemed so small. Such was the aggression of his play on TV that I had expected him to be about six foot seven. I couldn't believe this smiling, wiry sort of guy who introduced himself. On the field, though, it was a different story. He was quite magnificent, and in one game I learned more about half-back play in combination with a back row than I had learnt in my whole career. We had a chat for about three minutes before the game; he said that he would release me a couple of times and support. About five times in the game — very competitive, by the way — I found myself flying through gaps around the scrum and I couldn't believe it. Murray is one of the best players I have come across, and a few years later he played with Wanderers for half a season. Although he had his enemies in rugby, to us he was a true friend, a good club man and a wonderful player. I didn't agree with a lot of his thoughts on the Cavaliers tour a few years later, but that's another story.

I made the Transvaal side in 1982 and played in the first few games, but things did not go well. The new coach had a hell of a job reorganizing things and trying to establish discipline, and we lost games heavily. I had done fairly well, but then got sick, cried off the side and couldn't get back — a young serviceman called Harry Viljoen returned to Johannesburg, and he kept me out. He was a big strong guy in the Terry Holmes mould, and it was what the team needed.

How I got sick is quite funny. Like a large number of rugby players, I had suffered from haemorrhoids. The doctors tell me that it simply affects some people, but I'm sure big-match nerves had a lot to do with it. Now I should tell you that this story has become quite a rugby legend in Jo'burg circles, and I should preface it by saying that a lot of Wanderers players didn't believe that I was a real Irishman — my accent being east coast rather than the 'begorrah, bejapers' variety heard in music halls. One Saturday Wanderers had an away-game at the mining town of Randfontein. Now this is to Johannesburg rugby what Shannon away is to Ireland, and I'd imagine Pontypool away is (or was) in Wales — a very hard game. I got a kick on the head and concussion during the game. As chance would have it, over the same weekend, my haemorrhoid problem became very serious and I had to have an operation, and so I lost my place to Harry. But some good did come out of it — my mates now knew that I was a genuine Irishman, because only an Irishman could get a kick in the head and then have to have an operation up his backside.

So the first season started well but finished in disaster: I was a club player again. I must say that I hadn't been too impressed with South

One of the benefits of being a high-profile sportsman in South
Africa is sponsorship. I was given this car at the time when I
was dropped by Transvaal, and some wit suggested that the
lower door panel should read 'Transvaal doesn't.'
(Picture credit: Pierre Oosthuizen Beeld)

Hitting the top of the ball and rolling great distances — with
drop goals that became my trademark in South Africa.

Playing against Wales in 1981. I never should have played as my back was injured but the man behind me in the photo made up my mind for me.

Ireland v Gazelles 1981. Slats and Ronan Kearney watch as I clear. Little did I know that I would play many games with the Gazelles in the picture: Jannie Breedt, Vleis Visagie and Piet Kruger.

I used the Transvaal forward training nights to practise my own skills.
In 1987 I missed my fly-half twice in twenty-four games!

Naas and I as Judges in the SA Sports Photographer of the
Year competition.

With help from my back row I
was also more of a threat as a
runner.
This is a Currie Cup try
against Eastern Province.

Against Errol in the Bok trials
in 1985. Later in the game I
fouled him — and have
regretted it ever since!

At a promotion in Johannesburg Bok wicket keeper Ray Jennings, self, Gary Bailey and canoeist Oskar Chalupsky. All are good friends.

The final score in the 1988 Olympia superstars.

| JOHN ROBBIE | 89 | JOHAN FOURIE | 62 | ADRIAN KUIPER | 27 |
| ULI SCHMIDT | 87 | STEFAN KRUGER | 57 | PIET NORVAL | |

Meeting PW Botha before the 1986 Currie Cup final. Jannie
introduced me as the Irish-South African but PW walked past
without a word.

A cartoon from Rapport after I was dropped for Garth Wright.
I'm booted out the door by Dr Luyt along with my loyalty
record while Garth and other new players are welcomed in.

Coaching kids in Eldorado Park — A 'coloured' suburb of Johannesburg.

Fielding inside in the 1986 Currie Cup final.

Receiving a merit award at the SA Breweries Sports Journalist of the Year function. A year later I was one of the guest speakers - and that caused a hell of a row!

Caddying for David Frost at the stadium golf competition. I claim that I sorted out his swing that day.

Left: Jennie and the kids a few months after Suzie was born.

Below right: Jennie today at home in our Johannesburg home.

Below left: Johnnie and Suzie.

'No apology'

Robbie sticks to his guns on pay-fo[r]

Staff Re[porter]

AS WESTERN
take the fiel[d]
crucial Curri[e]
the former
player at th[e]
pay-for-pla[y]
to back d[own]

Former [
scrumhalf
day—

● Stuck t[
the teams
at Newlan[d]
to be West[
ened was [
fee was w[

● Denn[
gised to[
Pickar[d]
and ins[
tention[

● Sa[
surise[d]
and s[
sourc[e]
the [
alse[

WP pay [r]

Team threatened to strike

Staff Reporter

THE Western Province rugby team threatened a pay-for-play strike in their dressing-room before last week's Currie Cup match against Northern Transvaal.

This was claimed by a former provincial player and now commentator John Robbie, who told a Johannesburg audience on Tuesday night that several senior players had refused to go on the field unless their match fee was increased.

Yesterday WP captain Carel du Plessis hotly denied the allegation, saying it was "malicious rumour".

Expenses

Last night Mr Jan Pickard, chairman of the Western Province Rugby Union confirmed that players received an amount of R700 per match, but said that he knew nothing of the dressing-room "revolt" as he "was not there".

Mr Pickard said the money was for expenses.

This is the second time this season that the "pay-for-play" controversy has been raised in the WP camp.

Earlier this year WP players also demanded higher fees, while this issue has also been raised by the Eastern Province team.

Last night members of the team said they had formed a players' committee to oversee their interests.

Payment to players is banned by the world ruling body, the International Rugby Board (IRB).

The latest revelations could bring the South African Rugby Board into confrontation with the IRB.

"This could cause problems for the SARB," said Professor Fritz Eloff, who is president of the IRB this year.

As WP will probably play more than 20 games this season, the payments amount to at least R14 000 per player for the season.

According to the Cape Times' information, players of every province receive cash for playing, and:

● The amount varies vastly between the "rich" unions such as WP and Transvaal and the smaller unions. Players in the bigger unions receive hundreds in "expenses" for a match, a player in the Boland team will receive a maximum of R50.

● Payment to WP players was upped by R300 from last year. "At the beginning of last season we got R400 for a match," said former WP hooker Wessel Lightfoot. "During the year this was raised to R600. Now we are getting R700," he said.

● As far as is known, members of the Northern Transvaal team are paid R500 each after every team match. Some senior members of the Transvaal team received more than R1 300 per month in 1987.

According to a provincial coach, EP's current poor form is due to players' demands for higher "match fees".

On Tuesday Robbie, who was at Newlands on Saturday as the M-Net commenta[tor on the game] — alleged that one of the sides in last Saturday's match at Newlands threatened to stay in the dressing room unless the players' fee was increased.

Robbie made the allegation as guest speaker at the SAB Sportswriter of the Year awards.

Robbie is a former Transvaal, Ireland and British Lions scrumhalf who is in close contact with players country-wide.

Yesterday an Afrikaans daily newspaper in Johannesburg alleged Robbie's allegation.

According to Mr Pietman Retief, spokesman for the South African Rugby Board, it was legitimate to pay players for expenses.

"It is up to each province to decide how much players are given for expenses," he said. "As long as they are only being reimbursed on that basis, there's no problem."

Confrontation

The revelations about the amount payed to players could lead to a new confrontation between the SARB and the IRB.

In November 1987, when it was revealed that some Transvaal and Northern Transvaal players stood to earn nearly R10 000 a season, three members of the rugby body condemned the payments.

The revelations at the time put any prospects of an international tour to SA in jeopardy as the member countries said that they would be loathe to tour a country which breaks the amateur code.

In terms of the IRB ruling, players can be refunded only for legitimate expenses.

The pay-for-play issue first came to a head within the WP camp two months ago. In March, as players limbered up for the season, lawyers were brought in as players allegedly stipulated demands for higher cash payments.

JAN PICKARD: R700 a match

JOHN R[
The pl[
manded a[
● Cash pa[
cancelled pa[
● Contro[
amount that [
provincial u[

WP

y row

...match — has escalated to ...nternational level as a pro- ...d tour of South Africa by a ...ld XV later this year could be ...

...r Craven confirmed that he ...received a fax from the world ...ing body, the IRB, over the ...sue.

MAKE OR BREAK FOR WP IN WELKOM TODAY

LOUIS VAN WYK PREVIEWS THE MATCH. See PAGE 12

The IRB has a strict ruling against rugby union players receiving any money for play.

Dr Craven said he had already sent a reply to the IRB, but declined to disclose any details.

"This could damage our chances of a tour later this year," he said.

Earlier this week Mr Pickard, president of the WP Rugby Union, asked the Cape Times and the Burger, John Robbie and SATV for an apology concerning the alleged refusal of the Western Province team to take the field against Northern Transvaal last Saturday.

A Johannesburg newspaper yesterday reported that Robbie had apologised.

Speaking from Welkom, Mr Pickard last night denied earlier reports that he had claimed that Robbie had apologised to him

"I want to make it quite clear that I have not made contact with Mr Pickard. I have therefore not apologised and have no intention of doing so," Robbie said in a statement last night.

"I stand firmly by my remarks."

Robbie said that "several WP officials" had telephoned him on Wednesday night and Thursday morning. "These were Dr Cecil Moss (WP manager); Carel du Plessis (WP captain), and Dawie Snyman (WP coach).

"I refused to divulge to them my source of the allegation, despite pressure from them to so do."

Last night Dr Moss denied pressurising Robbie.

"I asked him who his source was because the story is not true," Dr Moss said.

He said he would not "pressurise" Robbie as he was a "personal friend".

After an urgent meeting between Mr Pickard, team management and the players after the disclosures on Thursday, Mr Pickard said he regarded the matter as "closed".

"The outburst came at the right time," he said. "The whole thing bonded them and could inspire them to give their best against Northern Free State."

According to Lieutenant Attie

JOHN ROBBIE gaan Saterdag Nuweland se Curriebeker-wedstryd tussen WP en Transvaal regstreeks op M-Net uitsaai. INLAS: Mnr. Jan Pickard. 'Robbie kan maar kom, maar hy is nie welkom nie.'

Pickard wil
Robbie nie hê

Maar kom wat wil, hý is op Nuweland, sê John

Deur JOHAN BOTHA
TV-beriggewer

JOHN ROBBIE kan Nuweland toe kom — maar hy is beslis nie welkom nie!

Hiertoe is die WP se rugbybaas baie beslis. Mnr. Jan Pickard, voorsitter van die WP se rugby-unie, het in die naweek met die woorde "klaar gepraat" oor die feit dat Robbie, 'n gewese Leeu-skrumskakel van Transvaal, Saterdag die rugbywedstryd tussen Westelike Provinsie en Transvaal op Nuweland vir M-Net gaan uitsaai.

Die wedstryd word regstreeks op dié betaalnetwerk uitgesaai.

Mnr. Pickard se skerp reaksie volg op 'n "omstrede stelling" van Robbie vroeër vandeesmaand in 'y toegeskrywe op 'n dinee in Johannesburg waar die SA Sportskrywers van die Jaar aangewys is.

Robbie het gesê hy het gehoor dat 'n provinsiale span "voor 'n wedstryd oor een man geweier het om op die veld te draf omdat hulle meer geld wou hê. Ná sy

toespraak is berig dat Robbie die Klaarblyklik na die WP span verwys het toe hulle op 6 Mei teen Noord-Transvaal te Nuweland gespeel het.

Robbie sê: "Die ding het nou heeltemal te ver gegaan. Ek het nooit gesê dit was die WP wat nie uit die kleedkamer wou kom nie. Ek het na 'n sekere provinsiale span verwys.

"Daar is ook gesê dat ek nou hettemal te ver gegaan. Ek het 'n provinsiale span verwys."

Robbie het gesê hy het "voor 'n wedstryd oor een man geweier het om op die veld te draf omdat hulle meer geld wou hê. Ná sy

Hy sê 'n nasionale keur-

der, dr. Cecil Moss, die WP se afrigter, mnr. Dawie Snyman, en die span se kaptein, Carel du Plessis, het hom oor die berigte gebel. "Al drie was boos, maar ek het toe presies verduidelik wat ek wel gesê het," sê Robbie.

Mnr. Pickard het middel-in die berrie gesê hy weet nie van so 'n voorval waarna sal spelers skors wat meer geld vir wedstryde vra. Volgens hom het Robbie duidelik geprobeer om onmin in WP-geledere te saai.

Du Plessis het ook ontken dat sy span die Curriebeker-wedstryd teen die Blou Bul het gesê: "Dit is net kwaadwillige gerugte." Ander nou nie oor die saak uitlaat nie.

Mnr. Pickard het intussen belowe hy sal ondersoek instel na enige geldkwessie in WP-geledere.

Op 'n vraag of hy na die spraak, of wie nou eintlik die "provinsiale span" is oor wie hy gepraat het, het Robbie aan Rapport gesê: "Ek wil my nie daaroor uitlaat nie. Ek staan nietemin by wat ek gesê het en ek sal g'n niemand om verduideling vra nie."

Mnr. Dawie Schoonraad, bestuurder van die WP-span, wou net sê: "As my voorsitter (mnr. Pickard) reeds sy sê gesê het, wil ek nie oor die saak praat nie."

André de Villiers, hoof-sportpublisiteit van M-Net, het van deesweke bevestig dat Robbie die wedstryd Saterdag uit te saai.

Mnr. Pickard het ook aan Rapport gesê: "Ek het M-Net toestemming gegee om die wedstryd regstreeks uit te saai, maar sedert die bekendraak kry ek baie klagtes van die publiek. Almal wat nie dekolverders het nie, klaar dat hulle nie die voorreg sal hê om die wedstryd te sien nie. As M-Net aanstaande jaar weer aansoek doen, sal intussen sê Robbie, hy kom of te nie. "As M-Net gaan Nuweland toe, welmy Saterdag op Nuweland wil hê, sal ek daar wees."

Trying to cool things down as happy fans invade the Newlands pitch after Western Province score against us in the 1986 Currie Cup final.

Scoring a try against Northern Transvaal in 1987 I dislocated a finger. Hell, I screamed when it was put back!

African rugby either. The provincial stuff was very hard, but the coaching was very unimaginative and there was no emphasis on having fun. About the only real tradition in this regard was the initiation given to new provincial players. This is known as the *borsel* (brush). Frank Quinn and I made our debut for Transvaal away to Griqualand West in Kimberley, and had no inkling of the *borsel*. We won well, Frank and I played reasonably, and we assumed it was drinks and bed just like at home. But we were told that all new caps had to wait outside the team room until summoned. We asked the other new caps — there were about five — what was involved, but they had obviously been told to say nothing.

Finally I got called in. The room had been altered and for all the world it was like a courtroom. All the players were dressed immaculately in their number one blazers, ties and pants and there were three 'judges' sitting at the front. Everyone was deadly serious and there wasn't a sound. I made some wisecrack as I walked in, and I was quickly told to shut up. It was all serious and I got nervous. I had to remove my shoes and stand on a chair in front of the dock. I was asked to tell the member what I thought of playing for the team. Again I made a joke. No one laughed. I was asked to sing a song which I did, no one clapped or did anything. Suddenly I was grabbed, turned upside down across one of the lock's shoulders with my backside up, and each member of the team with the flat of his hand gave me, in turn, a real smack across my bum. I couldn't believe it. The pain was excruciating. After they had stopped I was angry and nearly lost my temper. Luckily the judge — I think it was Tommy Bosch — just told me that this was tradition, and to say nothing. Then I was turned up and hit again. I was actually crying in pain and anger. But when it stopped, the judge made a genuine speech of welcome, I was told that now I was a true Transvaal player and each player shook my hand. During this escapade I also had to drink four or five full glasses of beer. At the end it was actually quite emotional.

I gather it's a fairly tame initiation by some provincial standards, but I must say I hated it and still do. But it's part and parcel of South African rugby tradition, and I confess that when Frank came in after me I belted him along with the rest of them. Since then I have seen how this *tugkomitee* or discipline committee works. Apart from newcomers, anyone who is late or doesn't conform to the team's agreed code of dress or whatever may be summoned and punished in this way. It's all a bit childish but it does keep discipline, I assure you. (Somehow I could never see it taking off in Ireland: the thought of the team walloping a Willie Duggan or a Moss Keane is outside the realms of reality. Each to their own, I suppose.)

For the first few weeks in South Africa we lived with the Walters family, then for three months we house-sat for a very wealthy business-man who was in Australia. After that we rented a flat. It all went very quickly and before we could sit down and take stock we had been liv-ing there for a year. I confess that we were extremely homesick. I think that's the case for most people who move from close families to other countries. And of course we weren't in England or in Northern Ireland, we were thousands of miles away. I secretly admitted that after two years we would be returning home. The rugby season had not gone so well for me, of course, and true to form this probably affected my feelings.

But the job was going well. I was studying hard at night school, and the ABC of business was all very new. I studied accounting, market-ing, finance, human resource management, decision-making and stra-tegic planning. I passed my exams and got a lot of satisfaction from that. I suppose for a businessman it was very basic, but I had to work and the college was very strict. I seem to remember that of the fifty or so who started the year's course, only about fifteen of us graduated. After leaving Cambridge without finishing my degree, and then failing to do so at home, this was important for me. (Failure to finish at Cam-bridge remains one of my greatest regrets, and the fact that I had done a lot of work and really only needed a bit of discipline to put it all together makes it worse.)

Living in a place is very different from touring there. On tour you really have only three responsibilities: play rugby, not be late for any-thing, and enjoy yourself. But now a living had to be made, and there weren't fans, liaison men and journalists surrounding you and taking care of your every need. I had to make my own way — and after all the publicity and especially after such a promising start, the rugby papers had to an extent written me off.

The standard of living for most white people is exceptional. We were amazed to hear many people complaining and wishing for the good old days. The first surprise was the lack of outward animosity between the races, the second the relative prosperity that is observed everywhere. I had expected most black people to be destitute, like the tinkers one sees on the street corners in Dublin. For the most part, black people in Johannesburg and the other cities have a well-developed dress sense and take a lot of care about appearance. I had been to other countries where a great gap exists between rich and poor, and I had been appalled at things I had seen. For example, in Portugal, where I toured with Cambridge, we had once gone to see the mighty Benfica play in the European Cup. To get to the magnificent stadium we had to walk through some really bad slum areas. Nowhere in South Africa have I ever seen conditions like those. In Bombay also, *en route* to New Zealand, I had seen poverty on a scale that I could not have contemplated.

Now please get me right on this one. I am not for one minute suggesting that all is wonderful in South Africa. It is not. There is poverty, and a form of oppression that I believe is totally wrong, and I believe the whole philosophy of the separate development plan is evil, particularly in the detailed way it has been worked out. Sure, white South Africans who might be racist in outlook are very careful to disguise this with newcomers and visitors. But the country is racist — I suppose people in many parts of the world are racist to a degree. The difference, of course, is that in South Africa this racism is enshrined in the laws — and that is evil.

The big question, of course, is how do you change that, when the people making the laws are scared stiff that they might lose not only power, but everything they possess and their ancestors lived for?

South Africa is a bit like life in general. When you have just arrived, it is like when you are young: you think you have all the answers. When you have been a while — when you get older — the complications have set in. Hell, even the questions become unclear.

What was clear to me was that South African rugby and I were not compatible. First of all, the training was very foreign. Part of South African rugby tradition is the *koppestamp*. This means competitive, opposed training, and it takes place in every school, club and province. On a Monday night the squad warms up and the first team plays the seconds. There are no holds barred, and it is every second team player's right to try and win his place on the Firsts. The Saturday match is usually easier than these sessions. True, if the first side is winning, the Monday games are less intense; nobody changes a winning team. But if the side has lost on the Saturday, then the Monday becomes a full trial. I have seen more fights on a Monday night than I have in Saturday games; often the referee is the second team coach as well, and, as you can imagine, this also has its problems.

By and large I am not a fan of South African coaches either. With a number of shining exceptions, like Cecil Moss, the Springbok coach, and Terry McGee from Wanderers, most South African coaches have no sense of humour at all. I have always believed that if training is en-

127

joyable players will run through brick walls for the team. I would say that most of the problems I have had with coaches, officials and even presidents of rugby unions have arisen from jokes I have made that have been taken up wrongly.

I was an ex-Transvaal player at the end of my first season, and also I had dislocated my shoulder in a club match, the result of the latest tackle I have ever received. I was fed up and seriously thought of calling it a day. The second summer in South Africa was fabulous and consisted of cricket (playing and watching) and a holiday at the coast in Durban. Work was fine, and I was moving successfully into the trading side of the business.

I played rugby the second year, 1983, but took it all easy. I didn't train pre-season, eased in slowly — and started playing well again. Harry Viljoen then got injured, and I was invited to the Transvaal trial and suddenly I was in the side again. My first game back we beat the strong Free State side at Ellis Park, and then beat them in Bloemfontein in a friendly. It was the first Transvaal win there in about twenty-five years, and I got my first drop goal for Transvaal. I had never been shy to try a drop goal, and in South Africa this became something of a trade mark. (I have discovered that in my eighty-four games for Transvaal I dropped twenty-three goals — not bad for a scrum-half.) I practised the skill a lot, and remembering old advice from Ollie Bourke — that a drop is the only score in rugby against which there is no defence — I started to use this tactic more often. In one season, my best with Transvaal, I scored nine drop goals in twenty-one games. All these came from the base of the scrum or from driven ball in the line-outs. Hardly any other scrum-halves used the tactic, and it was amazing how other sides used to try and counter it — which of course used up resources, and often opened up gaps which we could exploit.

I also made a decision that was to have a big effect on my rugby. I had always been of slight build, but had never really suffered. But in South Africa the commitment to the physical side of the game, from school right up to international level, is far more intense; coupled with the hard grounds on which most games are played, I reckoned I was too weak. So I started lifting weights. At first it was all very low-key, but I soon realized the benefits — and discovered the ignorance that surrounds it in rugby circles. So often I had heard the advice that weights would slow a nippy athlete down and make him muscle-bound (whatever that meant); in fact, the opposite applies. I was lucky to get friendly with a physio and former wrestler called Keith Gordon. Thanks to him

I regularly went on pre-season weight-lifting courses. I became more explosive, confident and resilient. I only regret that I didn't start at the age of about eighteen. In the next few years there will be a fitness and condition revolution in rugby, although looking at the All Blacks and the level they have reached I reckon this has already started.

At the end of the 1983 season I had another big surprise: I was eligible to play for the Springboks, something I had never given any serious thought to. I had ambitions in provincial rugby, I was playing well and I think was making quite a names. Divan Serfontein, my old rival from the Lions tour, was the Western Province scrum-half and number one in the country (if not the world, following the Bok tour to New Zealand). During the season there was a big exhibition game in Cape Town, Western Province against the Rest of South Africa, a side picked by the Springbok selectors. I was amazed when I was named at scrum-half. I assumed it was a gesture and a recognition of good form, and thought nothing of it. But some journalist took up the matter and asked Dr Danie Craven if I was eligible for the Springboks. Craven said I was: I had permanent residence and no plans to return to Ireland.

Doc Craven has always been a good friend. I met him on the Lions tour, and was amazed at his memory. Apparently he always makes a point of speaking to each player in the touring squad late in the tour, well after the initial introductions: he makes the contact and uses the players' names. I have heard the Doc speak on many occasions. After I emigrated I was a guest at a Pretoria golf club and the whole night was in Afrikaans. During his speech, Doc looked down and asked if it was me he saw. After that he spoke only in English, as a courtesy to a visitor.

I was staggered to learn that I was eligible. I knew I was behind Divan in the rankings, but I also considered myself as good as the rest; I was also a seasoned international and was younger than most of them. Men like Barry Wolmarans and Tommy du Plessis were coming to the end of their careers. Players like Harry Viljoen and Paul Lombard were big, strong and physical, and I thought they were of international standard — but the experts started punting me as Divan's understudy. In 1984 England and the South Americans were due, and so I decided to give it a real crack. Hell, I reckoned, I have a chance now to play for Ireland, the Lions and the Boks. For a guy with my ability, limited compared to the Gareth Edwardses, Sid Goings and Ken Catchpoles of the game, that would be something indeed.

My rugby fell into a pattern. My passing was excellent, possibly my strength. I had always been good off my right hand, but in the Five Nations I had always dived to the right or turned and used my right hand. In South Africa I soon realized that second team scrum-halves could all pass off either hand and that I must learn. With surprisingly little practice it came, and it was soon second nature. My kicking from the base of the scrum also improved. In Ireland, except for the up-and-under, I had been content to feed my fly-half for the tactical kicking, and with guys like Ollie, Wardie and Ian Burns that had been acceptable. Here, great pressure is put on the fly-half, especially if one's pack is battling. So I worked hard on my kicking and soon learned to use the shape of the ball to my advantage. I knew from Ollie Bourke that foot position is the most important factor in scrum-half play: all kicks and passes can be performed easily from a correct base.

Thanks to Murray Mexted at Wanderers, I learnt how a number eight and a scrum-half, given reasonable ball and a good understanding, can cause havoc. South African sides had not experienced play like this, and for a season or two I managed to score or set up loads of tries. The most important thing, though, was that my biggest weakness as a player — my limited threat as a runner — was now masked, if not eliminated. By using my number eight, opposition back rows had to look out for me.

My tackling had to improve. In South Africa they tackle hard; they also try to run right through you, and so I could no longer cover as another full-back. I soon learnt that I was never going to crash guys backwards, but I always tackled low and became quite keen on that aspect of the game.

I also learnt early that most South African scrum-halves complain a lot if they get bad ball. It is expected of them, and they are coached to kick up a row if the forwards are a bit sloppy. Now here I used my head. No self-respecting lock forward who is busting his gut just to get a hand to a ball in a line-out is going to take kindly to criticism from some clean-shorted dwarf who has an easy life anyway. So I always encouraged my forwards and never criticized them. If I got a suicide ball and got clobbered, I would tell the apologetic lock that it was no problem. This had an amazing effect on the forwards: soon I had their respect, and the percentage of bad ball I got went down.

Mind you, in South Africa the line-outs are a pleasure for a scrum-half. In Europe, any assistance for the jumper is frowned on; English refs especially seemed to take pride in penalizing sides all day, even if the game was ruined.

There is the letter of the law, but most players welcome the application of the spirit of the law as well. In South Africa they allow early binding at line-outs, which is another way of saying that props and flanks are allowed to assist the jumper. But it still requires skill, and the result is that the line-out more often than not results in a catch and the game can develop from a platform. In my whole career with Ireland I don't think I ever got a clean ball from the front or middle of the line-out. We won ball to the back from Willie Duggan, sure, but I had to scramble away scraps from the front.

I remember once being very irate against France in Dublin. I got a bad tap from the front, over my head; I ran back and fell on the ball in textbook style, got up, and was tackled by the French hooker who was built like a gorilla. I managed to hold onto the ball, but together with another forward I was bowled over into touch. Slattery the skipper said, 'Well done, but try and stay on your feet next time.' I nearly hit him, but instead started to laugh. It's amazing the rubbish captains talk sometimes. I was just as guilty as Slats when I was captaining the Irish universities against our New Zealand counterparts in Dunedin. We had narrowly lost the first 'Test' but rallied magnificently and we were about fifteen points ahead in the second. But the Kiwis were angry and really flinging everything into attack. They ran a short penalty and had some athletic-looking simian running hell for leather at the thin green line guarding our goal area. One of our props, a guy called Job Langbroek met this huge guy shoulder to shoulder and stopped him in his tracks. The ball flew loose, and from the scrum we cleared the danger. I remember, as skipper, blurting out that next time I wanted to see Job tackling low — talk about saying the wrong thing at the wrong time. (We ended up winning 18-4. I was also delighted when Job got his Irish cap at the first World Cup.)

In recent years there have been a number of changes to the laws of the game — but they won't even consider allowing early support in the line-outs. Every time I watch a Five Nations game I cringe at the poor old scrum-halves who have to risk life and limb tidying up bad ball from the shambles that is the modern line-out. I very much doubt if I could go back to that.

10

In 1984 trials were held in Port Elizabeth to select a Springbok side to play the visiting English. The week before, I played well in Transvaal's first win at Loftus in years, and I got the nod for the B side in the trial. I played satisfactorily and was, to my great delight, named on the bench for the first Test. In many ways I got more of a kick from this than from my first Irish and Lions caps. On both those occasions it came out of the blue; I'd had no time to build up for selection. Here I had been on the fringes for a couple of years, and I had played in the trial. Sure, I was only on the bench, but it meant I would at least get to wear a Springbok jersey and get one of those beautiful track suits.

Many years earlier, when I was still at school, I had gone to watch a provincial squad session; I had seen Kevin Mays, the giant Irish lock, wearing a Bok track suit; he'd apparently swapped with a South African at the Scottish Centenary Sevens at Murrayfield. I had always thought the dark green with the leaping Springbok looked beautiful: now I was getting one of my own.

Two days before the first Test, disaster struck: I came down with the flu. I was as weak as hell and couldn't even see properly. It seems that every few years South Africa gets a belt of the latest strain of flu that has hit the world, and to avoid it the Transvaal players had been given jabs sometime before. Well, mine worked perfectly because I got it and I could hardly stand! I was faced with a dreadful choice. I had a feeling that the Bok selectors would have picked me again as reserve for the second Test, if I did the honest thing by pulling out, but I couldn't be sure. I imagined that they would pick Gawie Visagie of Natal to replace me on the bench for the first Test; apart from his excellent rugby skills, I knew that he had a character second to none, and I kept imagining a big win for the Boks and Gawie making them laugh so much that they would keep him on the bench just for that. Also, of course, I had Emmett O'Rafferty's experience in mind, along with Pat Whelan's advice the year I should have cried off against Wales.

I ended up saying nothing and travelled to Port Elizabeth to meet up with the Boks. There was so much excitement that nobody noticed that I was under the weather. I did mention that I had a bit of flu, and Doc Augie Cohen pumped me up with vitamins. I then told Rob Louw, my best mate in South African rugby, about my dilemma, and we agreed to do a bit of running after the Thursday practice: I had to stop after two sprints. At one stage, Divan and fly-half Errol Tobias were sharpening up their kicking and I had to stand in at scrum-half for the team. I will never know how I pulled it off — I could hardly see the ball coming out of the line-out, but luckily it was windy and I positioned my fly-half — I think it was Gysie Pienaar — almost beside me. Somehow I got away with it, and sat on the bench for the Test.

I believe that if I had been asked to come onto the field I would have collapsed after the first bit of action. I was painfully aware that I would be castigated from on high if that happened, but I kept thinking of Emmett and I got away with it. It was the first time that I sat on the bench for an international, praying that I would not have to go on. Quite apart from feeling ill, I was also full of shame. I was being dishonest with guys who had put a lot of trust in me. Had I played and blown it, I would have been a Bok — but I would have lost forever the respect of Cecil Moss, Daan Swiegers and Dougie Dyers, to say nothing of Doc Craven. Looking back I would have probably made the same decision. But it was a hard one.

However, the Boks murdered England, everyone played well and so I got away unscathed. Rob Louw and I had a laugh about it afterwards and I had improved greatly for the second Test. I sat on the bench again, but this time I was praying for a run. It was not to be. Again I watched Errol Tobias mastermind a runaway win for South Africa.

I was thrilled with the win, and the knowledge that I was number two scrum-half was great. I must say, though, that I got really pissed off by the attitude of some of the British journalists who covered the tour. They criticized the Boks; they said the line-outs were unfair, they said the South African rucking was weak. Hell, the Boks had just beaten England twice by thirty points, scoring about a dozen tries to nil. I understand that the reporters were a bit shell-shocked, but I thought they might have been a bit more gracious in defeat. Still, the English players were great, and guys like Phil Blakeway, Dusty Hare and Huw Davies seemed genuinely pleased that things were going well for me in South Africa.

Later in the year the South Americans toured, and there were two

133

more Tests. I had the honour of captaining the B side in the trial, and had one of my better games. I tried a novel approach and put it to the B side that our aim was to get just one player picked from our side. If we did that, then we had made the selectors think again and we would have done our job. In the end Nick Mallett, Anton Barnard and Louis Moolman got selected and I was actually thanked by the selectors for my efforts. I remember that in order to get a bit of spirit going I gave the side an 'Irish' warm-up. As I talked, we exercised as a team and I kept barking out questions to specific players. It wasn't the full blood and guts stuff but it was on the way. I thought the motivation was good and after all the exercises I told the players they had a couple of minutes to do what they wanted — in terms of warming up specific areas of their bodies before we came together to run onto the field. All the players responded, except Louis Moolman who went back to his traditional methods — he sat down!

Well as I played, Divan was quite rightly named as captain of the Boks and he played well in the two wins. I always admired him as a player, and in many ways he never got the credit he deserved; for some reason the media never seemed to build him up. I always enjoyed our tussles. He was like Colin Patterson — you couldn't take your eyes off him for a second.

Divan also had a talent for copying signatures that used to amaze us all. Part and parcel of every international side is signing autographs. After about a day with the team, Divan could sign balls all on his own. Even the players couldn't tell which balls were genuine and which were faked. I also remember that Divan hit the hardest in the *borsels* — it was like a pistol shot. He also had great success as a skipper, and when he announced his retirement I was sorry that we wouldn't be in opposition again — but also delighted, as the general feeling was that I was next. I was in line to play for the Boks in 1985 and this was the big one — the All Blacks.

The whole approach to this tour was different. Selectors were everywhere, even appearing at club games. Normally, if you have a bad game, you know the next good performance can set it right. Early in the 1985 season Transvaal played a night game at Ellis Park — against Eastern Province, I think — and we won. But I received a bit of scrappy ball and fumbled a few times; I also chucked out a few dodgy passes. By that time my game was very steady and consistent; I rarely set a game alight, but I could control things and was very tidy. After the game I heard that Cecil Moss, the Springbok coach, was there. I was terrified that I had blown it and was very depressed. At the cocktail party he came to me and complimented me on the way I had been playing. I confided in him that I thought I had blown it and he laughed. He said they certainly didn't put much store on one game, and told me that I was certainly in their minds for the Boks.

Well, the change was fantastic — all was well with the world again. I think that is Cecil's biggest strength. He is careful about choosing players, but once a man has performed for him he is very slow to ditch. I have not met a more honourable man than Cecil; and with Daan Swiegers, chairman of selectors, he had the confidence of all involved.

It was obvious that they had meticulously planned the build-up to the All Black tour. All players were watched at provincial level and then a traditional Springbok trial was held. (This is very different to the Irish trials. Over a hundred players are invited — just about full sides from the bigger unions and representatives from all the junior provinces.) The trial was in Cape Town and when we arrived they had already had a number of sides taking part in junior-level trials. From these the best players graduated to the full trials held over the next week. (As well as being an intense rugby occasion, it's also good socially as the top players in the country are all together under one roof for a week.)

There were to be three days of trials with a rest day in between each; I was picked for the senior side to partner Naas Botha. We played out at Stellenbosch's beautiful Danie Craven stadium — the first time I had been there since sitting on the bench for the Lions in 1980. I remembered how traumatic that day had been: Fran Cotton had to leave the field with a suspected heart attack, and it had been a poor, ill-tempered game and the Lions won playing badly. I hoped the trial would be better, and it was. I gave Naas a good service, and afterwards he even said that I was the first scrum-half he had played with who could give him the special 'drift' ball that he likes occasionally to vary his line of running. Perhaps he was just being nice, but it gave me a lot of confidence. I made a few half-breaks as well, and overall I was happy.

The next day the Cape Town press gave me nothing, but all the Western Province guys were mentioned in dispatches. I remember being a bit disappointed at this provincialism, but a few chaps told me that it was par for the course and not to worry. The second trial was okay, but I missed Naas a few times — and I confess to doing something I wasn't proud of.

While Naas had been in America having a go at the gridiron game, Errol Tobias had forced his way into the Springbok side. I really took

135

my hat off to him; he had come from nowhere with a series of brilliant tour games against England. As well as getting his line going and kicking well, he had made a few searing breaks; in the Tests he had also played well and of course scored that fabulous try at Ellis Park. The way 70 000 white South Africans cheered him was very emotional, and the thought of something like that happening a few years earlier would have been impossible. Errol proved his ability beyond all doubt, and I was disappointed when guys like Gerald Bosch and De Wet Ras, former Bok fly-halves, criticized Errol's play and implied that, had he been white, he would not have been selected. The very idea was nonsense.

I agree with what Rob Louw wrote in his book: that the saddest thing about the whole issue is not knowing just how good Errol would have been if he had received a sporting education equal to that of most white players. I really thought Gerald and De Wet let themselves down with their remarks (assuming that the quotes were accurate).

Anyway, back to my shameful moment. With Naas returned from gridiron, the trial became a duel between the Golden Boy and his star stand-in. I don't think there was any doubt that Naas would get the nod, in terms of match-winning ability. But Errol was naturally keen to do well. In the second trial game someone had made a half-break and Errol was running hard to get into a supporting position. I was playing against Errol's side, with Naas, and I saw that if Errol could get into support, the guy breaking could release him and he would easily have been able to sprint from the halfway line — and Errol is as fast as hell.

So I obstructed him. As I turned to chase I grabbed his arm. He couldn't get into a supporting position, and the man who had broken was tackled. The normal guy would have hit me — it really was an unfair thing to do — but Errol just looked at me. I had ruined his one chance at the limelight. After the game I felt awful and apologized. Errol accepted it, but I knew he was as disappointed in me as I was in myself.

The final trial was to be held on the main pitch at Newlands. I was once again picked with Naas for the A side and we won well. Late in the game I got a shock when I was heavily tackled, high, after a break. I really thought I had broken my jaw but luckily it was okay. The trials were over, Naas had never been under pressure, and I knew my chances of making the side were good. This was further emphasized when Cecil Moss held a few clinics for a small number of players on the off day. I was there at scrum-half, and just the way I was brought into discussions made me think I was the man in possession.

136

We returned to Johannesburg, the feedback was good; we moved back into provincial rugby. But you could feel the tension in the air. Every day there were articles about the tour. Old Boks were recalling past series, and I could believe that the New Zealand vs South Africa clashes were the real world championships. Except for a couple of British Lion interludes (1971 in New Zealand and 1974 in South Africa), it was the way it always had been. Tickets were being printed and full houses predicted. I looked at the itinerary and worked out just when the different provinces would play against the All Blacks, to see how good or bad games could affect my standing.

I started to work harder at my game. On a Tuesday night the Transvaal forwards practised alone; as the poor old scrum-half I had to come along too, and would normally stand with the donkeys during line-out and loose maul drills. Now I started going off on my own to practise skills, especially my kicking. I would imagine various positions on the field against the All Blacks, and how I would save or win the game with a brilliant tactical kick. It was as if I was back in Ireland as a fourteen-year-old when I used to play imaginary Test matches in our old garage behind the house. (The neighbours complained that the thump, thump, thump of me playing football against the wall was driving them crazy. Mum explained to them that it wasn't a football but a rugby ball. I don't know quite how that changed things, but I can't remember being told to stop.) All normal dreamer stuff, I suppose, for a sports-mad kid, but a bit childish for a twenty-nine-year-old married man with two kids. Now the big thing in sports psychology is visualization, and it really is supposed to work. Well, at that time all I could see was myself in a dark green jersey playing against men in black ones. I was torn between believing that I was in line for a Bok cap, and not daring to do so. In short, I was in a perfect frame of mind to play. When the tour was cancelled I was shattered.

There had been a lot of stories in the papers indicating problems, but it had all happened before with other tours. It seemed that two New Zealand lawyers were genuinely trying to find legal loopholes to stop the tour, but surely they had no chance. After all, the tickets for the first game in Welkom were already being sold. Then out of the blue, with two weeks to go, the tour was cancelled after a court injunction.

It's strange, but all I could remember for ages was the reaction of one of the Transvaal players. He was a bit of a lad, and during the Bok trials in Cape Town he had gone out on the tiles; when we came down to breakfast we would meet him coming in from a wild night. When the news of the cancellation came through, he started to laugh — he claimed he was the only one who had got anything out of the trials week. Perhaps he was right.

But almost at once, in order to salvage something, it was announced that a Springbok squad would be chosen, and that they would go on an internal tour of South Africa. We were also led to believe that full Bok colours would be awarded, so I was still in with a shout. Okay, it would be a loss not to play the All Blacks — but I could still see that cap perched on my head. The other thing I wanted dearly was to see my name hand-painted on the honours board at the Wanderers, where all club members who played for the Boks in any sport are recorded. Today when I walk past that board and see the list there I still get a pang of regret. I missed out by a whisker.

For reasons I'm still not sure of, it was decided that the tour would go ahead and Springbok jerseys would be worn — but that neither full colours nor caps would be awarded. Apparently a few old Springboks complained and said that international colours should never be awarded for games against opposition from within one's own country. I felt this was wrong. It wasn't the players' fault the tour had been cancelled; besides, New Zealand had given full caps for the internal tour they ran after a Springbok tour was cancelled in the 1970s. I gather that certain officials (including Louis Luyt, the Transvaal president) tried hard, even well after the tour, to get them to revert to the original idea; the officials argued that anyone who wears the South African jersey is good enough to be given a South African cap.

So it was a huge disappointment — but nothing to compare with the disaster that was the tour itself. I have had many highs in the game and a few lows, like breaking my leg and getting dropped by Ireland and then, at the end of my career, by Transvaal. But that internal tour will go down as the absolute nadir: there was nothing lower in my rugby life.

The idea was that the Springbok squad would travel around the country and play three games against regionally based Barbarian sides. The fourth and final game would be against a full South African Barbarian side, made up of the players who had performed best in the regional matches. For the Boks, this was a recipe for disaster. The top players were in shock over the cancelled tour, and to the experienced Springboks the substitute tour was a joke: they weren't really interested. The old guard had their caps safely tucked away; the rest of us didn't count.

But I was in the party, and it was a strong one on paper. I was the number one scrum-half at the beginning, and was kept for the second game against the powerful Cape Town-based side. We lost and I had a nightmare; I still have no idea why my passing let me down. Having a new number eight with precious little experience didn't help either, and once when I went to dive-pass the ball from a scrum, he chose at the last moment to put his foot on the ball. Obviously he was trying to protect me, but it meant I ended up doing a beautiful dive pass without the ball. The crowd started to laugh and I just felt foolish.

To make matters far worse, the curtain-raiser was between a local side and the visiting invitation side from Wales, the Crawshays XV. In it were a number of former Lions colleagues and also other top Welsh players. I was so keen to do well and show them that I had improved since emigrating that the result was even more disastrous. It was the worst performance of my career, bar none, and of course the press — the Cape Town press — had a field day. 'Pathetic' was the word that came up a few times, no mention of bad ball at all.

In the next game I did better in a scrappy win, but by now I was number two — and Christo Ferreira, the young Free State scrum-half, was playing well, which made things worse. It's ironic that the following year in the two Tests against the Cavaliers he went through many of the agonies that I experienced on the internal tour: my heart went out to him, I knew how he felt — but the big difference was that he had two Springbok caps in his cupboard, I had — and still have — none.

The internal tour disaster took place against a background of massive political in-fighting. As a tour it was devoid of the normal spirit and camaraderie. I still don't know the full background, but this is how I saw it.

Nelie Smith had been the Springbok coach against the Lions in 1980 and also on the 1981 tour to New Zealand. I must say that all dealings I had with him were very straightforward and I found him to be a very polite, pleasant man. I had given a few scrum-half clinics for him at big schools coaching courses. However, it seemed that not everyone was overfond of him. Wynand Claasen, the captain of the touring side in New Zealand, had written a book in which he was very critical of Smith, and alleged that all sorts of political motives were behind many of his coaching decisions, especially in selection. Now it seemed that on this internal tour certain players had been told, or had taken it on themselves, to try and change this image of Smith and to discredit what had been written in the book.

I read the book and enjoyed it. I had also met and played against Wynand many times and had always admired him as a player, captain and person. But I felt that his views, even if correct, should not have been aired at the time he was a national selector. He made comments about the political leanings of players who were still available for the Boks, and I felt that this was a bit much.

So, right from the start, apart from the unsatisfactory origin of the internal tour, I could feel that things were not right: there were obvious sub-groups within the party. I felt that a lot of the blame for this should have fallen on Naas Botha; after all, he was the one big change in the squad from the very happy bunch that had walloped England. With hindsight I feel I may have been a bit unfair. Naas is not by nature a guy who mixes straightaway, and he is not 'one of the crowd'. Also, he had just returned to the country and had replaced one of the star players from the previous series. That he tended to stick with his good provincial mates was perhaps understandable.

One day I was walking through the hotel, aware of the lack of players around, and I started to get worried. After all, if you miss any meeting your backside gets a hiding that you can't forget. I rushed to the team-room — and was horrified to find a big meeting in progress. I ran in and apologized — and was then asked to leave, as the meeting was only for those who had been in New Zealand. I left, but I was far from happy. I was a new player for the Boks, although I had been in the squad the previous year, and I had just had a shocking game and it was obvious that I needed building up. Instead I had run slap-bang into a situation that I did not understand.

In Ireland where, let's face it, there is a spectrum of political beliefs as wide as in South Africa, I had never once encountered any political undertones. Hell, after matches on tour we used to sing 'The Sash My Father Wore' and follow this with the most republican ballads imaginable. It was good fun and helped build team spirit. Looking back, I think I should have spoken up, and gone to skipper Theuns Stofberg and told him of my unhappiness. I also knew that a lot of other players could feel the atmosphere, and that strong leadership was needed. But because of my disaster at Newlands I was acutely aware that I had still a lot to prove and so I held my tongue. I cannot give enough praise to Rob Louw for his support at this time. I think he was the only one who knew how I felt, and at all times he gave me encouragement and also kept me in the picture. Ray Mordt was also very sympathetic.

Rob and I went back a long way. After the Lions series we were both invited to be part of a world squad to play Wales in the Welsh centenary celebrations. We had hit it off. I also remember that the day after the South Africa Test against Ireland in the following year, he had in-

140

vited Freddie McLennon and I to play golf with him in Cape Town. Afterwards he had come back to our hotel and had a few drinks with the Irish team. I remember Ronnie Dawson being particularly delighted at this: it reminded him of the camaraderie that should exist in rugby, right up to top level.

In fact, while talking about Ronnie Dawson, let me share something with you about him. Ronnie is of course a former Irish and Lions captain who has become an outstanding administrator at national and IRB level. He is very conservative in a rugby sense, but he is a very honourable man. I was always aware of his presence, but had never been particularly close. Then when I went to Cambridge, after my broken leg, Ireland seemed for a while to forget me. I was away from home, out of the squad and feeling a bit neglected. Then out of the blue I received a number of letters from Ronnie. They were assurances that I was not forgotten. They contained much advice and encouragement, and were the basis of a friendship. I realized that when things are going well, lots of people write and want contact. When I was in the pits, Ronnie chose to write. I will never forget that.

Rob Louw was, and still is, a real mate and although we always played hard against each other, no matter how close the game was we always managed to have a laugh. Once at Newlands, when I was taking off to put pressure on the WP fly-half, he just grabbed me by the jersey under my armpit and said: 'Robbie, you're getting slow.' Next year in the first scrum, before putting the ball in, I looked at him and in a voice that only Rob, Divan, the ref and I could hear, said: 'God, are they still picking you at your age?' He is that sort of guy, and he epitomises what a top rugby player should be, on and off the field. I also admire him for the way he is colour-blind. Rob sees people, not skins, and he did that long before it was fashionable.

I once caught him beautifully. It was a few years later. Rob had returned from rugby league and was invited to be one of the captains in the South African TV sports quiz. Rob had to spend a week in Jo'burg filming and naturally I gave him a shout. We had a champagne breakfast at our house, Rob and I went to a game in Pretoria and then we picked up Jennie and went out on the tear. On the way to Pretoria Rob told me that he was amazed at the number of gay people working at the SABC, the South African Broadcasting Corporation. He had nothing against them, but felt it was interesting. I told him that in today's world this was commonplace and especially in the creative professions. I also mentioned that one of the Transvaal players was gay. Rob was shocked, he couldn't believe it. After a minute he asked who it was, and I replied: 'Give us a kiss and I'll tell you.' Hook, line and sinker, and we laughed all the way there.

I still don't know just what happened at that team meeting on the internal tour. Apparently a petition was produced trying to get Nelie Smith back as Springbok coach, inspired by the right wing supporters involved in rugby. I don't know — but I won't say that I don't care, because I believe that rigid conservatism is the greatest evil in South Africa. I believe that were it not for small-minded, insecure people, the process of reform would be far further down the road than it is.

The 'Boks' were on a hiding to nothing. The opposition sides were highly motivated, wanting to prove the selectors wrong. It was apathy all round, and the man I really felt sorry for was Cecil Moss, the Springbok coach. He had put so much effort into the year, he had been so meticulous; this was dashed, and he then had to contend with a squad which had other things on its mind. I felt so bad about the whole thing, and so ashamed at my performance, that I wrote to him. It was the first time I had ever done such a thing.

Mind you, although Cecil is a mild-mannered gentleman he also has a temper. A few years earlier I had been picked as reserve to Divan in a side to play a touring invitation team in Cape Town. It was the first time I had met Cecil, and the day before the match we were to meet at a hotel — two o'clock sharp. The mood was very relaxed and there was a lot of horsing about. A number of the guys from provinces other than Transvaal got a laugh at my inability to speak Afrikaans. As a result I tried to use it at every opportunity, just for a laugh. Anyway, a few of us ordered some obscure dessert at lunch and there was a delay, so we were late for the team meeting. We weren't worried and Ockie Oosthuizen, the Bok prop and Transvaal skipper at the time, told me the Afrikaans phrase for poor service.

We walked into the team room and I said, 'Jammer, Doc, maar die diens is kak'. Only a few guys laughed, and then I realized that we'd misread the situation. Doc Moss was worried at the attitude of the team, and was furious at the late arrivals. When I came out with this it was the last straw and he exploded. He told me that he didn't give a damn about the service in the hotel, but he did care about the attitude of the players and, with his eyes fixed on me, he said he was not interested in players with the wrong attitude. I must have been as red as a Welsh jersey, and I was almost in tears. I had just broken into representative

South African rugby, and now I felt my chance was gone forever.

After the game Doc spoke to me and assured me that I had done no harm to my chances. He told me that he had been worried about the casual approach of the side, and he was waiting for a chance to nip it in the bud. He said I was the unlucky guy. His tactic worked, though, and the side suddenly became very serious about the job in hand and won well. I remember late that night sitting chatting to Ray Mordt in his room when Doc walked past on his way to bed. He popped in and we had a long chat.

He was interested in his players as people as well as pieces of meat, and this was again one of his strengths. During the Test against England the Bok full-back, Johan Heunis, got a knock. We were up about twenty points at the time, and Doc told our reserve full-back, Liaan Kirkham, to warm up. Liaan was on the sideline, waiting for his first cap, when Johan recovered and went on to play well in the victory. Liaan later suffered a serious hamstring injury and although he still played very well at top level, he never fully recovered the blistering pace that made him one of the best broken play runners in the game. Later I was chatting to Cecil and Liaan's name came up. Cecil told me that although he had been delighted that Johan had recovered, he always wished that Liaan had got his cap.

To have been that close and not to have got it seems very unjust. I must say that I agreed, as Liaan is the bravest of players. Mind you, I also feel sorry for myself. I make no bones about how much I wanted that Bok cap.

I remember getting very annoyed a few years later. It was when there had been a lot of uncertainty over the future of official tours to South Africa. The Cavaliers had come and gone; the next season saw the sudden arrival of the South Sea Barbarians. These were mainly Fijians and Tongans and they did quite well. However a number of players, Carel Du Plessis included, had been negotiating to bring out an Australian side. Carel started to appear in the media acting as a sort of unofficial, self-appointed Bok spokesman. He said the Boks didn't want to play against sub-standard sides as it demeaned the jersey and so on. I was furious. It was fine for him — he had the cap and the jersey. What about the many of us who were on the fringe and had been there for a number of years?

I actually tackled Carel on it and asked him to put himself in our situation, to imagine himself capless. He talked to me the next day and said he had never looked at it quite like that, and that he sympathized.

Carel is a funny guy. I like him but, like Naas, he has a facade that is hard to get behind. But since I retired Carel has been a great help in doing interviews and so on, which have helped me in my new career as a journalist. He also is a truly great player.

Following Christo Ferreira's brilliant play on the internal tour he was the obvious choice for the Cavaliers Test series. However he played well below par in the first two Tests, and so the Boks were a bit stuck. Unfortunately I had torn rib cartilages and had missed the start of the season. I played a third team game, my first after the injury, just before the third Test. I later heard that the South African selectors actually enquired about my fitness, as they were worried about the third Test. In the end they went for the EP youngster Garth Wright, who the previous year had been discarded after the junior trials. It's history that he played brilliantly and scored the last try against the New Zealanders in the final Test. He was magnificent — but I still wonder whether I would have got the nod if I had been fit. I like to think that I would have.

That Cavaliers series caused a mountain of controversy. Of course the seeds were sown the previous year when the official All Black tour was cancelled. This came as a hell of a blow to many of the Kiwis, especially the more senior players. Guys like Andy Dalton, Andy Haden, Murray Mexted and Gary Knight had been All Blacks for years and were legends in world rugby. About the only challenge left for them was to defeat the Springboks in South Africa.

I think, quite rightly, that they saw that achievement as the one thing that would have set their great side above all the other great New Zealand sides of old. We heard reports that they had tried to press on with the tour even after it had officially been called off. I believe that the day the 1985 All Blacks finally had to concede that the tour was off, arrangements for the rebel Cavaliers of 1986 began.

The shock waves of the tour spread through the rugby world immediately, and ended the era of total administration power. Until the Cavaliers tour, the rugby establishment had ruled supreme. It would have been unheard of for players to go against the IRB, and it would certainly have been beyond comprehension for such rebels to have got away with it. That's what the Cavaliers did, demonstrating that never again could the views of players be ignored by the rule-makers.

A number of things should be mentioned. First of all — and let it be underlined, lest people who were against the tour, or who have tried to discredit it subsequently, try to twist the truth — the standard of rugby was extremely high. The level of commitment was frightening;

however, judged against previous series, it was not particularly dirty. Also, from a South African viewpoint, it was the real thing. It was the Boks against the All Blacks for the unofficial championship of the world.

The Boks won and deservedly so. The Kiwis think they were robbed, but they weren't. They were beaten by a side that, in addition to having the will to win, had just too much pace in the back line to allow the All Blacks to run in tries from situations that would normally have yielded such results.

For all the New Zealand superior forward play, by drifting the defence in the back line the Springboks were never vulnerable on the outside. I do not believe that in modern times a three-quarter line has had, man for man, the speed of the Boks of 1986 — Garth Wright, Naas Botha, Danie Gerber, Michael du Plessis, Carel du Plessis, Jaco Reinach and even Johan Heunis at full-back. Without exception each of those guys could have played international rugby on the wing, and never have been shown up for pace. I know because I have chased the heels of all of them on occasion; and I am also in a good position to comment on the series as I did match analysis for TV, and saw every minute from the best seat in the house.

Time and time again the All Blacks — and I call them that deliberately, because that is how South Africa saw them (and had the Cavaliers won, it's how New Zealand would have seen them) — won superb second-phase ball. They'd then spin it wide having sucked in a back or two. Normally, with straight running, an overlap would be created and a try scored. Time and again they moved it wide with a half-overlap. But the Boks, marshalled by Michael du Plessis in midfield, pushed across and then Carel du Plessis and Jaco Reinach, on the outside, were able to turn and tackle; if the New Zealanders cut back, Jannie Breedt, Wahl Baartman and Gert Smal were there to make the tackles.

It was a simple case of homework being done; and in Michael du Plessis the Boks had the best defensive centre I have ever seen. His talent was really brought home the following year, when he came to Transvaal; in the whole season not one break was made through our midfield. He has a gift for defensive alignment and also for communicating this to a team. The fact that he is as odd as two left feet tends to cloud opinions of him, but I like him and feel that the decision of sports writers not to make him Player of the Year in 1988 was very wrong. He had one off day, in the Currie Cup final. But it was his protest against the political system in South Africa by moving during the playing of the National Anthem that sealed his fate. He didn't make the top five.

145

Never have I seen three men tackle like Wahl, Jannie and Gert. It makes me laugh when I read European selections of great players of that era. The back rows invariably have Mexted, Shaw, Mourie, Rives, Winterbottom and so on, and certainly they were amongst the best. However, based on performance in that series, nobody could discount the claims of the Bok trio. And when you consider that all were getting their first caps in the first Test, the achievement is all the more incredible. The reaction to the video of the series, which I sent home, backs up my contention that if you talk about the 1980s, that was the outstanding series.

But this book is not really about the technical side of the game, or even about scores and results. No, I think the issues of that tour lie off the field. Much has been said about it — but much more has not been said. In fact, apart from the odd derogatory reference to it, it has almost been wiped off the slate, swept under the establishment carpet.

Why is this? I'd like to give some thoughts on it, reflecting how I saw things at the time. Perhaps players more closely involved in the tour, especially from the Cavalier side, have other views; if so, it's clear that they are not talking too much. It's only natural that the rest of us have formed our own opinions.

Why did the Cavaliers defy the IRB and come on a rebel tour? The answer they give is that they wanted to play the Boks in South Africa, and as the 1985 tour was cancelled at the last minute they decided to take matters into their own hands. That was the basic reason for their coming. However, I don't believe that this alone caused thirty players to risk their very membership of rugby union and go against the express wish of the establishment.

A lot of money was involved. The Cavaliers were guaranteed large sums to come and to complete the tour; they also made a lot of money on the tour. Mind you, that has been a part and parcel of major tours for ages. The ticket pool alone in a country like South Africa or New Zealand would have realized plenty. How does the pool work? Very simple. For each game, each tourist receives a number of complimentary tickets. These are pooled and sold, often at a profit to locals who need the tickets. The money then goes into the players' pool. It's banked and divided up at the end of the tour. This way the players can buy presents for going home. What if the touring player really does have an Auntie Edith living in Jo'burg? Well, he then buys back the ticket from the pool at face value. It's as old as the hills. In recent years supermarket visits, business lunches and other promotions have also been added, but they are politely ignored by authority. Everyone scores and the touring side become better known to the fans in the host country.

But the Cavaliers took this to new heights in South Africa — I suppose because they took part in the first professional tour. How much were they paid to come? I have no precise idea on that one, but figures of thirty to forty thousand US dollars a man have been bandied about. After the tour I even read a report in which Colin Meads, who had been an official of the Cavaliers, admitted that money had been received. And what happened? Were the players banned for life like players who go to rugby league? Not on your life. They missed a game or so for the All Blacks, and were then cleared and returned to the fold. It was also reported that a number of them bought new houses or did building extensions, but none of them spilt the beans. Of course they didn't — they had broken the rules and got away with it, and good luck to them.

Naturally, the South African players weren't too chuffed at all this. Sure, they had a series but what about some expenses for their efforts? Top South African players cast an eye at other sportsmen on a similar level, and they noticed the big Mercs and other perks. It boiled over before the fourth Test. The All Blacks took the field in front of 70 000 spectators. At the same time a deal was being thrashed out in the Springbok dressing-room. An amount for the series was agreed, and proportionate compensation was also negotiated for those who only played a few games. Only after this was settled did the players agree to take the field — and they won well.

The All Blacks had been whingeing ever since the third Test defeat, which meant they could at best only share the series. They were complaining that the referee was biased against them, and that the Boks were cheating in the line-outs, and so on. I thought it was all sour grapes, but I suppose that's the way all losing tourists behave. The New Zealanders just didn't appreciate that the pattern they employed was good enough to beat the rest of the world but not good enough to beat South Africa.

Anyway, after that final Test there were the usual speeches. Andy Dalton, who hadn't played, stood up and we expected the usual stuff about a good game and congrats to the winners. Instead he said that, in all his rugby career, he had never accused a referee of being a cheat — until today. There was a stunned silence. I was appalled. I had known Ken Rowlands, the Welsh ref, for years; indeed, he had refereed the Cambridge/All Blacks match all those years ago. I had known him to be very straight, and also a very nice, sensitive man. I booed loudly, it just came out — and Alan Whetton, the big All Black flanker, spun round in front of me. I thought, 'My God, he's going to smack me.' But I think when he saw who it was he decided not to. I said something to the effect that Dalton was offside, and Whetton turned back.

The speech was in very bad taste. Naas replied for the Boks, and handled it beautifully. He thanked the Cavaliers for the game, and reminded them that the Boks felt that Welsh referee Clive Norling had cost them the series in New Zealand in 1981. However, the Boks had kept quiet and congratulated New Zealand. Naas said that cowboys don't cry, and that he felt sorry for them: then he paused, and added that actually he didn't. It was a sad end to a great series.

I felt sorry for Andy Dalton. He had been injured, a broken jaw from a cowardly punch by Burger Geldenhuys in the Northern Transvaal game. He had stayed on tour, and it must have been difficult. He had obviously heard all the moaning from his players, and mistakenly thought that to speak out was in their interests.

A few days later I met Murray Mexted in Johannesburg. Now as I've said Murray and I had become good friends during his stay a few years earlier in Johannesburg. He had got on well with Jennie and me, and we were very keen to meet his lovely new wife. There was a big 'do' arranged at a former Wanderers skipper's house. I made a point of speaking to Murray, and telling him exactly what I thought of the Cavalier players' attitude to the series.

He argued the other way, and came up with all sorts of accusations against the ref and the South African board for paying him off. I said that was nonsense, as both teams were also getting paid. Just in time Murray saw the trap, and with a big smile told me that was not so, that they never got a cent. That was the closest I ever got to breaking the veil of silence.

The whole question of payment of rugby players has been discussed over and over again. In all the books I have read, the issue comes under the spotlight — and in all the books the writer very daringly proposes that some greater compensation for top players is needed. At the same time, the writer neatly sidesteps any admission that he himself has received money.

Well, I'll say it up front. I have received money for playing rugby. Not a lot, I'll admit, but certainly enough to put me outside the fold as far as the rugby board are concerned. And before you think that all this took place in dastardly South Africa, where we all know that this evil practice goes on, let me state that I've received money in Ireland,

England and New Zealand. However before the rugby bailiffs arrive, let me also add that I've never received a cent that did not come either from rugby officialdom or with their certain knowledge. I've already told how I used to feel about this, but like all old players — or the vast majority, anyway — my views have changed.

I'll never forget the first time I received money that wasn't legal. It was in Ireland at the opening of the new Saint Mary's clubhouse in Dublin in 1976. They picked an Irish Fifteen, selected from players who had been to New Zealand, plus Willie John McBride, to play against the club side. It was great fun, a nice day and a big crowd. I twinged a hamstring and went off early: Rodney O'Donnell, then a very junior player in the club, organized ice for me. I can remember thinking that it was a pity that he was never going to make it to the top level after all his promise at school. Four years later he made me eat my words when he got selected for the British Lions in South Africa.

I had travelled in to the St Mary's game with Mum and Dad. Afterwards, Tom Grace, the Mary's skipper, gave me an envelope. I said to him that I had no expenses. He told me to take it, but I insisted that it should go to the club. In the end Tom told me it was more of a nuisance to take it back — and that was that. I had taken tainted money, and I must confess I worried about it for ages. Now, of course, I look back and laugh. (The amount I took from St Mary's? The princely sum of five pounds.)

I have no proof that the Cavaliers were paid. I have no proof that the row took place in the Springbok dressing-room before the last Test. But I know — people have told me, people who were involved.

The following year there was also a row. Out of the blue, a side from the South Sea Islands arrived. They were mostly Tongans and Fijians, and a colourful lot they were. The two big games were supposed to be Tests, and with Garth Wright injured I got the nod. Test caps at last — but no way. Later on, under threat from the IRB (or at least under perceived threat), the South African side took the field as the Barbarians.

The night before the first 'Test' there was a meeting. Suddenly, far from preparing for the game, the team meeting became a forum for debate. All the senior guys said they would not play unless they were paid. They believed that the opposition were picking up big bucks and that — and this is important — after the agreement reached after the player-power talks before the Cavaliers Test, money was due to the South Africans as well.

I must confess I talked strongly against the blackmail. I felt that if

149

the players had a case it would stand up afterwards, and that brinkman-ship, especially against Chick Henderson and his Barbarian commit-tee, who have always played to the traditional rules, was very unfair. Most of the senior players, including skipper Naas Botha, took the opposite view. I must add that a lot of the debate was in Afrikaans and too quick for me. But, although I was by then in favour of getting all the bucks going, I was against the gun-to-the-head tactics. The next day more rugby officials arrived; in the morning they patiently listened to all the arguments — and I confess I was furious.

Gone were all the brave demands from the previous evening. All the leaders were meek as lambs now, and I felt even Naas was giving the impression that he had been against the motion the previous evening. The only player I know for sure was with me was Burger Geldenhuys, but the vote was something like fourteen for cash and six against. Any-way, the officials had to act quickly and they promised to look into the matter. I felt sorry for them as they were in an invidious position. If they flatly refused, then the game would be off and the whole saga would come out in the wash. If they didn't, then they were giving in to player demands.

In the end we played, won, and won again in Durban. The crazy thing about the Durban game is that while we were changing, the South Sea men were on strike in their dressing room. It seems that they didn't trust their manager with all their allowances.

I suppose the situation the South African officials found themselves in is similar to that of the IRB. They are the defenders of the amateur faith, and as such must take an official hard line on all payments. But everyone knows that players are paid, no, sorry, reimbursed in coun-tries like France and Italy as well as South Africa.

Some of the big English clubs are now doing it, too, and it's funny that only the poor old Welsh seem to have an official question mark against the practice. They were the originators of 'boot money'.

The hypocrisy is mind boggling. But just like the South African offi-cials before the tour games, the IRB knows that if it cracks the whip the whole lot will come tumbling down. Imagine being the first famous player to be nailed for receiving cash. Hell, he'd blow the top off the whole thing and down it would come. Why do you think the Cavaliers were cleared? If they had been banned for life for receiving payment, they would have produced tons of evidence to insist that the same tough measures be applied in France and Italy.

I know one senior international player who has actually kept a photocopy of a cheque received from a rugby authority, simply as security against anyone in the future trying to have him banned for breaching amateur rules. I also heard the other day, from a very reliable source, about a member of the RFU committee (that's the boys at Twickers) who is paying out £2 000 a month to players brought in to strengthen his club.

So the big winners were the Cavaliers. They broke the rules, had a hell of a series (with their wives along), got paid, and then were received back into the fold in time for a number of them to help win the World Cup. For all South Africans, *that* was a hollow victory — how can you have a World Cup without the strongest team in the world? In fairness I believe the All Blacks would still have won on home turf. But I know for sure the Boks were the only side that would have given them a real go.

Am I a professional at heart? Not at all. I've often said that although the game will go professional, and so it must, I'm equally glad that the vast majority of my career was as a true-blue amateur — with the exception of the odd five quid here and there. How can this be? Surely this statement is as Irish as Paddy's pig? Not at all.

Rugby is almost perfect. Schools, youth and club rugby must never change. It's great fun, people don't kill (although they can), and it embodies the amateur ideal. By the way, in this scenario I don't include the top Welsh or French clubs. What I mean is that the junior ranks of the game are fine. The big problems occur at the top: with World Cups, Welsh Cups and certainly Currie Cups, the pressure to win is enormous.

As each side gets better, so they put up the required standard to compete. In fact, I believe the strength of the current All Blacks will do more to push the game towards professionalism than anything else. Last year Wales, having shared the Five Nations, were absolutely destroyed in New Zealand, and now British rugby has a decision to make. Does it stay second division to the southern hemisphere, or does it get competitive? Well, just look at the national training squads in Wales and England for your answer. In the old days they used to meet a day before an international. Now they go on training camps to Spain and Portugal. The players are having to work harder and harder.

Meanwhile, up the road in the Rugby League, all is different — that game has been transformed, partly through TV. The players are making bucks and enjoying a great game and now national stardom. League names are just as big in England as Union ones are. And after the tenth cap for Wales or the sixtieth, what's the difference? Jonathan Davies has gone to League, so has Adrian Hadley — my bet is that more will go too, because League is fulfilling a need. It offers another step further up the ladder for the top player. A cap is no longer enough reward for all the hours of training.

South Africa needs rugby. There's also no doubt that South Africa has the best climate for rugby and the best facilities — and the game is backed by the big corporations. Add to that the increasing isolation, and it's an ideal spawning ground for the professional game. There's also another factor. In Europe, the IRB is held in some awe. The way of the amateur is genuinely felt to be the way to proceed in the game. When the IRB makes an announcement, it is received by most rugby men with the same deference that would be accorded a papal encyclical among Catholics. In South Africa that is not the case — the IRB is seen as a group of well-meaning people who are totally out of touch with the game. And, rightly or wrongly, the body is widely believed to have betrayed South Africa over promised tours.

'To hell with the IRB' is a common cry. 'Let the game go professional' is another. After all, it's widely believed that players receive perks in South Africa, just like in France, Italy and Wales — so why not go the whole hog? Especially sickening to South Africa was the first so-called World Cup. Okay, it was impractical for South Africa to take part, that was accepted. But to hear various foreign rugby officials lauding the success of the event, and even indicating that South Africa wasn't needed or wanted, made many of us sick.

So let's look at a possible scenario. As I write, South Africa has endured two seasons in which official tours were promised and none took place. Players, public and officials are annoyed and frustrated. Forget politics: the SARB has undoubtedly cleaned up its act, and after the early attempts at window-dressing, the reform in terms of a non-racial game is now genuine. This year is the SARB centenary. Once again, there is talk of a fully sanctioned official tour. If it doesn't come off, then I believe even Doc Craven will not be able to prevent the start of the revolution.

The first stage will be a rebel tour. It will consist of top players, the guys who are dissatisfied with life at the top. They will come and they will be paid; the IRB will this time have to expel South Africa and the rebel tourists, and all hell will break loose. In South Africa, the Turks will gain control and the Currie Cup will go professional. School and club rugby will be the same, but the eight top provincial sides will be sponsored and will agree terms with the top players. In addition to the locals, the rebel players, plus others from overseas will be taken into the system — as they are in cricket.

Satellite channels in Europe and around the world will buy the TV coverage, despite condemnation from the IRB. The world will watch the top players in the world play out the Currie Cup under perfect blue skies and in front of capacity crowds at Ellis Park, Loftus Versfeld and Newlands. And in the following season, the top players left within the official game will be queueing up to play. Before long, some entrepreneur will put together a side in, say, Sydney to play in the series. Perhaps it will be backed by something like the Mark McCormack group. After all, that body has no qualms about representing South Africans who have demonstrated beyond all doubt that they do not support racial discrimination in any form. If you don't believe me, ask Gary Player.

Perhaps some of the money generated could be used in community projects within South Africa. Imagine if this series provided funds to build a new hospital in Soweto or a school in Mamelodi. A lot of people would sit up and take notice, and the players would at least feel that some concrete advantage would accrue to some victims of apartheid. Fanciful perhaps, but projects like that could tip the scales as far as players in the rest of the world are concerned.

After a few years the Five Nations, still strictly amateur, would be to the South African series what the amateur soccer internationals in Britain are to the soccer World Cup. Rugby would be the same at grassroots, but at the top it would be fantastic. Players who have given their lives to the sport would have a place to go. Refereeing and discipline would be strict. With TV cameras, instant replays and adjudications, dirty play would be kept to a minimum. Players would be massively insured, just like the top soccer players.

Perhaps I'm dreaming. Perhaps the vision I've seen is far-fetched, and perhaps the players in the rest of the world would never go for it. But Kerry Packer and the Wimbledon boycott by professionals took place: so ignore South Africa and its professional aspirations at your peril.

I passionately believe that the game must go at least semi-professional. It's the only way for it to remain honest, and indeed it's the only way for top players to exist without a future full of poverty, cynicism and disillusionment. However, I concede that if the game goes pro, some of the fun will go out of it. Just like soccer, it will become a career for many; but at least at lower level all would remain the same. *The Art of Coarse Rugby* will be just as relevant in the future as when it was written.

153

11

One of the funny things about the major South African rugby grounds is that they each have a different smell. I first noticed it on the Lions tour.

I was used to Lansdowne Road, Twickers, Murrayfield and the Arms Park, and Parc des Princes, too. I know that each of those grounds is different — but they all smell the same. There is a dampness and a richness of the soil that, because I was so used to it, I never noticed or considered. Then I went to South Africa and, especially when you move away from the coast, you are aware of a change.

On the highveld the dryness hits you, not just in the atmosphere. It's in the turf, in the concrete; hell, it's even in the people. I love it, and my favourite ground in all the world is Loftus Versfeld in Pretoria. It's also my lucky ground, which helps. I first saw Loftus when the Lions played Northerns in 1980. I had replaced Colin Patterson who had flu; I was terrified, and will never forget the roar as we ran onto the field. I played well, though, and barring that bone-shaking mistake I made in taking on Pierre Edwards, it remains a treasured memory.

Ellis Park is also a highveld ground, but at a greater altitude than Pretoria. At Ellis Park I always detected a slight staleness in the air — and the pitch smells different. I once mentioned this to someone, and they explained that it was because of all the shit Transvaal play on it. But I think it's due to being situated in the old, run-down part of the city and also the totally enclosed design. Loftus has that huge open side and I think that lets the air in.

Bloemfontein's Free State stadium is depressing. I think all players hate playing on grounds that have an athletics track around them, because the crowd is so far away. In Bloem you also have a cycling track to contend with, and you feel the lack of atmosphere immediately. Mind you, that could also be because there is rarely a full-house feeling there — even 20 000 or so get lost in its vastness. I always think of the pitch as yellow and hard, with a very sandy texture. I hated it.

Then we move to the coast. The city of Durban itself has a smell all of its own. I don't know if it's the humidity or the vegetation, but when you get out of the plane in Durban all this, mixed with the smell of the sea, produces a very spicy aroma. The ground is also very 'Durban' and of course as you leave it after a game the delicious smell of smoke and braaied meat creates a lasting memory.

Boet Erasmus in Port Elizabeth is a beautiful ground, but somehow the smell is of a small country rugby pitch. Somehow you don't smell buildings, you smell grass. It is sort of cut into a hill and there is a lot of earth around, and no doubt that's where the feeling comes from. It's huge, but doesn't smell huge.

Then, of course, there is Newlands. What a perfect ground for rugby. Even with the new stands and the perfect pitch they now have, it just smells of tradition. On reflection, there's also in my memory a paint smell. They are always painting something at Newlands on match day, always in blue and white and always by a rabid Province fan. That's the smell at Newlands: the paint of fanaticism.

Of all the provincial grounds I've been in, Newlands has the best people. You get the impression that all of them — the chap who directs you off the team bus, the lady who has just cleaned out the dressing-room, the programme sellers, union president Jan Pickard himself — all are happy and they are all Western Province fans. You don't get that at other grounds. Even at Loftus and at the Arms Park, it's hard to tell whether the people are working there out of love or for the pay. At Newlands you feel that the pay is not important, you really do. I loved playing at Newlands.

Transvaal played Western Province there in the Currie Cup Final in 1986. It was our first final in about fourteen years, and when we arrived we saw where the paint would go. On the grandstand there was a line of dates representing the years in which Province had won the trophy; the first three numbers of 1986 were already painted in. After the game and our defeat, they handed out plaques to both teams on which the winner's name, 'Western Province' was already painted. They knew they were going to win. We gave it a hell of a go, but inside I think we always knew that Province were too good.

After the game it was all smiles in the dressing room. After all, we had won the Lion Cup knockout and reached the Currie Cup final. Transvaal hadn't known such success for years. Later the players and wives were even taken to Mauritius on holiday. I suppose it was officially a 'coaching course' but it was a hell of a setting — or so I'm told, because Jennie and I were in Italy. (At school when we won the Under-14

Leinster cricket cup, our side was taken on a day trip to Butlin's holiday camp; some parents at one of the Dublin schools accused us of professionalism. I'm sure that's what certain rugby people would say about the Mauritius trip, but in South Africa it's common. In fact, have a look at some of the top English and Welsh clubs and their choice of venues for summer tours. After winning a Welsh Cup, for example, a free 'rugby' trip to the States or Hong Kong is not all that arduous. It's the British equivalent of a trip to Mauritius.)

Yes, at the end of the 1986 season the Transvaal camp was happy. 'Wait until next year' was the defiant talk by the officials at the function after the game. Well, next year came and it remains one of the highlights of my career. We had a great season, played good rugby and were a very happy bunch of players. We took the Lion Cup again at Ellis Park and qualified to meet Northern Transvaal in the Currie Cup Final, again at Ellis Park.

This was a Test match. It was an international in everything but name, and to watch the tape of the game with visitors from Britain or Ireland is very enjoyable. They have rarely seen anything like it. It was fabulous.

After the game, sitting in the dressing room at Ellis Park, I remember staring down at my sodden boots and starting to laugh. It was crazy. All around grown men were crying. Officials were stomping around, terrified to look anything other than stern — and I was laughing. I wasn't hysterical, either. I genuinely felt elated. We had played a game of rugby, in a magnificent new modern stadium, in front of 70 000 people, in weather that defied description (rain and hail will do for now, but not one soul left his seat).

At halftime we were 15-6 ahead. Then, in the driving rain, their forwards began to get more ball and Naas kicked us to death; our magnificent pack lost control. We would win a few loose balls and work our way up the pitch; Naas Botha would get one ball and, bang, sixty yards back. Then line-out to Transvaal — crooked throw-in or a knock-on, scrum to Northerns, drop-goal from Naas. It was as simple as that. Four penalties and four drop goals he got, in a display of kicking that would have been considered too far-fetched for the *Hornet*. At the end he got a bad ball, dodged to one side and with his wrong foot, as bodies fell around him, he dropped the goal. As it went over I grabbed him and said something like 'Well done, you bastard.' It was merely a remark of respect to a genius. Later I heard that the gesture was not appreciated by certain Transvaal officials. It was never mentioned to my face, of course.

We had led for most of the game, been caught with a minute of official time to go, and then lost in injury time. We had scored two tries to none, but Northerns had beaten us 24-18, courtesy of Naas Botha's kicking genius. It was a game of rugby in the epic tradition — unforgettable for everyone who was there. So I felt good, and that was why I laughed.

I must also mention how, before the Cape Town final, I met State President PW Botha for the first time. I thought beforehand that as a South African he would want to chat a bit and take an interest in one of the big days on the sporting calendar. Not on your life — he seemed to be in a trance as he walked along meeting the players. He wasn't interested at all. Even with all the adrenalin pumping, I felt disappointed. If I ever make it to State President of South Africa or to the monarchy in England, I'll be different.

PW wasn't the first 'royal' I'd encountered, though. I met Queen Elizabeth and Prince Philip in 1980, before the Welsh Centenary match at Cardiff Arms Park. I was disappointed to see that they were very much on automatic pilot when the players were introduced: the smiles were there all right, but the minds were elsewhere. Prince Philip asked me if I was fit, but before I had a chance to answer he moved on. That game sticks in my memory: the two composite sides were Wales/England vs Scotland/Ireland. Being just after the Lions tour, it was a sort of re-union and I must say that the Welsh Rugby Union did us all proud. Wives were invited, and nothing was spared to give us all a good time The fact that we laid on a really good game somehow justified it all.

We learned that we would be meeting the Queen beforehand, and that this would involve standing on the pitch for a while in the cold weather. This of course was liable to cause pulled hamstrings, so our skipper, Andy Irvine, requested that we get tracksuits. These were duly arranged, and we stood meeting royalty resplendent in our beautiful green and blue tracksuits. (The Welsh and England side froze in their playing kit.)

Afterwards, despite the instruction that we must return the tracksuits, most of us just put them in our bags and forgot about them. This was fine, until a few weeks later we were all contacted by our unions. We were led to believe that there was a holy war going on over the tracksuits, and that keeping them meant infringing our amateur status and that we would have to return them pronto. Absurd, isn't it? But I had mine laundered and returned it to the secretary of the IRFU — only to be told that they had sent the letter, not really thinking that anyone would heed it. I then asked if I could have the tracksuit back. Sorry,

157

he said, then I would be infringing the rules. I was furious, as in those days a fancy tracksuit really was something — and this one was a once-off production for a single game. If it had been South Africa, the teams would probably have been given tracksuits and blazers as well to commemorate the occasion.

Mind you, the Irish official in question really was a dyed-in-the-wool amateur of the old school. After my first international in 1976, he did a really mean thing to me. As luck would have it, I had the ball in my hand when the ref blew the final whistle. Great, I thought, planning to have it autographed, sealed and displayed on the mantelpiece for ever. Remember I was just twenty, mentally a schoolboy and fulfilling my life's ambition. So there I was in the dressing-room after the game, considering my dilemma about swapping my jersey. Rod Hauser, the Aussie scrum-half, naturally wanted an Irish one, but I felt that my first jersey should be kept. Tony Ensor, the Irish fullback, saved the day by giving me his jersey. He told me this was traditional, for a senior player to do this for a new cap; later I would give my jerseys to other debutants with the same problem. So I had the match ball, an Aussie jersey and an Irish jersey — what a feeling!

Then this official sidled up to me and asked for the ball. I said that I wanted to keep it. He smiled and said that the IRFU needed it for squad sessions etc, and to let me keep it would be infringing the rules. Knowing what I know now, I would have laughed at him and called one of the senior players who would have told him to get lost. Being a youngster, I handed it over without a murmur. Quite what motivated that official to be so small-minded I do not know; I was very disappointed.

But I suppose that, even in the 1970s, it was a different era. In those days the Irish jerseys felt like canvas sacks. They were made by some firm in Cork who had been doing them for years. We were only allowed to keep two jerseys a season, which meant that if you played in all four championship games and wanted to swap each time, you had to buy two of your own jerseys. For playing for Ireland you received your cap, at the end of the season and usually by post; and you also got a blazer badge — which you had sewn on after you'd bought the blazer yourself. (Elsewhere in this book there is a snap of my meeting with Billy Beaumont on my first day as a Lion. That's my Irish blazer I'm wearing, bought by my dad and with the presented badge sewn on.)

Nowadays the pettiness all seems so daft. In fact, during my first season one of the senior players — Tom Grace, I think — leaked the story about the two-jersey limit to the papers and after that we were given one per

158

match.

Getting back to that Currie Cup final in 1987: why should I have felt sad? All my life I had wondered what it would be like to play in a classic: now I had. Apart from international players, I don't believe any rugby player from outside South Africa can experience anything like a Currie Cup final. If you think I'm exaggerating, do yourself a favour and get your cousin in Johannesburg (no doubt the black sheep of the family) to send you a tape, and judge for yourself.

After a while, though, my post-match elation turned more to annoyance. We had put up a magnificent show, far better than the previous year, but there were no congratulations. The dressing room was like a morgue. There were a few half-hearted words. Only one selector, Hughie Bladen (the former Transvaal and Junior Bok centre), actually took the trouble to speak personally to each player. All else was beetle-brows and muttering. There was no talk of Mauritius, either, or looking forward to next year. I began to realize that we were in disgrace.

There is a saying in South African rugby that winning is not the important thing — it's the only thing. It's nonsense, of course, but I learnt that certain officials take nonsense seriously.

I should have known that this would happen, mind you. The previous week we had won a very tough semifinal against South West Africa in windy Windhoek by a three-point margin. It had been a physical, dirty game. I had been late-tackled on numerous occasions and once, after the ref had blown up, I even threw the ball, gridiron fashion, at my assailant as he raced away. To my dismay the ball flew the fifteen metres or so like an arrow and hit the guy, all six foot six and sixteen stone of him, right on the back of his head. I thought I was going to get killed. But the guy, Sarel du Toit, just laughed and the ref changed his decision against me. We'd won and were in the final again. It was to be at Ellis Park, surely we were heroes.

In the Windhoek dressing-room it was like an ambulance after a bomb blast. Every one of us had blood somewhere, and there was more pack ice than at the North Pole. We stood in the customary circle and waited for the officials. Our president, Louis Luyt, came in and looked at us for a minute. Then he said '*Pateties*. Pathetic'. I saw red, took off my jersey, threw it down and walked out. I went to the South West dressing-room and had a beer with them. Later I learnt that my annoyance had registered, and so I talked to Luyt; he apologized to the team.

But that wasn't the end of it — I should have known just what winning the Currie Cup is all about. To many union officials it is an obsession. In Ireland we would have been praised to the heavens for having done the job we set out to do — getting to the final. Here, the narrow squeak meant that for the first time the officials thought we might actually lose the final.

We had a week to go, a week to cure all the bruises and bumps of Windhoek. Northerns had two weeks from their last game, and perhaps that gave them an advantage. Even if it didn't, we gave them that advantage with the stupidest week of training I ever did see. Instead of resting and recuperating and possibly doing some light sharpening work, we were put through the mill. We had a game practice early, and had the guts run out of us again and again. It was murderous. To my grave I will believe that if anything other than the Lord Almighty cost us the Currie Cup that year, it was the week leading up to the final.

I believe that with sensible and not suicidal preparation we would have kept control up front in the final, and we would have celebrated a Currie Cup win. I know now that the defeat marked the end, or at least the beginning of the end, of my rugby career.

The next season I decided to really give it another go. I worked hard at the weights in the off-season, and was as keen as mustard to have a last shot at a real Bok cap as well as another season in the limelight with Transvaal. But I should have known that the knives were out for a number of senior players. The key thing that we all failed to realize was that the success of the previous year was not universally agreed upon. We had played great football, won the Lion Cup in style and drawn record crowds (average 35 000) — and we'd given Johannesburg a classic final, the first at Ellis Park for well over a decade.

'We lost to a genius, sure — but overall, what a season'... John, you were fooling yourself. For three years the senior players in that side had run it. We had a coach, Professor Pa Pelser, who spent long hours training the side. He was a traditionalist who ran us up and down hills, and believed that hamstrings were in the head. He also had a habit of ninety-minute team talks before games. We didn't mind him too much, but take it from me that the players ran things.

We had Jannie Breedt as skipper — laid back, fun, but what a player. He never went in for talks or motivational stuff at all. To him, when that whistle went you gave your all, no question. If you couldn't do that, then bye-bye, you didn't have what it takes. I was his vice-captain — and the comedian of the side, taking a delight in making the players laugh. It was necessary, as the South African way is far too serious off the field. I think that some of the Transvaal players learnt for the first time that the rugby atmosphere can be fun as well as intense.

Chris Rogers had a major say in the forwards (as a Bok hooker he had the respect of all), and Schalk Naude, with me as a sort of check and balance, ran the backs. That was the unofficial way the Transvaal team had evolved, and what a side it became. (Peter Winterbottom, the England and Lions flanker, couldn't make the team at a time when he was playing superbly.) We had a love of the jersey, a pride in our team and a mutual respect — even love — for one another that was above anything else I've encountered. Okay, perhaps the casual approach we had off the field, and our habit of treating officials as never more than equals, were annoying to some — but what the hell? We were heroes in the clubs and in the province; we were invited to functions, a few of us had horse races named after us and we gave a bit of pride back to the union. How we misread things in 1988, though.

There is a brand of official, in all countries, who believes that the game is for him and not the players. In the bad old days in the Transvaal these types held sway; then, if you looked sideways at an official you were liable to be dropped. But now it seemed to be different — at least for a while.

The 1988 season started badly. Carel du Plessis and Michael, his brother, went back to Cape Town. I suppose they had made the most of their season in Jo'burg, and then — of course for business reasons — went home. They are both great players and were popular, even though some players felt that they received special treatment from the coach. If one of them had a twinge, it was rest and ice packs; other players, unless it was bad, were told to continue running. But this wasn't serious. Then Jannie Breedt got injured, and that was the real blow. I was made skipper for the first friendly of the season.

We lost to one of the B Section sides, Western Transvaal. Instead of kicking a last-minute penalty, from an easy position, Schalk Naude spotted that their backs were turned, and had a go at a tap and run. He didn't make it, we lost by two points and he was dropped. I was next.

We took a weak side to Port Elizabeth for the EP Centenary celebrations, and were walloped by a fired-up, full-strength Western Province. I decided that if we were going to go down fighting then I was going to be in front. I tackled my guts out, and after the game was actually thanked by my pack — that was a real compliment, as any scrum-half in the world will tell you. At one stage in the game one of our flanks, new cap Cheese van Tonder, kicked one of their men. It was not in keeping with our way, and the ref saw it. I was worried Cheese might be sent off, so in full view of the crowd I took him aside and wagged the finger at him while holding the scruff of his neck. The ref then came and said thanks, and the game proceeded. What I actually said to Cheese was: 'Listen, the ref has seen you, I am doing this to try and keep you on the field, sorry about it, but do me a favour and cut out the kicking.'

That night I was in trouble. Firstly, because of that incident my captaincy was in question; secondly — and this really pissed me off — my play was being questioned. On the Monday I was dropped. I was furious, but what can you say? I remembered the gracious way that Johnny Moloney reacted when I took his place on the Irish side all those years before. At the time I had thought little of it; after all, he was 'old'. But he was only twenty-six, and it must have hurt like hell, just as it did with me. But I congratulated the new scrum-half, Pieter du Randt, and sat on the bench.

The Transvaal side lost, I think, about eight of the next ten games. I was then recalled for the very tough game in Windhoek against the surprise side of the season, newly promoted South West Africa. This was a real crunch game, and of course after our bruising win in the semifinal the previous year there was a lot of talk of revenge. I was touched when Jannie Breedt, back as captain, said publicly that the spirit of the side was restored after my return, and that he was confident of a win. Well, we had a hard and close game, but we won: no doubt that we were back in business.

Then came one of the most ridiculous incidents of my rugby career. On the Monday morning at work, I was called by coach Pa Pelser. He was very worried. He said that at the selection meeting it had been stated that I was never again to be picked for the Transvaal side. What on earth could he mean? Everything was back on course, we'd had a great win and a happy visit to Windhoek, and were now looking forward to the rest of the season with confidence.

The story was that I had told the president of the union, Louis Luyt, to 'f--k off' after the match. And it was true — in a sense.

You'll remember that Luyt angered us the previous year by telling us in the Windhoek dressing-room that we were pathetic, and I had stormed out. Now, a year later, we were in Windhoek again, with the experiments regarding younger players having failed and John Robbie and Schalk Naude back in the side. As a result, it was to be a watershed game.

The night before the match, Schalk and I were walking down to the team meeting when we met Louis Luyt. He was in good form, but a bit the worse for wear after a function. No problem, as he wasn't involved in the team meeting and had been at a dinner with the South West officials. We joked about the incident the year before; he promised that even if we won by a point he would be more than happy, and that we wouldn't be 'pathetic'. He went on to tell Schalk and me how important we were and so on — all good fun.

Anyway, the team won, Schalk and I played well and we were in the dressing-room waiting for the officials to come in before saying our prayers and singing — South African rugby traditions. For some reason the officials were late, and this was a nuisance. The team was in high spirits and we wanted to celebrate without delay. As we waited and waited, I couldn't resist the chance to act the fool. I started to go into my impersonation of our president. 'Pateties,' I said, and all those who had played the year before knew exactly what I was on about. Just as the laughter reached a crescendo, in walked the officials. So everyone laughed even more — how would Robbie get away with this? Well, I naturally kept up the act. To Louis Luyt I said, in broken pidgin-Afrikaans, that he had asked for a one-point win and we'd gave him three (our winning margin) — it was therefore not 'pateties'. And I confess I finished off with a 'f--k you!' in Afrikaans for good measure.

Everyone laughed, and the requisite prayers and songs were done. We had a hell of a night and trip back the next day, and the general mood was excellent. And then came the call on Monday with the news.

Now I was confused. My initial reaction was to say nothing and let them ban me — it would backfire on the union for breaking up the winning team. I believed I had done nothing wrong — on the contrary, I had contributed to an important win and a huge improvement in morale. But still, I had always enjoyed a good relationship with the president, and if there was a problem — and obviously there was — then maybe I should see him. Pa Pelser said the president wouldn't see me, but I suspect Luyt had set all this up, knowing full well that I would go and see him to sort it out, and I did.

He told me that my swearing at him had upset him. Now, without going into all the details, and after talking everything through with Jannie Breedt and my team-mates, I have a fair idea of what happened. You see, Jannie told me that Luyt laughed as much as anyone at the time. However, there were a number of other officials present, including the South West African rugby president; but it seemed that the Transvaal officials were the ones who had made the fuss.

One thing about Dr Luyt is that he has always enjoyed good relations with the players. He has always had an open-door policy and on a number of occasions has helped people who were having career problems, or given advice in businesses. The night before each home Currie Cup game, he and his gracious wife always lay on a meal for the players and their wives at his magnificent home — for South African rugby, this is very progressive.

But I believe that certain officials complained to Luyt about my remarks; he then formed the opinion that, far from acting the fool, as he himself had originally thought, I was actually taking a cheap shot at him and was using the win to drag up the previous year's incident. He must have thought that I had never accepted his apology, and that even our friendly chat the night before was only an act. I can see that, after the complaints from certain officials (possibly people who harboured a grudge against senior players in the side), Luyt had put two and two together, got five, and felt hurt and angry.

I assured him this was not the case. I assured him, just as I had always done, that if there was a problem I would speak to him first — a trait he said he had always admired in me. I said that even if he did ban me for life, I was more concerned with him knowing that I was simply acting the fool in the general euphoria of the winning dressing room.

There was even an explanation to the Afrikaans 'f--k you' I had used. The reason I had said it in Afrikaans was because it had been a standard joke in the squad that the phrase represented my total vocabulary in the language. If I had really wanted to tell the good president where to go, I would have told him in English.

So Dr Luyt and I ended up having a good laugh, and I was selected again for the next week. However, I have no doubt that I was now beyond the pale as far as certain officials were concerned. At the first opportunity there were a number of them — and I now know who they are — who would put in the knife. But I was blissfully unaware of it then, and as we won well the next week and then beat Free State by thirty points at Ellis Park, it was almost like old times. We had turned the corner.

Then Garth Wright, the Springbok scrum-half, arrived from Eastern Province. It was a blow, I'll admit, as Garth is a super player and had taken his chance against the Cavaliers in 1986 with both hands. But he had a poor 1987 season, by his standards, and in the yearbook (a sort of South African rugby Wisden) I was one of the five Players of the Year, chosen by all the rugby writers in the country — a very high honour indeed.

But Garth was a young player to be respected, and I knew I had a hell of a fight on my hands. Garth and I had always got on exceptionally well, and when he arrived we had a good chat and agreed that whatever happened in terms of selection we would remain friends. I also knew, of course, that after a disastrous spell Transvaal had now won three games on the trot and that I was playing well, and more important was getting a lot of publicity for it. He would have to fight for my place.

We had to play Natal next in Durban, and as he would not even have the chance to play a club game before that one, I was safe. On the Monday there was a trial, the usual hard Monday practice, and I was especially keyed up. I did well, too, but at half-time Garth was switched into the A team. Once again, though, I did well on the B side and was soon switched back: I had comprehensively outplayed him. After the trial all the players came and said well done, and so did a number of officials and journalists. As chance would have it, I had to speak at a dinner that night. The MC in his welcome asked me how I had done at the trial, and with total confidence I assured the gathering that I had seen off the challenge, at least for the moment.

The next morning I heard on Radio 702 at 6 am that Garth had been named at scrum-half for Transvaal. Never before had I felt so angry. I was stunned speechless, and for me that is quite something. Then the phone started to ring: it was like my selection for Ireland, but in reverse. Eleven of the selected Transvaal side phoned to say the decision stank. It didn't help: I was well and truly dropped. My initial reaction was to tell the Transvaal selectors to get knotted, blow my stack in the newspaper, and then call it a day. However, I decided that this was the reaction certain officials would have enjoyed, and — once again keeping Johnnie Moloney's example in my head — I played it cool. Named as replacement, I went to practice that night.

There was an atmosphere you could cut with a knife: hardly any talk, and players gathered round in little groups. Normally there would be lots of fun and leg-pulling before practice started. Then Garth arrived. He came straight over. I congratulated him, and then he made an amazing offer. He said he totally disagreed with what had happened, that this was not the way he wanted to get his place. He offered, to Jannie and I, to stand down there and then. Of course I told him not to, it was nothing to do with him — but I will never forget his gesture. He had been placed in a very difficult position, and through it all he behaved impeccably and our friendship has endured.

165

My contempt and inner anger was directed at the selectors. Here was a group of rugby people, one former Bok and half a dozen ex-provincial players, who had broken one of the most sacrosanct rules of sport — a new player must prove himself and play his way in. Jannie Breedt was asked by Pa Pelser to welcome Garth in front of the team; Jannie refused. He welcomed Garth in private.

Pelser, the selectors and the officials said not one word to me at that practice. Pelser even had the audacity to gather the side and call for more team spirit. It was unreal. If it hadn't totally broken the spirit of a side — and we all felt it just drain away that night — then it would have been very strange. The side was beaten by Natal in Durban, and lost all but one of the remaining eight games. It was a sad end to an era, if you can call three great happy years an era — and it signalled the end of my career.

I had expected to be dropped. Garth was the incumbent Bok scrum-half and was in his mid-twenties. In my early thirties, I knew I would be replaced before long. But I had been determined to make Garth win his place — and then I would then have gone down with all the grace in the world (and the side, though they might have been sympathetic, would have accepted it).

Even as I write, I can feel the bitterness rise in my guts, and the sorrow that I felt for Transvaal rugby returns. Of course my incident wasn't an isolated one — it was only the most dramatic. The way they treated Charles Pieterse, Andre Skinner, Schalk Naude and Chris Rogers, and then at different times Hempas Rademeyer and Hugo van As, was disgusting. I don't know which individual was to blame; I have my suspicions, but I'll say nothing. All I know is that if I were on a selection committee that acted as that 1988 Transvaal committee did, I would resign on the spot. The fact that two rejects, Chris and Andre, declared for Northerns on being dropped and then fought their way into the strongest pack in the country, is evidence of Transvaal's foolishness.

There, the story is told. Many people have said that Afrikaner politics was the reason I was dropped, because I am English-speaking. But I don't believe there's any truth in that. After all, I had won almost ninety caps for Transvaal in seven years. By South African standards that's a huge total, and I must be one of the most capped — if not the most capped — Transvaal scrum-half. No, I believe what happened was a total misreading of a situation. A hugely successful season the year before was, because of our final defeat, considered a failure. I also believe that the fact that our side refused to bow down to certain officials and to a large degree acted as adults, doing our own thing off the field, contributed to our downfall.

In almost all the cases where there was an alternative player available to the senior men in the 1988 season, the senior player was dropped. In most cases it soon became clear that the moves were not successful and, as with me and Peter Durandt, the senior was recalled. All in all, the season was a total disaster. My only pleasure came from the reaction of my fellow players, the public and — in most cases — the media. One of the reasons why I tried at all times to avoid undignified rantings was that others were fighting my case for me.

I am still a big Transvaal fan. I still go to the games, and I'm still very friendly with the union. They now have a fine young side and, although I don't believe they compare with our great side, they will do well. Garth will do a good job: he is still as quick and skilful as ever, and would be on my short list as one of the best scrum-halves I have played against.

My great hope is that the lessons of 1988 are learned. No officials have the right to mess around with time-honoured principles. There's another lesson of team sports: that the sum of the parts does not equal the strength of the team. Something else — spirit — binds a side together; keeping that is the way to success, and you mess with it at your peril.

I also learnt that to maintain a sense of proportion and values is important. During this very traumatic time, friends and family stuck with me. I look back with many regrets at the season, but now have put it down to experience. I had been lucky to get many great highs in the game, and I suppose I needed to sink to the depths to round things off. I was also able to play for Wanderers for a spell at the end of the season, surprising many who thought I would jack it in early. I know I was respected for that.

In the last game of the season we were beaten at the strong Alberton club in the south of Johannesburg. I got a bad gash behind my ear, and had a hell of a night in the Alberton bar. At some point I noticed that their splendid jersey and blazer collection was one short, and I offered to donate my Lions blazer to the club. I think that was symbolic — and at that moment I knew that I had played my last game of rugby.

12

Right at the beginning I mentioned that I have read just about all the rugby books. I loved them, even the ones that were too full of statistics to allow the reader to get into the subject's head. However, in all of them I particularly liked the compulsory chapter on the player's favourite players, or his best team. I always spent ages reading those. Of course, being a great fan, I knew the decisions that had to be made. Was Peter Wheeler better than Bobby Windsor at hooker? Should Mike Gibson be at fly-half or in the centre? And how the hell could you choose between Barry John and Phil Bennett, let alone between Ray McLaughlin and Ian McLachlan? Somehow they did, and I always imagined picking my best-ever side.

Now it's my turn, and I'm going to have fun. This is where I enjoy myself, picking the players whom the stupid selectors never seemed to put together. This is going to be easy....

And now it's days later and I still haven't started. What's the problem? It's that, having played for so long at different levels and in so many places, the exercise is proving harder than I imagined. The chapter needs a structure, and that's how I'm going to get through it.

I've always fancied myself as a selector. Years ago I was named to lead the Irish Universities against the Irish Wolfhounds. It was in 1977, a month or so before the game against France in which I broke my leg. Ireland had been having a poor season, and so the universities game took on a new importance — it became a trial for the French game.

I was at a club game at Lansdowne Road a few days before the fixture. The Wolfhound side was named, and it was a strong one on paper. But I knew that we were a much better unit, and would win easily. At this club game, though, one of the Irish selectors, Ray Carroll, came up and commiserated with me. Why, I asked. It became clear that he thought we were to be murdered. I was a little rude, and asked him if he knew anything about the players in Ireland — I told him we would

win easily. And we did, about 15-0, and had we not got a bit complacent at the end it could have been a lot more. His face was a picture afterwards, but I said nothing.

The point is that I have always reckoned that the mix of players — how they get on as a bunch — is just as important as the individual strengths and weaknesses. Often selectors don't take this into account when doing their job.

I am going to pick a number of sides as well, ending with my all-time best team. This will be the side that I select to play against Mars, and available for selection will be all those I've ever played with or against. They will be judged on how their play was at the time I encountered them. For example, although I sat on the bench when he played, I never encountered Gareth Edwards and so he is not eligible. I played against Willie John McBride, but right at the end of his career, and so it's on that form that I have to judge him for this exercise. That's a pity, as he was always one of my biggest heroes, but 'rules is rules'.

I love lists, and first I want to pick an Irish side. The same rules apply, and I am not allowed to play. But I am the coach and sole selector, which means I can select players to fit into my pattern. Hell, the power is frightening.

FULL-BACK

The candidates are Tony Ensor, Hugo Macneil, Johnny Murphy and Kevin O'Brien. Tony was a very elegant player and a good attacker. He was very fast as well, and suffered in playing at the same time as JPR Williams and Andy Irvine. Tony would have been outstanding on a Lions tour.

Johnny Murphy is one of those guys with talent to burn. He went with Liam Brady, David O'Leary and Frank Stapleton to Arsenal and would no doubt have made it. But he was homesick and returned to make it to international level in rugby. However, I don't believe Johnny was ever really fit enough to show his true potential.

Kevin O'Brien was a favourite of mine, and in the right side would have been dynamite. For Lancashire he was magnificent and was a little unlucky for Ireland. He scored a good try against South Africa in the second Test in 1981 and I was pleased for him. He'd had to live with a lot of criticism after his debut a year earlier.

Notice that all the players on offer are attackers. They would have to be in my side, and that's why Rodney O'Donnell didn't get a nod. He was one of the bravest and certainly he did well in a green jersey

169

— but full-back has become the key to all attacking play and so Rodney doesn't get my vote.

Hugo is a real mate. He is an intellectual, but has a great sense of fun as well. I loved playing on the same side as Hugo, and when he got picked he certainly made the most of it with tries in his first two internationals. He was also brave and resolute in defence. It's a toss-up between Hugo and Tony but, because of his last line of defence, Hugo gets the nod.

WINGS

In my side they have to be flyers. On occasion I've played in sides with guys who, if they get put away will score, whether they get the ball on our line or the opposition's. There are many footballing wings, but in the right side I go for speed every time — the playmakers will do the hard work for them. Tom Grace picks himself on the right — no real contenders with his size, speed and football, and he would also be my skipper. Left wing is harder to pick — Frank Quinn, Wallace McMaster, Terry Kennedy, Freddie McLennon and Vinny Becker spring to mind. There's also Keith Crossan, Moss Finn and Trevor Ringland.

Now Vinny was the quickest of the lot and would have got loads more caps but for a number of defensive shortcomings. I remember watching him playing in a cup match for Lansdowne. It was a blustery day and the opposition scrum-half put up a high Garryowen over a line-out. Vinny was there underneath the spiralling ball, running in ever-decreasing circles; the crowd held its breath. In the end the ball landed on top of his head and bounced high into the stand. A voice shouted: 'All the skills, Vinny, all the skills!' It was a moment of typical Irish club rugby humour.

Back to serious matters. Bearing in mind the style of play my side is going to adopt, I'll go for Vinny. Sure, he might give a try away, but look inside at the team-mates he'll have and ask just how many he'll score from anywhere on the field. We all laughed at the man, but when we played against Lansdowne he was the guy we were frightened of.

CENTRE

Centre is in my opinion the hardest position on the rugby field. To have to make decisions while watching the fly-half inside you giving the ball is tricky. However, when you know that there's some psychopath running at you from ten yards away with one aim in mind — to separate your torso from your legs — and then still be expected to make split-second decisions, is crazy. But good centres do it all the time and think nothing of it. My choice is between Mike Gibson, Paul McNaughton, Davie Irwin and Ray Finn.

Ray only got a single cap but he was one of Ollie Bourke's men and that's important. Mike Gibson is a must. His work-rate, speed and sharpness were amazing, even when I encountered him when he was supposedly over the hill. Last year, at that touch-rugby tournament at Sun City, he was still one of the stars — at about forty-five. Also, of course, Mike was sentenced to play most of his career in plodding defensive sides. Have a look at the films of the 1971 Lions, and his genius is apparent.

Alongside Gibbo I go for Paul McNaughton. Paul was a team player and with his timing, straightening and defensive play would have been a perfect foil. He also would be the team character, and nobody would be allowed to become big headed. As we say in Ireland, there would be great slagging — good-natured teasing — that to the outsider can look cruel. Paul was a master of this — but suffered one year after spilling a pass with the line at his mercy against Wales in Dublin. Quick as a flash, Paul was rechristened Paul McKnockon by the boys, and that can still be heard down Greystones way. It's hard to leave out Davie Irwin, but it's a Gibson/McNaughton midfield for me.

FLY-HALF

Now for the big one. Never before in Irish Rugby was there such a controversy as there was in 1979 when the selectors, on tour, picked Ollie Campbell ahead of the European Player of the Year, Tony Ward. On the billboards in Dublin they announced 'WARD DROPPED' in letters of a size last used when the dreadful news about the 'Irish' president, JF Kennedy, broke in 1963. It was unbelievable. The whole nation was split and today, with both players retired, the debate goes on. (Ollie wrote a lovely tribute to Tony on the latter's retirement, in which he says that he hopes Wardie meets as many Campbell fans as he has Wardie fans. Ollie also told a lovely story about giving an old lady a lift, way down in the country. The lady asked Ollie if he played sport. Ollie said he played a bit of rugby. The old lady told him that she knew nothing about the game but that the selectors were mad to have dropped Ward.)

171

Obviously both are in contention for place in my side. However, Ian Burns, Micky Quinn and a guy called Daragh Coakley must also be looked at. Ian probably had the most talent of the lot, but never quite fulfilled it. He is still an excellent player, but those of us who remember him at school expected more.

Micky Quinn is one of the best-loved rugby guys around. He was like a big brother to me when I hit the scene and through ups and downs has never changed. He was a hell of a player as well, but in some ways suffered because he played all his club rugby in a very strong side. Micky is Naas Botha's best friend, and it was a dream come true for them to play against each other in an international.

Daragh would have played international rugby but for his size. He had a heart as big as himself and a will to win that was total. He played in that Under-19 side that I loved so much, and was a Bourke disciple.

But it comes down to just two, and I go unashamedly for Ollie Campbell. He was one of the best players I have ever encountered; he also had a rugby brain second to none. Tony had bewildering skill, but to my mind could never read situations as Ollie could. One year, Hugo Macneill, as Oxford skipper, flew me back to captain the Stanley's side against the Varsity. Wardie was fly-half and late in the game we had a three-to-two situation near their line. It was a simple matter for Tony to straighten and pass on the overlap — instead Tony ran across and tried a scissors with the wing, and no try came of it. However, in a tight spot Tony could be magnificent. That day against Wales he created two tries out of nothing. Both were rare players, both have been good friends since we opposed each other at school.

SCRUM-HALF

No, I can't do it. I had intended to pick another scrum-half but I can't. This is my side and I want to play. Johnny Moloney, Donal Canniffe, Robbie McGrath and Colin Patterson, you are going to have to pick your own teams. But I'm not in on merit, I might add, I'm in because it's my book.

PROPS

Forwards are more difficult. Donkeys have a tradition and a value system all of their own. Perhaps it's presumptuous of me even to pick the forwards, but I'm going to try.

Phil Orr picks himself as loose-head — none better when he was in his prime. Imagine the selectors dropping him after forty-nine consecutive caps — mad as hatters. At tight-head I go for Mick Fitzpatrick: mobile and strong, sure, but also a big mate of Phillie's, and that's important in the front row. Phil O'Callaghan, Roger Clegg and Tom Feighery were all considered, but I'm happy.

Phil O'Callaghan is a real rugby legend. He was the player who, when told by the ref that he was boring, replied that the ref wasn't so flipping entertaining himself. The story has been credited to many, but Phil was the original. He also is reputed to have made the definitive *faux pas* at a rugby function. On a tour the Irish players were to meet some Governor-General who apparently suffered from Parkinson's Disease. The players were warned, and of course no one was to mention it or stare. Apparently Phil, on being introduced, said '…and it's nice to meet you, Mr Parkinson.'

HOOKER

Hookers are all mad. I've come to that conclusion and nothing will change my mind. It's bad enough to be in the forwards, but to go in with both arms pinned and to stand on one leg into the bargain — that's plain crazy. My criterion for hookers is simple: when I put the ball in, does it come out where and when I want it? I don't know and don't care about scrumming ability; it's the ball that counts for me. With that in mind I'm afraid that Pat Whelan, Ciaran Fitzgerald and all the others must take a back seat to Johnnie Cantrell, and Dessie O'Leary, my Greystones hooker. Both gave me 'channel one' ball off a conveyor belt, no matter what. For my team, Johnnie gets the nod.

LOCKS

Locks were always a problem in Ireland. We never quite seemed to have the big ones that other countries did. Moss Keane is an exception, and in he goes. He was to the late 1970s and early 1980s what Willie John and Bill Mulcahy were before. Moss was also a great wit, and after a few jars totally unintelligible. One day we were playing for the Wolfhounds, and in the side were Moss and Charlie Kent, the big blond English centre. Now Charlie is a diabetic, and at half-time this rather puffed ambulance man arrived in our huddle and tapped Moss on the shoulder. The man asked Moss if he was the man who wanted a sugar

173

lump; Moss said, 'ArraJaysus. Who do you think I am, Nijinsky?' (referring to the famous racehorse). I would say that of all the Irish players I played with, Moss was far and away the most popular. He was to Irish rugby what Vince van der Bijl was to South African cricket.

His partner is a problem. Donal Spring was a retreaded number eight, Emmet O'Rafferty, Brendan Foley and Mick Molloy were secondary jumpers; so I go for Donal Lenihan. When I left he was just starting to make the grade, and in those days was without peer.

LOOSE FORWARDS

The back row is crucial to any side, but for my running game it's even more important. I need ball players and I need tacklers; I also need speed to the breakdown. Fergus Slattery is a must, on his speed and also his performances in South Africa. Reluctantly, I therefore have to leave out Stewart McKinney, the late great Shay Deering — and Pierce Power, who was the most under-rated flank in the country for many years.

My blindside flanker is a former number eight, Harry Steele. He was the sort of player a scrum-half dreams about. I remember on that New Zealand tour, in the game against Canterbury, falling on a loose ball behind our scrum. I got rucked to bits, and Harry picked me up and told me that was his job. He suffered in the shadow of others, but for me he would be a great foil for Slats on the side of the scrum. Others were John O'Driscoll and Colm Tucker, both fine players and Lions Test caps to boot.

At number eight it's a choice between four: Willie Duggan, Mike Gibson, Donal Spring and Denis Hickie. Denis was a great favourite and I played my first big senior game with him. As a nineteen-year-old I played in the pouring rain for a Portlaoise selection against the Wolfhounds. In their side for this Mickey Mouse game (to them, but life's highlight for me) were Andy Ripley, Jean-Pierre Rives and Steve Smith. I didn't sleep for days and was scared stiff. But we had Denis Hickie and it was a pleasure. I got a couple of loose taps away early, and he said, Well done. He was great.

I actually played little with Donal at number eight, and so it's a choice between Willie Duggan and Mike Gibson. Willie was very hard and durable, and no doubt for the majority of Irish teams he would be in. But I remember the young Gibbo, he of the soaring leaps and the huge side-steps; I also know his effect on the side. So he's in.

174 That's my side, and I'd back it against all others.

Hugo Macneil
Tom Grace (c)
Mike Gibson
Paul McNaughton
Vinny Becker
Ollie Campbell
John Robbie
Phil Orr
Johnnie Cantrell
Mick Fitzpatrick
Moss Keane
Donal Lenihan
Fergus Slattery
Harry Steele
Mike Gibson

My coach would be Ollie Bourke, of course, with Roly Meates as an advisor. I notice that there are eleven Leinster players on the side. I suppose I'm biased, but also remember that I played in a dominant Leinster side. Anyway, that's it and I stick to it; I also imagine it would be a good side to tour with — plenty of laughs.

But now let's move on. Without as much discussion, it's time to pick my Lions side.This is going to be very difficult indeed. Again, it's a running side to play as a team, so the way characters mix is very important.

FULL-BACK

It has to be Andy Irvine. A question mark about hitting the line from set play, but remember my side will be running from everywhere. He edges out Hugo Macneil. Although I played against JPR Williams, it was near the end. In an all-time team, of course, he would get the nod over them all.

WINGS

Tom Grace again, and Gerald Davies. I played against him when he was near the end of his career and captaining Cardiff. I remember once I was covering and he got a ball near the touchline. I had him in my sights. This was to be savoured: JR crunching one of the world's greatest

wings. He leaned into me as if he was going to go on the outside —
then bang! — he sidestepped inside me and away.

(The only other time I had felt so stupid was on that Irish tour to New
Zealand. I came on as a reserve against North Auckland who had the
great Sid Going at scrum-half. They called a short line-out and threw
over the back to Sid. I read it and had those same fantasy headlines
— 'JR crunches Sid.' Next second his hips moved away and seemingly
without looking at me he hit me with a hand-off that left me on my backside. Such moments give you a better understanding of what rugby great-
ness is all about.)

CENTRES

Mike Gibson gets the centre berth again, along with Ray Gravell. Ray,
that lovable loony, was a fine player and would bring a physical presence
to the midfield. He would also bring a psychopathic presence to the
dressing room.

Jim Renwick, Clive Woodward, Dai Richards, Paul McNaughton (who
should have been a Lion) and Paul Dodge would be considered.

HALF-BACKS

Ollie Campbell again at fly-half, and even I cannot select myself for
this one. Terry Holmes would have to be scrum-half, with Colin Patterson as reserve. (It's funny but I don't mind not playing in this side
— yet I can't leave myself out of the Irish selection. Perhaps it would
be the only way for me to get that elusive first win in an Irish jersey.)

FORWARDS

Phil Orr would be loose-head, Peter Wheeler the hooker and Graeme
Price the tight-head. My other Pontypool colleagues, Bobby Windsor
and Charlie Faulkner, would go close, as would Clive Williams. Billy
Beaumont and Maurice Colclough would lock the scrum: nobody else
really comes close.

The back row: again it would be Slattery, with John O'Driscoll on
the other side with Jeff Squire at number eight. (Curious that I pick
John O'Driscoll for my Lions side but not for the Irish one — but I'm
not changing that. They look fine.) If I were playing for the Lions selection, I would have Eddie Butler at number eight. We had a good part-

176

nership and I enjoyed playing with him. He was very underrated — but not by his scrum-halves.

So there you are. My Lions selection would be:

Andy Irvine
Tom Grace
Mike Gibson
Ray Gravell
Gerald Davies
Ollie Campbell
Terry Holmes
Phil Orr
Peter Wheeler
Graeme Price
Billy Beaumont (c)
Maurice Colclough
Fergus Slattery
John O'Driscoll
Jeff Squire

Noel Murphy would coach with, of course, 'Mallet Head' (Syd Millar) as manager.

Next I'm going to pick my best Springbok side, based on my rules above and drawn from those I've played with and against. Then, bringing in anyone else I want, it's that World side to play against Mars.

FULL-BACK

Only two real contenders: Gysie Pienaar and Johan Heunis. Both brilliant in different ways — Gysie of the broken running, against Johan of the knife-like burst. It's difficult, but I go for Johan. His defence, kicking and just his presence in a side are inspirational.

WINGS

Well, despite Gerrie Germishuys's tries against the Lions, it's Ray Mordt and Carel du Plessis. What a pair, and what a prospect to try and mark them. I must have played against Ray a dozen times in provincial and club rugby, and despite many attempts I don't think I ever tackled him.

(Funnily enough, I recently was shown a tape of the 1980 fourth Test, and in it I managed to tackle him twice. Perhaps later on I knew him better and was beaten before I started.)

CENTRES

Who plays with Danie Gerber? It's actually a choice between Michael and Willie du Plessis. Michael gets the nod, and with his defensive organization that's the midfield sewn up. Nobody would get through, and what a pair in attack. Michael would be a perfect foil for the attacking genius of Gerber.

FLY-HALF

There's Naas Botha, Errol Tobias and Schalk Naude. I loved playing with Schalk; in the 1987 season someone worked out from the videos that only two passes went astray between us in twenty games. Like Ollie he was prepared to take on the back row as well. Errol was magnificent in 1984 against England, but I never really played with him. However, it has to be Naas at fly-half — but it is the Naas of later years, far more likely to run from his own twenty-two metre line than in days gone by. I've talked about him at length before, and I realize that as a person he is not everyone's cup of tea. I really like him, have glimpsed behind the facade; and I feel it's just a pity that he has never really had the chance to show the rugby world what he is capable of.

SCRUM-HALF

Between Divan Serfontein and Garth Wright. Divan gets the nod, on experience. But Garth is a fine player and, along with Ray Mordt, a guy who has a fitness level far above anything else I've ever seen in rugby. Others considered were Tommy du Plessis, Harry Viljoen and Gawie Visagie. Freddie Ferreira has been unlucky with injuries, and of the younger brigade Robert du Preez could turn out to be the best of the lot. But from my career it's Divan at number nine.

FORWARDS

The props would be Martiens le Roux and Jan Lock. I don't have any evidence other than the comments of props who have played against

178

them. Piet Kruger, Hempies du Toit, Ockie Oosthuizen and Frans Erasmus would also come up.

Hookers: only two for me, Chris Rogers and Uli Schmidt. Uli gets the nod based on his terrific work-rate in the loose. He has no weakness except, perhaps, a tendency to overstep the mark in the aggression stakes. I had one run-in with him in a Transvaal/Northerns game. He late-tackled me and I had a bit of a swipe at him; he waited his turn, and from a bad line-out tap he managed to get me and the ball at the same time. I was hit by a hell of a shoulder charge, but tried not to show it. A year later in the Superstars, where we were first and second, I told him how much it had hurt. He just laughed and I think I hadn't fooled him at all. In the scrums Chris was supreme, though, and the respect he enjoyed from all players is a tribute to him. He has also done very well in business. It just proves that donkeys are born with brains as well.

Louis Moolman is one lock in my team, and what a pleasure it would be to see his battles with Maurice Colclough again. Kevin de Klerk and Moaner van Heerden would be there, but remember I saw them near the ends of their careers. Until he had the car crash Andre Skinner would be considered — but I have to look at the balance of the side, and I go for the living beanpole Adolf Malan. Nobody will get a ball off him, and although in the loose he'd battle he also scrums well. In modern rugby, to have a guy like Adolf who will win all of his own ball is a gift from heaven. In that Springbok trial in Pretoria I had both of them as locks, and in the line-outs they destroyed Schalk Burger and Vleis Visagie. They were that good.

Rob Louw owns the open side — no contenders there. At number eight I go for Jannie Breedt — yes, even above Morne du Plessis. To play with Jannie is an experience for a scrum-half, and with his line-outs and open-play running, it's no contest. Although Naas is in the side, Jannie would be captain.

The other back row spot is also not easy. Wahl Bartmann, Burger Geldenhuys and Theuns Stoffberg are my contenders — Wahl gets in, because if he wasn't picked then the side might have to play against him, and that's too terrible to contemplate. Charles Pieterse would also come into contention — he's another player who never got the credit he deserved...

Burger Geldenhuys is an unusual bloke. He's been called the rudest man in the world, but I think it's all for effect. When a point of principle is involved he's never been afraid to nail his colours to the mast.

Also, in my experience, he has always got the facts before making a decision. After the pay-for-play row following my speech at the SAB Sportswriters Awards dinner, Burger felt I had deliberately tried to stir up a controversy. This wasn't true, and I respect him for coming to me for the facts before deciding on the issue. One of my happiest moments was on the golf course the day before the South Sea Barbarian 'Test' in Durban. Jannie Breedt (off an eight handicap), Schalk Naude (scratch), Burger (five) and myself (twelve) had a game for money. For some reason God was smiling, and I managed to shoot a two over for the nine we played and I won the bucks. That really annoyed Burger, but for the rest of us it was hugely amusing — he hates to lose. However, Wahl just shades him in my side.

So there you are, my Springbok side. Interesting, but not really surprising, that it's made up of more contemporary players than the Boks I encountered in 1980.

Johan Heunis
Ray Mordt
Michael du Plessis
Danie Gerber
Carel du Plessis
Naas Botha
Divan Serfontein
Jan Lock
Uli Schmidt
Martiens le Roux
Rob Louw
Louis Moolman
Adolf Malan
Wahl Bartmann
Jannie Breedt (c)

Before I even consider the World team, I see dilemmas all over the place. How the hell do you pick between Murray Mexted and Jannie Breedt, Andy Irvine and Johan Heunis, or Rob Louw and Slats? That's before you even consider Ollie, Naas and Hugo Porta. I suppose in the end we have to rely on gut feelings.

At full-back it's Johan Heunis. His defence gets him the nod but I know inside he's an HO de Villiers who just needs a side like mine to break out. (Serge Blanco pulled out of the French side with flu in 1981, and so I never played against him.)

What a choice of wings. Gerald Davies, Tom Grace, Carel, Ray and John Kirwan. I go for Carel and Ray. (I can't pick Kirwan anyway, I've just remembered, because I never played against him — thank God.) Even with his brilliance, I must decide on Gerald Davies when he was at the end of his career; Tom Grace was a favourite — but my guts tell me Carel and Ray.

At centre it's really a choice between Danie and the two Michaels. It's close but I go for Danie Gerber and Mike Gibson — what a combination!

Ollie Campbell is fly-half. His defence and running are better than Naas's, and even though Naas is the greatest tactical kicker I've ever encountered, that's not quite as important in my side. Hugo Porta would be close. I played against him when he guested for the South African Barbarians against the Lions in 1980. He was outstanding but I only played against him once.

Scrum-half goes to super Sid Going. Even the odd wayward pass wouldn't go against him, either. Pierre Berbizier, Divan and Garth Wright were considered.

Phil Orr gets in again at prop: remember I played with him when he ran in the loose like a rampaging bull. Uli Schmidt hooks between him and Graeme Price. At lock it's Billy Beaumont, skipper as usual, and I put him with Andy Haden. That's not the older version, but the Haden I encountered in 1976.

Possibly a slight weakness in the line-outs: against an Adolf Malan or a Moolman we might battle; but I stick to my guns. (I have a soft spot for Jean-Francois Imbernon, though. He played against me for France and also for Perpignan. I remember as a youngster being very impressed when, after a Perpignan/Leinster game, I saw him drinking fruit juice all evening. It was only when he fell over that I realized he had been skulling Pernod — pints of it — all night. A good guy and a good lock.)

Number eight is the hardest choice of the lot. I played many games with both Murray Mexted and Jannie Breedt. The easy way out would be to stick one on the flank, and I'm very tempted — as I did with Harry Steele in the Irish side. But that would be ducking and diving and I'm not like that — well, not too often. I go for Jannie at number eight. Possibly he's a bit looser, but he makes up in the line-outs and in this side that gets him the vote.

Jean-Claude Skrela gets the blindside flank job — even if he did break my leg all those years ago; Wahl and Burger came into contention. On the open side, it's Graeme Mourie, Slats and Rob Louw. Again, many reasons for all of them, but in the end it's Slats again. He did outplay Rob on the Irish tour. Also, he has Jannie and Wahl inside him, so the odd missed tackle would not be so crucial. I only played against Mourie once, and remember Billy is skipper, so leadership is not really a factor.

So there you are. That's John Robbie's team to play Mars. I have no doubt it's not the best available. But they're the men, based on my career experiences, that I would select. Self-indulgent, but fun.

Johan Heunis
Ray Mordt
Mike Gibson
Danie Gerber
Carel du Plessis
Ollie Campbell
Sid Going
Phil Orr
Uli Schmidt
Graeme Price
Bill Beaumont(c)
Andy Haden
Fergus Slattery
Jean-Claude Skrela
Jannie Breedt

The coach would be me, and what an easy job.

13

A while ago Jennie and I were invited to a wedding in Johannesburg. The well-known TV presenter and renowned bachelor Derek Watts was finally taking the plunge. After the formalities were over, the accent was on enjoyment.

Derek had for a number of years worked for the SABC, before his move over to M-Net, the independent subscription channel. As a result there were many TV and radio people present. Often showbiz functions are a bit of a pain, with people trying to act the part and usually not quite making it. This was different, with everyone relaxed and posing kept to a minimum.

We grabbed a table with Chris Gibbons and his wife (Chris is my boss at Radio 702). We were joined by Gary Bailey and his wife Kate. Gary, of course, kept goal for Manchester United before an injury finished his English career; he returned to South Africa, and after a successful operation he's been captaining Kaiser Chiefs — the Liverpool of South African soccer. He also is a successful businessman, and a nice guy.

The wine was flowing freely. We had a great chat that went from sport to business, and ended up solving the problems of the world — normal Saturday night stuff. (I might add that the next day I had a normal Sunday morning head, but it was worth it.)

Later Chris spoke to me. He said it was amazing watching Gary and I talking to each other. He was at the other end of the table, and so wasn't really part of our conversation. But he had picked up something that I had never really considered. He was watching two guys who had met each other a few times before but couldn't really be called close friends, who were chatting like long-lost brothers. It must have been obvious that the conversation was totally open and uninhibited, and devoid of small talk. It hit subjects and factors in sport and life that would normally be offsides between anyone but close friends. Someone, I suppose a bit dramatically, once talked about the brotherhood that exists between top sports people — and I think this was what Chris had perceived.

You look at the life of a top sportsman — someone who has played in an environment where his sport is followed by lots of people. Look at the way he behaves in public: most of the time, unless he's with friends, he operates behind a mask — usually a facade of polite quietness, almost always pretty neutral. It's often seen on the television: a man is interviewed and you form an impression of him. But if ever you meet him, you find that the real person is totally different. I know that I slip into that persona myself with strangers. It's not deliberate, I think it's an unconscious defence mechanism. In the same way as show business people play a role, so do sportsmen.

Naas Botha is the classic example. If I had a rand for every time someone has said to me that they respect Naas as a player but hate him as a person, I'd be rich. To most South Africans, Naas is an enigma. He's a great player, possibly the greatest match-winner that rugby has seen — although because of isolation, the Brits and the New Zealanders have never seen him dominate matches and whole seasons the way he does in perhaps the toughest league of all.

As a result, Naas has a life I would hate. He cannot go for a bag of chips in Pretoria without being mobbed. Once I went by car with him to a physio in Pretoria, before a North vs South game. When his car stopped at traffic lights, the windows of the car alongside were rolled down and out would come the bit of paper and a pen. As a result of all this adulation — in other places, open hostility — Naas has developed a public face that is unfortunate. Also, he is such a competitor on the field that when things don't go well he often gets petulant, and this doesn't help his image.

In fact, Naas is an OK guy. I like him a lot. He can also be very funny indeed. His cousin, Hendrik Kruger, was married in Ireland a few years ago and as I was in the country on a flying visit I was invited. Hendrik married a lovely Irish girl from a well-known Dundalk family, and so it was a very big, posh wedding. Now can you imagine the job Naas had as best man: I must say that I wouldn't have fancied it in my first language, let alone my second, which is what English is for him. I needn't have worried. Naas carried it off beautifully, and had the audience in stitches.

The point is that Naas rarely gives that sort of glimpse to outsiders, and so is misunderstood. However, to another sportsman he's different, and this is what I'm getting at. When I was talking to Gary Bailey the barriers were down. We were talking as men who had this common bond, based on a common understanding of the hard work, passion and fears involved in sport at top level. I suspect, too, that there's also a silent agreement on the cruel side of sport — the hardness that comes from realizing that the schoolboy perception of sport is at times very different from the reality. It's an unspoken password that says, look, we both know that the image we sportsmen have of life is totally different, so let's cut the bullshit. We, at least, can talk to each other as we want to talk. It's difficult to explain more fully, as that is really just a feeling, a recognition or a respect that somehow comes through.

A few days after that wedding, I was asked to play in a pro-am golf day with visiting lady professional golfers here to play the South African LPGA circuit. I played with an English girl, Claire Waite, who had competed at the highest level. There was no talk of rugby or my career, as it was very much a golf day; our four-ball was very chatty, though, and the golf was good. After a few holes she turned to me and asked me what sport I had played, and at what level. One of the businessmen answered for me (and exaggerated a bit in my favour, but that's beside the point). She told me that she knew that I was a sportsman.

Something had told her in the way I spoke about ladies' golf. All I had done was ask a few questions about how she had got started, and how she had made the decision to turn pro. There had been no mention of my sport — but she had known, and I think it was that sort of Masonic bond coming through again.

It's interesting, and now I'm keen to see if this understanding continues after retirement. I rather think it does with one's contemporaries, but I wonder how it will be as the generation gap widens.

Getting back to that chat with Gary Bailey. I have been a Manchester United supporter for many years, and like so many people in Ireland tend to regard the top professional players as heroes. Talking to Gary, it became obvious that the life of a top soccer pro is very different in reality. I was horrified to learn of the problems that many of the household names of British soccer had encountered after retirement. Stories of bankruptcy, divorce and criminal activity were not uncommon. Also, with so much money involved in the game, it is clear that the camaraderie that exists in most rugby set-ups is rare. Gary had received a number of lucrative offers to play top soccer in Europe after his successful operation, but he wasn't tempted. He now has a career outside football, and to him that's precious. I doubt if anyone but another sportsman would have got so many insights from Gary.

185

Talking of all-round sports interest, one of my happiest memories is the Superstars. I was lucky enough to win the South African event in 1988, after finishing second the previous two years. It was great fun, very lucrative and the spirit of the South African event — serious but not win at all costs — is just about right. Once again, the event enabled me to meet a wide number of top sportsmen from all over South Africa over the two days.

I met the athletes and learned about real fitness. Johan Fourie, a man who with international competition would have been right up there with the Coes and Ovetts, was typical. I beat him quite easily in the 150 metre sprint, and expressed surprise: he told me that he didn't have great speed, but his endurance was his strength. He had run a 400 metres flat out in forty-nine seconds, after warming up and stretching; he had also been timed at fifty-two seconds on the last lap of a 5 000 metre race. Now to anyone who had played any sort of sport where fitness is a factor, that is staggering. Year in, year out, athletes build up endurance that a rugby player could only guess at.

The boxers were an amazing bunch. Without exception they were the gentlest of all the competitors. Every time I watch heavyweight Pierre Coetzee pounding some unfortunate into pulp, I remember him chatting to my young son and entertaining us all on the springboard. It was also noticeable that none of the boxers ever gave up in an event. Welterweight Harold Volbrecht and Pierre ran and cycled themselves into the ground; other big names certainly didn't.

Jimmy Cook, the tall Transvaal and Springbok cricketer, took part one year, along with Baby Jake Matlala, the tiny boxer. One of the last events each year is the obstacle course. This changes each time, but it always involves a two metre wall which has to be negotiated. Now Baby Jake is about half that size, and all of us were a bit scared that he would be unable to get over this wall at all and it would look very unfair. He was drawn to run against Jimmy in his heat. Jimmy got to the wall first, bent down, Jake got on his shoulders, and up and over he went. It was a priceless, spontaneous moment, and it made the event.

Clive Rice also took part one year. He had just returned from holiday in Spain, but true to form spent every available moment of the preceding week in practice. He didn't get among the top three, but he came close. He brought the house down in the basketball event by netting from a full ten metres, when there was no time left to reach the basket for a last score.

I have also met a number of the real sports heroes in South Africa.

I had always thought that rugby is the national game of the country, and I had experienced the limelight that is given to top provincial players. But I had no idea, until Superstars, just how minor all this is in comparison to the worship that is reserved for the black soccer stars. They are treated as gods.

One year the Superstars competitors were invited to the TV studios to do a preview for the event. I arrived at the same time as Carel du Plessis. I must admit that I was a bit flattered when a number of people came up to us in the lobby of the SABC to chat and ask for autographs. I suppose it was nice to appear modestly embarrassed in front of the athletes, boxers and other sportsmen who were present. Then Marks Maponyane arrived, and the whole place went mad. Marks is the biggest star in the Kaiser Chiefs team, and every technician, secretary or whatever was suddenly there clamouring for an autograph, a conversation or even just a touch. Our little bit of glamour paled in comparison.

The soccer scene in South Africa is incredible. I went to a Chiefs vs Orlando Pirates final last year at Ellis Park (which is also used for big soccer): there were 92 000 people inside the stadium and another 30 000 locked outside. Every weekend the lives of a huge percentage of the population are governed by how their team has performed. I had no idea just how popular the game is until I organized twenty-five tickets for a soccer final for a number of friends in National Trading Company; I asked them to distribute the remainder as they saw fit. Well, there was nearly a riot, the trade union ended up getting involved and there was actually a punch-up. I was told politely not to try to organize any more tickets.

Many of these top South African sports stars are now my friends. The bond that exists allows me to talk to them as few other journalists can. This is a hell of an advantage in my new career.

How did I get into journalism? Well, as usual the whole thing just seemed to fall into place. I was working as a sales manager with NTC, and very happy there as well. I was involved with many large companies, and certainly my rugby helped and I used it. The American company we represented had an incentive scheme, and three times in four years I qualified. Jennie and I went all expenses paid to Tahiti and Rome, and we even had the luxury of turning down a trip to Hawaii.

One day I got a call from Radio 702 news and sports editor Chris Gibbons. He's one of the most respected newsmen in the country and I was honoured to meet him. Over lunch and a few beers he asked if I would be interested in joining the morning team as a freelance sports reporter. It would be two mornings a week, would involve an early start, and at first would be for very little pay. Typical Irishman, I accepted.

The first morning I arrived at the studio, I expected to be handed a neatly written report to read. I got a hell of a shock when I was confronted by a huge pile of telex paper hot off the wires. From this I had to sort and compile the reports — and I was also expected to type it all out. I can't type, I said. Learn, they said, and that was it. So for two-and-a-half years, on two and then three mornings a week, I got up at 4.30 am and started work at about 5.20, going on air at six and finishing at eight. Then it was off to NTC; after work, in the winter, it was rugby training. On Mondays, Wednesdays and Fridays I only saw my kids when they were asleep in bed; often we were playing away from home, and so I only saw them on Tuesday and Thursday mornings and — with a battered body and a hangover — on Sunday afternoons. It was a crazy schedule and at first the money was minimal.

Why did I do it? I loved it, I really did. To get on the air talking about sport was a dream. Also it opened all sorts of other avenues. I was amazed to learn that, for all the profile rugby had given me, just having my voice on the radio gave me more. One day I was at the Hyperama, a huge shopping complex, to buy a video machine. The manager of the department was Chinese. As I started to talk, he asked me if I was John Robbie. He said that he'd never seen a rugby game in his life — but he listened to Radio 702. He even gave me a whack off the machine.

A year and a half later, I was nominated for a broadcasting award and won, to my amazement. It was a great honour, and coming just after I had been booted out of the Transvaal team, a boost when I badly needed it. Radio wasn't work, either; it was a chance to report, comment and joke about sport in the way that most people do on a Saturday night over a drink. But I was getting paid and adding to a profile which gave me a lot of benefits. NTC were happy, and the rugby people had no problems.

Incidentally, a year later the SAB awards landed me in a big row. It was one of those things where a minor situation was blown out of all proportion — with upsetting results. It got a lot of publicity in South Africa and, believe it or not, I also got TV and press enquiries from as far away as Australia. Here's what happened.

The centenary of both the South African Cricket and Rugby administrations falls in 1989. The organizer of the SAB awards dinner, Gary May, invited myself and Eddie Barlow, the famous cricketer, to be the

188

guest speakers. He particularly asked that our addresses should be a bit meatier than the normal superficial talks on these occasions. I set out to speak humorously on the origins of rugby, but then got more serious when casting forward to the future.

The main point I had to make was that both the die-hard amateurs and the top players in the world have a common belief that the game has qualities that are unique in modern sport. In addition to the physical game there is a tradition of fun, high spirits and camaraderie; and in the future this should be safeguarded. However, the official belief that this can only be achieved within a totally amateur game is resulting in a lot of dishonesty and militance.

Now the week before I had been doing a TV commentary for M-Net at a game in Cape Town between Western Province and Northern Transvaal. Before the game a former Western Province player and a man very much involved in the game in the Cape, warned me that the Western Province side were involved in a row about expenses and had threatened not to take the field. He was warning me to save me getting unnecessarily worked up for the game, as I was wont to do at the time in my TV broadcasts. I have since heard that the dispute occurred at an earlier date. Anyway, nothing happened and the game and my commentary went on as planned.

During my speech, when I was alluding to the militance within the game, off the top of my head, I mentioned (as but one of many examples) that at a major game in South Africa the previous week one of the sides had threatened not to take the field unless demands were met. That was all I said, mentioning no names or provinces. I tied up my speech calling for more honesty in facing this big-money question, so that at least the inevitable change to semi-professionalism would be achieved with the minimum of antagonism. That was all, and the night proceeded well.

The next day the storm broke. A journalist wrote a story under a heading that said I had blown the lid off Western Province and their professional rugby players. It was all cheap and sensational and taken out of context. In fact, I had been referring to Western Province, but at no time in the speech had I mentioned them.

That night I received calls from Carel du Plessis, the WP skipper, and Doc Moss, their convenor of selectors. Dawie Snyman, their coach, called next morning. All claimed that nothing had happened and wanted to know what I was doing. I explained how the whole thing had come about, and said that if it wasn't true they should deny it and let the press come back to me. I explained how the reference had been arrived at, and stressed that it had been made only as a tiny part of what was, for me, a major speech. I had not mentioned Western Province at all. I assured them that I regretted that it had all become nasty down in the Cape and they were obviously worried at the developments there. I was worried as well, as I liked all three men very much and would certainly not have risked friendships that I valued. In particular, Doc Moss is a man for whom I have the greatest respect and affection.

Both Carel and Dawie were particularly keen that I tell them who my source was. I refused to reveal that, but stressed that the allegation against Province had only been made to me to save me sweat in preparing for my commentary. I am convinced the guy wasn't trying to cause any trouble. However, there was obviously going to be a witch-hunt and I didn't want the guy who had told me of the unrest to suffer. (In fact, I later learnt that a Cape journalist had written an article on the same lines as what I had been told, about a week before I got the story.)

Anyway, the whole thing would surely die a natural death. Province claimed there was no truth in it. I was glad that they accepted that no mischief-making had been intended on my part, and I even offered to phone Jan Pickard, the WP president, to explain things in detail. Doc Moss said that he didn't think this was necessary, but that if it subsequently proved so, he would let me know.

However the issue wouldn't die. It looked like a lot of smoke with perhaps some fire, the way the Western Province guys were acting.

Then in one of the papers I read that Pickard was demanding an apology from me. Demanding, mind you. I tried to phone Doc Moss that night to find out what was going on, but I couldn't get hold of him. The next day I saw in the papers that Pickard was claiming that he had in fact received an apology from me.

Now I started to get a bit fed up with the whole incident. I made a press statement in which I denied that I had spoken to Pickard. It followed that I had not apologized and that, furthermore, I had no intention of doing so. I again laid out what had happened, and added that as far as I was concerned the matter was now closed. There were more headlines and Pickard denied that he had claimed that I had apologized. It was all a bit silly, and I admit that what I should have done — although perhaps he was a bit bull-headed himself ('Bull' was actually his playing nickname, can you believe it) — was to have phoned up and talked personally.

That was that, until a few weeks later when I was due to go down to Newlands for another commentary. Pickard said in the press that he had decided to allow me in but stressed that I was not welcome there. I toyed with the idea of not going, but decided in the end to make the trip. In fact I was very well received by all my good friends there.

At the time of writing things are fairly quiet and I certainly hope Jan Pickard and I have the chance to maybe chat it out over a beer or two. One of the ironies of the whole affair is that my friend and fellow commentator on the Afrikaans button is former Springbok lock Schalk Burger. He is a senior management employee of — you've guessed it — Jan Pickard.

A year after the first awards dinner, I had left NTC to work with a few guys who had bought out a division of the company. Then one day Radio 702 asked if I would consider going full-time with them. It came out of the blue, and after some negotiation I decided to give it a crack. I joined as Sports Editor, but on a consultancy basis. This gave me the scope to develop the TV rugby commentary side on M-Net, and also the sponsorship interests and public relations work I was doing. In short, I would be as busy as hell, but involved with sport rather than engineering products.

I was also delighted not to be involved with the SABC. Although I had done a few bits of work with the parastatal corporation, including coverage of the Cavalier tour, I knew it was a huge bureaucracy, and the news service it gives out verges on government propaganda. Radio 702, though, is the only independent broadcasting station in southern Africa. Although they have to work under the State of Emergency laws, their reporting has always been fair and unbiased. Right of reply and coverage is afforded to Right, Middle and Left, without prejudice. Luckily, on the sports side they encourage comment, opinion and even a bit of bias in favour of the teams of our region (Johannesburg and Pretoria).

I enjoy it greatly, and am learning all the time — and hell, do the sports contacts I've made come in useful. Hunting people and stories for reports is difficult at the best of times, but a network of contacts makes it a lot easier. Let me give you an example or two.

First, after the Hillsborough soccer disaster, the newspapers, TV and radio were full of it. The magnitude of the horror, and the fact that we had seen it live on M-Net (who were covering the game), brought it home graphically to South African audiences. So we needed to get a report from people who were informed.

I immediately thought of Bruce Grobbelaar, the Liverpool goalkeeper. (This was on a Monday morning, with our news actuality programme on live at noon). I needed a contact man. Gary Bailey was out of town, in the sticks running a training course on motivation. Ray Mordt knew Bruce from their Rhodesian days — but Ray was out and I couldn't get him. I then thought of the Irish connection in the Liverpool team, and tried that route.

From my years in Irish rugby I knew all the journalists, and was particularly friendly with a guy called David Walsh. I phoned his paper, a Sunday publication, but of course being Monday it was his day off. The lady at the paper wouldn't give out the number — but to John Robbie she did. I got him and we talked: he told me that the Liverpool players, understandably, were not keen to comment. He said I needed an expert on security. He suggested John Stalker, the ex-Deputy Chief Constable of Manchester, who advises Millwall.

I phoned Millwall, and they wouldn't tell me his number at first. They told me in the end and I called his office in Manchester: he had left but his secretary called him up from the car park. Hell, I thought, this guy will be furious and tell me to get lost. I knew that John Stalker had been in the news a lot over the Royal Ulster Constabulary shoot-to-kill controversy, and that he had written a book — who was I to mess up his day?

Anyway, he came on the line. It was now after 11.30 am, and I knew that this was my last chance to get someone of status on the show. Perhaps it was my imagination, but I thought he was a bit irritated when he came on. I explained that football is big in South Africa — and he told me that he was a friend of Gary Bailey, so he knew. Gary Bailey, I said, hell, I was at a wedding with Gary a few days previously. Now I was chatting to a friend, and I got a smashing interview that went out half an hour later and was from a man who spoke with authority on the tragedy, its repercussions, lessons and responsibility. It was good radio — and I managed it because I was a sportsman. I got a real buzz from doing the job well. It was like a game: I had to get the interview to win; if I didn't, I lost. It was simple and invigorating.

After the interview I managed to get a copy of John Stalker's most excellent book about his trials and tribulations over the (shoot-to-kill) investigation. Imagine how surprised I was to see the name of Peter Murtagh appear as perhaps the most incisive and best of the journalists who covered the affair. He was the guy who indirectly led to me coming to live in South Africa. Funny how things move in circles!

Another good interview was with Springbok opener Jimmy Cook. After many years of top cricket in South Africa, Jimmy decided to play county cricket and was signed up to play for Somerset. We were all delighted when he hit seventy-five in his opening game against Hampshire. It would obviously be appropriate to get him on the radio. I had a few old mates from Cambridge; by using them I managed to track down Alistair Hignell, my former Varsity skipper who, on finishing his county cricket career, was in journalism. I got through to BBC Radio 2, but he had left; I managed to track him to HTV in Bristol. He was delighted to hear from me and hunted up the Hampshire number. I was able to get Jimmy Cook on the line from the dressing-room to talk us through his innings.

One of my most enjoyable radio reporting moments so far, and not tinged by disaster, was the 1989 Currie Cup cricket final in Port Elizabeth. A five-day game, it was the highlight of the SACU Centenary season. The game was exciting, crowds were big, and to cap it all there were hundreds of cricket legends present from all over the world.

I was the new journalist. I had been full-time for about two weeks, and boy, did the players help me. I knew Clive Rice, the Transvaal skipper, from Superstars; and as a Transvaal rugby player, all the guys were willing to help me out. I was a guest in the players' dressing-room, and I was so nervous getting my first interview that the players sat me down, fixed up the equipment and almost asked their own questions.

Mind you, I couldn't help acting the fool as well. There were many journalists in the press box who also covered rugby: at first, as the former player, I had my leg pulled. But I got some of them back.

One of the key Eastern Province players is left-arm spinner Tim Shaw. He's tall, very dark-haired and one of the EP heroes. The day after his first bowling spell, I was at the ground early and I saw him walking towards me. I introduced myself, and congratulated him on his bowling. He said thanks — and then laughed: he revealed that he wasn't Tim but another EP cricketer, a club player helping out with the administration at the final. He told me that people were always mistaking him for Tim Shaw.

Then we hatched a plot. We would go into the press box, he with his back to the main area. As the other journalists came in, I would interview him. It worked like a charm. As they started to arrive, I was interviewing Tim Shaw the EP hero, there in the press box. After a minute I started asking him a load of questions concerning the bad blood between the sides, and the socially unacceptable behaviour of the Transvalers. He played the role well, and I could see the other journalists' eyes out on stalks at this scoop; a couple reached for their pens. It was

193

only when he revealed that one of the Transvaal players had been sick over the president's balcony the night before that one of the locals walked over, had a good look, and said: 'That's not bloody Tim Shaw!' It was brilliant. The old hands pretended that they hadn't been taken in at all. But the rest were; afterwards a couple told me in private that I had caught the lot, hook, line and sinker. The players even got to hear about it.

While we were there I had another funny moment with all the dignitaries. There was a huge formal banquet one evening to celebrate the centenary. Tony Lewis, the former Glamorgan and England captain, and Christopher Martin-Jenkins were among the speakers; Compton, Miller, Greig, Boycott, Reid — you name them, they were there.

I had hired a dress suit for the banquet — but the hotel lost my laundry. I had no white shirt, and I was late. Very embarrassed, I wore a white, round-neck Adidas T-shirt turned back to front, with a bow tie round my neck. Under the dinner jacket it looked ridiculous. As chance would have it, one of the big knobs' buses was late, and Ali Bacher saw I was waiting for a taxi. He insisted I get on the bus with all the resplendent dignitaries. I was mortified — but to my amazement they all thought this was a new fashion in evening wear, and about a dozen asked me where they could get these collarless, buttonless shirts. I remember Geoff Boycott was particularly interested, and the fact that you would never have to replace any buttons he found very fascinating. Perhaps I should go into business.

At the time of writing, Radio 702 is going from strength to strength. It is a well-run business with a social conscience. Apart from the music, for which it is known, it also has the news and sport departments and the John Berks show. Berksie is one of South Africa's great characters — a sort of Terry Wogan — and he has a great ability to communicate with people from all walks of life. He asks the questions that the listener would ask, and with his sense of humour and sheer South African-ness is very popular. I'm proud to work with such a company, and hope that the fun I get each day in going in to work will remain — I think it will.

My biggest worry, I think, concerns my family. It's ironic: after all the years of getting me back late after training and being on their own, my family are now seeing less of me since I quit rugby. I must say Jennie has never asked me to quit, and has many times told me that if I went to play again she has no objections. She has been like a rock behind me all the way. Although, like all teams, we have the odd spat, our marriage has been a great success. I suppose the fact that Jennie is my best friend as well as my wife is the reason for that.

My kids, Johnnie and Susie, have also seen too little of me. We have been lucky with friends like the Klasens, Watersons, Wilsons, Stubbses and Kirks who have often entertained my family when I was away. I have never been particularly great with young kids, although I love them. I'm sure that as they get older we will discover more to do together. Because we had kids young, I believe that in a few years they will be like brother and sister to Jennie and I.

I love my family to bits. Why have I neglected them, at least in terms of time? Once again, it's been that driving desire, that passion for the game of rugby that's done it. Now the target is sports coverage. I wonder if I'll ever really grow up. I hope not — it's much more fun being a little boy.